Alex Miller was born in Czechoslovakia in 1924 into an impoverished Jewish family. After surviving both the privations of childhood and the horrors of World War II, in 1945 he met his wife, Eva, and after spending nearly two years in Displaced Persons camps in Austria they moved to Israel with their one-year-old daughter. After seventeen years the family moved to Australia with their two Israeli-born sons, changing their name to Sage.

Alex now lives in Melbourne, where he is writing a second book.

FOR ESTHER

This is the moving story of a Jewish boy born into a life of poverty in Czechoslovakia. Left to his own devices at the age of eight, Alex scrounged hospitality wherever he could find it, always trying to keep one step ahead of the authorities. He survived childhood only to find himself dangerously caught up in the events surrounding World War II. Eventually he was taken prisoner and sent to the notorious German death camp at Mauthausen. If starvation didn't get him, the gas chamber surely would. But Alex was lucky . . . Through letters to his beloved grand-daughter, Esther, the tale of Alex's past unfolds.

ALEX SAGE

FOR ESTHER

Complete and Unabridged

ULVERSCROFT
Leicester

First published in Australia in 2000 by
HarperCollins Publishers Pty Limited
Australia

First Large Print Edition
published 2002
by arrangement with
HarperCollins Publishers Pty Limited
Sydney
Australia

British Library CIP Data

Sage, Alex
    For Esther.—Large print ed.—
    Ulverscroft large print series: non-fiction
    1. World War, *1939 – 1945* —Personal narratives
    2. Large type books
    I. Title
    940.5'481

    ISBN 0–7089–4686–0

Published by
F. A. Thorpe (Publishing) Ltd.
Anstey, Leicestershire

Set by Words & Graphics Ltd.
Anstey, Leicestershire
Printed and bound in Great Britain by
T. J. International Ltd., Padstow, Cornwall

This book is printed on acid-free paper

This book is dedicated to my children,
Yehoodit, Yeegol and Ilan,
despite all that happened.

Author's Note

Ever since I returned from the Mauthausen concentration camp I have had an urge to tell the world at large about the terrible sights I witnessed and the horrible things I experienced there. Alas, in my early days I lacked the tools needed to tell my story. Although I was conversant in five languages, my knowledge of them was insufficient for the task.

It was very frustrating. I made many attempts to begin, but didn't get far before getting stuck. Then it occurred to me that I had had a fairly unusual childhood, the story of which might be of interest to people, and I began work on that. The words came more easily.

For years I struggled with the telling of my story, yet the urge to do it kept nagging at me. In 1965, a year after my arrival in Australia, I managed to write some five or six pages, and I asked my elder son's friend, who is now our GP, to read it and tell me what he thought of it. He was too embarrassed to voice an opinion on something he could hardly decipher.

I decided to make an effort to study English in order to gain the necessary grammar and vocabulary to write my story. In 1975 I learned to touch type and spent two hours of every day practising my English.

For twenty years after that I worked on my story, writing and rewriting it again and again. In 1995 I began studying English at the College of Adult Education in Melbourne, and, after completing a course of English as a second language, I went on to study English at a Year 12 level. What I learned there helped me to overcome many a problem in my writing.

When I decided to rewrite my story yet again, the idea occurred to me to use a fictional grand-daughter who asks me to tell her my story. So I invented an exchange of letters with her, telling her all.

By 1997 I had finished the latest rewrite and believed it to be the best that I could do. I asked my teacher, Mrs Barbara Boxhall, to read it and tell me what she thought. She liked it. So did HarperCollins when I submitted it to them. I put the manuscript in the hands of my editors, and at the turn of the new century it was published as the book you now hold in your hands.

The journey I have taken in writing this book has been long, as has the journey of my life. But I wouldn't have missed a single twist or turn of it.

A.S.

Acknowledgments

The person to whom I owe most for this book, and much else, is my beloved wife of fifty-five years, Eva. Without her support, love, devotion and trust I could never have written it.

I am also most grateful to my English teacher and friend, Barbara Boxhall. Without her immense help and encouragement it is doubtful I would have seen my book published so soon, if ever. My thanks also go to Ms Robin Freeman, commissioning editor at HarperCollins (Melbourne), at the time my manuscript was accepted, for the help and kindness she showed me. To Mr Brendan Cohen, who did the primary editing, I also extend my thanks. And I must not forget Mrs Barbara Wolf Colliner who, while treating me in her physiotherapy clinic for my back ailments, also helped me by correcting my English and encouraging me to keep up the good work. Also, her assistant in the seventies, Robin Kilgower, for her assessment and advice.

To all you people, my eternal gratitude.

Esther, my dear grand-daughter,

How can I begin to answer your letter? You say that you feel you do not know me; that you would like to learn about my life in Europe. In Hungary. These are not stories so easily told.

For years I have worked in the Postal Commission, sending other people's stories back and forth around the globe. Now, finally in my retirement, I have a chance to tell my story. But although I remember those days as if they happened yesterday, they do not translate so easily into words.

I have been struggling for some time now with the idea of writing down my story. Your grandmother does not want me to do so — she is afraid for my health. I have been reluctant, too, as my command of English restricts me, and I am not sure I could ever finish the task.

But now you write to me out of the blue and say you want to know me. This, per-haps, is the prompt I have needed.

I know your mother could not tell you much about my past, for the simple reason that I told her very little. Somehow we never talked much about that subject, all those years in Israel. By the time your mother grew up and got married your savta and I left Israel and came here. There was no opportunity for talks about our pasts.

Well, the best I can do until we have time together is to send you chapters of my story as I write it, in the hope that they can shed some light on my past. The thought of you reading them strengthens my resolve to revisit these dark memories, and to struggle now with the words which must convey them.

Mazel-tov on your eighteenth birthday, my dear grandchild. I wish you a safe and successful time in the army, which I know you must now join.

Write again soon.

Your loving grandfather,
Alex

1

The Apple and the Toy

I was born Alex Miller in a small village called Novoselice, some 60 kilometres east of Chust, into a Chasidic family. My village was in Ruthenia, a region of Eastern Europe which became part of Czechoslovakia after the end of World War I. I was the sixth child, but a sister some four or five years older died a year before I was born. Another was to die a couple of years after my birth. Both died of malnutrition. My parents, Moshe and Dvorah Miller, both suffered from tuberculosis. So did the eldest girl, Chava, and the third born, my brother Baruch. The first born son, Gavriel, together with my sister Leah, seemed to escape the disease; but the seventh child, Feigel, was a weak and underdeveloped little thing who remained sick most of her short life. There was no doctor in the village, and our family had no money for doctors anyway. So nobody really knew what was wrong with her. My parents, being deeply religious, trusted in God. They did their best for the child and hoped that God in His mercy

1

would help her. He didn't.

I was about three years old when my second sister died. I remember the time because I happened to be underfoot as my aunt was carrying a pail of hot water to wash the body in preparation for her burial. My aunt tripped and spilled some of the boiling water onto my left elbow, which left a scar that one can still see today.

Despite immense poverty, our family was fruitful and multiplied, bringing a new child into the world almost every year — as God commanded of His people. Never mind that there was not enough food for those already there.

All of this was some five or six years after the end of World War I, but the family had not always been as poor as that. Before the war, my mother's family had been quite comfortably off. She came from a well-to-do family, her father owning a pub and a grocery shop, and lot of land with many cattle and quite a few horses. When my mother was old enough to be married, her father did not seek a husband of financial standing, someone who would be able to look after his daughter and grandchildren-to-be. Rather, as was the custom in such cases, he looked for a God-fearing youngster who was well versed in the Torah and whose diligence in religion and the service of God would cause the Lord to look favourably on them, and their families.

When word got around in the surrounding villages that the rich Yitzhak Kaufman was looking for a husband for his beautiful younger daughter Dvorah, many eligible boys were marched off by their fathers to appear before Reb Yitzhak. My father didn't have any decent clothes or shoes in which to show himself on such occasion, so his relations banded together and lent him a reasonably good suit and a pair of shoes.

Of all the boys Dvorah was shown through the keyhole, Moshe Miller was the only one she liked. So when Reb Yitzhak asked Moshe to recite a verse from the Talmud, and he did it easily, explaining it very well in addition, Yitzhak had no hesitation in accepting his daughter's choice.

Moshe was provided not only with two new outfits of clothing, including underwear, which he had never before owned, but also received a new tallith (prayer shawl), a new caftan made of velvet and a shtreimel, the special fur hat Chasidic Jews wear on the Sabbath and holy days.

After a wedding befitting Reb Yitzhak's status, a big sum of money was deposited in the bank, the interest of which was enough to feed and clothe the young couple and pay for

3

any reasonable expenses they might encounter. It was foreseen that in case of any extra need, Reb Yitzhak's hand would be open for them.

My father was in seventh heaven. There was always food on the table when he returned from the prayer house where he went twice a day to pray and study the Torah. He had decent clothes to wear, shoes for summer and boots for winter. He was most grateful to God for providing all of this fortune. That was in 1912. The next two years were the best of his life. He was happy with his young wife, who did her best to please him, and he thanked God, the giver of all good things, for this wonderful new life. He prayed that it would never change.

But two years later, World War I broke out. Moshe, like many other young Jewish men who led a religious lifestyle, was considered unfit for military service. However, neither he nor anybody else was unaffected by the war. Early on, the Russian army broke through the Austro-Hungarian lines, and the Cossacks came swarming in. After some weeks they were beaten back, but they left nothing standing when they retreated. What they couldn't take with them they destroyed.

Reb Yitzhak was left destitute. What remained of his livestock after the Austrians took what they needed, the Cossacks either took away or killed. His pub, shop and home were burned almost to the ground. There were neither the materials nor the skilled men to rebuild them. He repaired what he could of his home to make it livable, but that was all he could do. When the war eventually ended in 1918, Reb Yitzhak had only his land left. But nobody would buy land, unless very cheap. The money in the bank was worthless.

And so the good times ended not only for Yitzhak Kaufman but for the Miller family too. There was a fairly big piece of land behind my parents' house on which it would have been possible to grow most of the vegetables and some of the staple foods the family needed, but alas, my father had neither the energy nor the inclination to do that. Children, however, he could produce. And they kept coming, one every year or two. By the time the war ended, Moshe was assured of a Kaddish, the prayer said for the dead, recited by a male. He had two sons and a daughter.

The situation went from bad to worse. My parents sold everything of value that my mother had brought with her or had since received from her parents. The coming of the Czechs, who took over this part of the Austro-Hungarian Empire, did nothing to improve our lot. Father spent most of his time in the prayer house, just as he had before, praying diligently for help from the only source that he believed help could come. But to no avail.

Mother begged Father to find some employment as a religious teacher, but there was nothing to be found. 'Then do what your sister has done for years,' she pleaded with him. 'Go begging.' But Father was shy, and he was no good even as a beggarman.

For my father, the bad turn of the family's fortunes only meant a return to familiar conditions. For some wonderful few years he had lived in a dream. When it came to an end, he accepted it as the normal flow of events and settled down to the familiar regime of fasting every Monday and Thursday, and eating gratefully whatever Mother put in front of him on the remaining days. He was grateful to God for the good years and accepted with resignation the return to the bad old days. This was God's will; he would not rebel against it. He would accept it with love, and hope for the coming of the Messiah, who would put things right and reward the righteous.

Mother, although also deeply religious, could not accept the situation. She persisted in trying to make Father realise his obligation to his family. Once she managed to talk him into turning over a small plot of land behind the house so she could grow a few vegetables. It took him a very long time and exhausted him to the extent that he refused to listen to her pleas to do more. 'I haven't got the strength,' he told her, 'I am not made for this kind of work. I am made to serve God,' and left for the prayer house.

Both my parents had relatives in Chust, a country town some 60 kilometres west of their village. When their situation in Novoselice became such that staying on there meant watching their children starve to death, they decided to move to Chust. Mother thought there might be some chance of finding employment there. So the house was sold and my father was sent to buy a house with the money that they had received. He came back several days later with the news that he had found a home for the family, ready to move in. The family packed its meagre belongings and hired one of their neighbours to take them in his horsedrawn cart to Chust.

I have few memories of Novoselice. I remember being scalded by my aunt, I remember being hungry most of the time, and I remember the only toy my father ever made for me: the lid of a shoe-polish box, nailed to the end of a piece of wood. I went out to play with it. After a while a neighbour's kid came out with a beautiful red apple and offered to exchange it for my toy. Hungry as always, I made the deal. But when I'd finished eating the apple I came home crying for my lost toy.

2

A Hunger to Survive

There is a saying in Yiddish which says that if you send a silly one to the market, the merchants will have a ball. My father, as a buyer, was no better than he was as a farmer. When Dvorah saw the house he had bought for us her face fell. 'Moshe, tell me this is not the house you bought for us!'

The house was supposed to have three rooms and a kitchen. But there was only one room completed, and the kitchen. The other two rooms only had the structural timber frame and the roof; neither the inner nor the outside walls had been built. When Dvorah admonished him for his incompetence, Father grinned with embarrassment. He stood there shifting his meagre weight from one foot to the other, eventually offering, 'We will finish the two rooms later; you'll see.' Mother just stood there, tears running down her face. She knew the rooms would never be finished. We turned around and started to unload the cart.

Our new home was of mud bricks with a

9

thatched roof. The entrance led into the kitchen, which had an oven built into it and took up most of the space. In the far corner were a ladder and a manhole leading up to the roof. To the left of the entrance into the house a door led into the only complete room, which was about 4 metres square. Our furniture consisted of one battered cabinet, one timber bed, and another bed in two parts which could be pulled together and used as a table during the day. There were two wooden chairs, a bench seating four, and a table. There was a square iron stove standing on iron legs near the door with four cooking spots. Two windows looked out onto the front garden and one onto the wall facing the yard. All of our belongings, except the cabinet, fitted nicely into the one room, and the family grew used to living out of a space which served as kitchen, living-room and bedroom. Naturally, there was no plumbing. Water was carried from our Jewish neighbour's open well, two houses away. (There was an open well next door, but that belonged to a Christian.) The floor was Mother Earth, and it was scrubbed clean every Friday.

By then my eldest brother, Gavriel, had been apprenticed to a locksmith in Chust and was living with his master's family. The next boy, Baruch, who was about ten at the time, left home to fend for himself.

Chava, our first-born girl, remained in Novoselice to look after the house of our father's unmarried sister while she was away begging. Having no other way of existing, Aunt Golda went begging from village to village during the months that the weather permitted. There were many Jewish beggars in that part of the world wandering around collecting alms, but not many women beggars.

Thus there were only two children at home — me and Leah — when the family shifted to Chust. But Mother was pregnant and in a few months Bassia was born.

My mother fed the family by going from house to house offering to clip hair or wash and clean. I remember her returning after sunset with food that kind people had given her. And if she worked some place where they gave her lunch, she would bring most of that home too, to feed her hungry family.

On Fridays Mum went to the houses of her two cousins and Father's cousin, where she received the heads, feet and other small parts of the poultry they had slaughtered for the Sabbath. That was the meat the Miller family had for Sabbath. On Thursday night Mum bought flour and yeast and baked bread for the following week. It was mostly maize flour, which was the cheapest, plus a little white flour to bake the challah, the ritual bread eaten at the Sabbath.

Things were never too bad until Mum's time of birthing. After giving birth to Bassia, Mum had to stay indoors for a whole month, and the family was forced to rely on thoughtful people to provide us with food. They didn't always remember to.

We children were at home most of the day on our own. Father left very early for the mikvah, the baths for ritual purification, before going to the prayer house or beit hamidrash to pray and study the Torah. He returned home close to midday to eat something — if there was anything to eat — then he'd lie down for an hour or so before going back to the prayer house to study some more Torah and stay for the evening prayer. He'd return home well after sunset.

Both my parents suffered from tuberculosis. Mum was coughing a lot, especially in the mornings and evenings. As she was coming home at night we could hear her coughing from a distance and we would eagerly run towards her, knowing she had some food for us in her bags. There was seldom food in the house before Mum got home.

I always had a great curiosity and was

constantly wandering off to explore the surrounding area. Leah, who was some three years my senior, was responsible for me, and she often had to search around and bring me home from a neighbour's yard. I was only three at the time.

When I was four, father took me to the Talmud Torah, a Jewish religious school where children were taught to read Hebrew and study the weekly portion of the Old Testament. Like my father I was shy and skinny. But unlike my father I was wiry and fairly strong. Because of my diet, however, I was underdeveloped, and so, looking weak and vulnerable, was often bullied and beaten by some of the bigger boys. When I hit back, my teacher — a sadistic little fellow with a red goatee beard — was quick to use his stick, especially on us poor children, whose parents didn't matter. 'Uny hasoov kameth' — 'A poor man is as good as dead', our sages stated. So I felt punished from both sides. But what bothered me more than the bullying and the cane was seeing most of the children unwrap nice sandwiches made with appetising slices of bread with butter or jam. Some children even had some sweets. I, on the other hand, stared at a single piece of maize bread and one cube of sugar.

The Talmud Torah in which I was enrolled

consisted of six classes, grouped according to age from four-year-olds to thirteen-year-olds. Those who did well in this school could go on to a yeshiva (an orthodox Jewish college) and eventually become a rabbi. My father had some hopes that this third son of his would achieve smicha (authorisation to teach as a rabbi). He was resigned to the fact that the older two were lost to Torah, even to Judaism. Gavriel, the eldest boy, had stopped praying and had even joined an atheistic Zionist youth organisation. The next boy, Baruch, had left home a year earlier, and what we heard of him was anything but encouraging, so far as adherence to the Torah and mitzvoth (religious commandments) were concerned.

As Mother went on having a child every year or two, there was always less and less food for the many hungry mouths. I must have been about six when times got so bad that there was no sugar in the house. Being of that age, I had little understanding of my mother's difficulties. When my mother told me there was no sugar and gave me my piece of bread and told me to go to school, I did not dare to say anything until I was out of the house and out of reach of my parents' hands. I stopped under the window, stamping my foot, and yelled, 'I want my sugar cube.' My mother's voice was strained when she told me, 'There is no sugar in the house, my child.'

But her pleading did not satisfy me; I kept demanding my sugar cube. 'I am not going to cheder [Hebrew school] without it,' I yelled. As soon as the door opened and my father stepped out to deal with me, I ran for my life, and he had no chance on earth to catch up with me. I went to cheder without my sugar cube.

There were times when even the maize bread ran out and there was no food at all for a day or two. At such times, I had to go to school with nothing. Yet I had, even at that early age, a strong instinct for survival. I soon found friends with whom I went to steal food from the market. During summer, when many fruits were in season, we would help ourselves to them from wherever they were not well guarded. As I grew older and stronger I'd try to earn a few haller by carrying women's shopping baskets from the market, or a salesman's samples from shop to shop so that I could buy some bread and marmalade. Of course, when on such excursions I missed school, and got into a lot of trouble because of it. But I was unrepentant. I had made up my mind to survive.

3

The Rooster

From late autumn to late spring it was already dark by the time school finished. Having been brought up in a superstitious household, I was afraid of the dark. None of the children of the Talmud Torah lived my way and so I had to go home alone. The school was only about a ten-minute walk from our place on Reti Street. I only had to walk to the upper end of the street, turn left, and after some three more minutes I was there.

My courage lasted up to the last street lamp, 100 metres or so from our home. There I stopped. No matter how cold it was, I would not move until someone came along whom I could follow to the gate of our home. In time I noticed that the policeman who lived a few houses further up the street knocked off work at seven o'clock and I could follow him home. After a while it became a pattern.

When I was about eight, I would play truant on Sundays whenever my football team played at home. On Mondays I would be afraid to go to cheder for fear of the beating I was assured to get from our teacher, Reb Borech. By Monday night I knew that Reb Borech had notified my father of my absence for the last two days. Now I was afraid to go home for fear of my father's wrath. So instead of going home around seven, I walked the main street, waiting for my father to find me and take me home where he would deal out what was, in his view, my well-deserved punishment. This way I got a double beating, because the teacher would not forgo his prerogative to use his cane on me when his turn came. That, however, did not deter me from reoffending the next Sunday, if my team played at home.

There were two soccer teams in Chust. One was a Hungarian team called the HSC, which had several Jewish players in it, among them the two Ackermans, sons of the grocer in Reti Street. The other team, the SK Russ, was made up of Ruthenians. Like most Jews who followed the game, I supported the Hungarians. Ruthenian kids, if they were interested in soccer, attended only their team's games. They never bothered with the Hungarian team. Sometimes I managed to slip in to watch the game by carrying the gear of one of the Jewish players. But most times I had to climb the fence to get in. It was not easy. Some days I'd get caught climbing in by the bigger kids, who were let in to watch the fence against such intruders. There were many Jewish kids who wanted to see the match but couldn't produce the twenty-haller entrance fee.

For me, watching the soccer game was the only fun I could have. During the week, all daylight hours were taken up with study, or my efforts to satisfy my hunger. On Saturdays, when I was free, play was forbidden. And anyway, I was ashamed to leave home in the rags I wore during the week, and I had no other clothes to wear.

Thursday was market day in Chust. On that day, peasants from the town and neighbouring villages brought whatever produce they had to sell to the market, which was situated behind the synagogue. Craftsmen came to sell their handiwork, farmers came to sell their produce and merchants sold a whole range of products (I recall one man yelling 'Vaselina pichy mastiti!' — 'Vaseline to smear the vagina!'). I never went hungry on market days. I was always there, usually accompanied by at least one of my friends, knocking off some fruit here, a loaf of bread there. Provided the weather was suitable, we would have a picnic on the banks of the River Tissa a few kilometres out of town. Otherwise we would find ourselves a quiet corner in the synagogue yard where we'd savour our ill-gotten meal.

It never occurred to me to share my bounty with my brothers or sisters, who were at least as hungry as I was. Fear of my father, who would not have looked at all favourably on his son's thievery, no doubt played a part in it.

My fear of being caught by those I stole from was never as great as my hunger. The peasants, and even more so the merchants, were alert to thieves, and at times I was almost caught in the act. But never quite, and so I was not deterred from trying again. I was lucky most of my life in this respect; I usually succeeded on the second or third attempt.

The market days began around April each year and ended in October. By the end of October, winter would have begun to set in, bringing cold winds during the days and frosts at night. The following six months were cold and lean in every way for me. Not only were there no market days but the little entertainment that the soccer season represented was also out. There were very few ways to earn a penny for bread and marmalade. The food available at home, never sufficient, was even less in winter time. Like most of the poor, the Miller family dreaded the winter, which brought nothing but cold, hunger and misery.

Being poorly clothed, I suffered terribly from the cold. And in that part of the world the temperature sometimes fell to -36 degrees Celsius. Having no gloves, my hands froze by the time I got to cheder in the morning and froze again by the time I got home in the evening. The thawing out was a painful experience. I would stand in front of the stove, in cheder or at home, warming my frozen hands with tears running down my face, moaning softly.

Wood for heating at home was not easy to obtain. We had no money with which to buy it. The only way to get wood was either to beg for it or steal it. I did it both ways, but I preferred the second option. Though small and skinny, I was fairly strong (all that stolen food certainly helped). I learned to use an axe well, and from time to time I'd go to a nearby wood, select a nice sapling, cut it down, tie it to the end of a rope and drag it home. With the help of my bigger sister, my father and I would saw it to the required size.

One night I broke into a timber yard and brought home enough timber to build a sleigh. With that sleigh, my younger sister and little brother would go to the neighbours by day to beg a few pieces of firewood. At night

my older sister and I would set off to steal a
sleigh full of firewood from the stacks of
better-off people. In this manner the Miller
family managed to pass the winter without
freezing to death. The stealing had to be done
without our father's knowledge, of course, for
he did not approve of theft. The Torah
forbade it.

Although there was no market in winter, I
continued to take the Thursday off and go
out in search of food, or the means to buy
some. I would often go to the railway station,
which was 2 kilometres or so from the town
centre, to carry the baggage of those who
could not afford the hansom fare. For half a
koruna I would be able to buy 300 grams of
bread and 50 grams of marmalade — enough
to sustain me for most of the day. Sometimes
the bag or suitcase I'd be employed to carry
was bigger and a great deal heavier than I
was, and after a few paces I'd find I could not
carry it further. On those occasions I'd go
hungry.

Some days, when the regular paper boy was
not available, I'd get a job delivering the
afternoon paper. This way I usually managed
to eat my fill at least once a week. At some
point I discovered that the Kahan family, who
owned a furniture factory in Chust, cooked a
big kettle of bean soup with sauerkraut once a

week on Thursdays. Any poor Jew could come in and have a dishful of the delicious, nourishing soup with a nice piece of maize bread. I made sure to be there whenever the food was given out, leaving school at lunch break on a Thursday to partake of the generous meal. My father, however, was too proud to show up, preferring to go hungry rather than be seen eating there. In this respect I wasn't my father's son; my pride was not so great that I'd miss the opportunity to quell the rumbling in my belly.

Both my parents would also rather have starved to death than touch food that had not been prepared in accordance with Jewish dietary laws. Non-kosher food, in particular any part of the pig, was anathema to them. But I found bacon very nourishing and not too expensive; my hunger had no religious scruples. At some stage I began buying bacon, whenever I was able to, from a Ruthenian peasant neighbour for about half of what it would cost me at the butcher's shop.

When the time came for me to start my secular education, I was enrolled in the Russian school. As the world around me began to open up, I found that everything was a matter of degree. Though there were many poor people in Chust, none were as poor as we. There wasn't another child who didn't have some sort of a sandwich to bring to school. The Ruthenian children would bring a slice of maize bread with some bacon, some of the better-off ones would have a bit of ham with brown bread for their lunch. Few children had white bread, which was the most expensive. I was the only child who had nothing but a slice of maize bread, and even that not of very generous proportions. My mother baked only so many loaves of bread a week. When they were eaten there was no more till the next bake.

It seemed to my father that I was getting more and more out of control. I hardly attended school and did not spend many days at cheder. I was misbehaving both in state school and at religious school. But Father could not pull me into line, so he responded in the only way he knew how: he refused to talk to me. Though he had spoken very little to me in the past, this new silence was galling. I felt that my father despised me and hated having me around, and I returned the compliment in the same fashion. There was nothing either of us could have done to change this unfortunate situation; we had to live together in our cramped house, hemmed in by circumstances beyond our control.

Mother implored me to understand the

situation. She pointed out that I seemed capable of looking after myself. 'Your elder brothers left home at your age to seek better lives for themselves,' she said. 'I think you should go too. You can see we are unable to provide enough food for all of you; we have the little ones to look after. Your father cannot find employment. He never has, and I don't think he ever will.'

That was in spring of 1932. I was eight years old.

By then there were two more children in the Miller family: two little brothers, Yisrael and Chayim.

My older sister Leah was a very obedient girl. From an early age she did as she was told, practically doing all of the home chores. She'd wash up the dishes, clean the house and look after the little ones while Mother was away trying to earn a crust for the family. Father was seldom home, since he was still spending most of his time in the prayer house.

One day Father came home around midday, as was his custom, to eat a little something before returning to the prayer house. Usually he'd find Leah at home looking after her younger sister and brothers. However, on that day he found little Bassia alone with the two toddlers, playing in the yard. Father asked Bassia where Leah was.

'She went somewhere with Frida.'

'Who is Frida?'

'Leah's friend. She often comes here to play.'

When Leah arrived home a few minutes later, flustered and gasping for breath from running, Father already had a good-sized branch at the ready, and he began beating her back, bottom and legs, shouting, 'This is for neglecting your little brothers and your duty to your parents.'

Luckily for Leah he soon ran out of breath and had to stop and sit down.

The previous winter had been the worst I could remember. Food was so scarce that I would have starved if not for the little extra I could steal. My brothers and sisters and our parents hungered bitterly. The little ones had no shoes, but for the begging of firewood they wrapped their feet in rags and a piece of rubber cut from old tyres.

Things had been ominous at the very start of that winter. Every year since our family moved to Chust I had received a pair of new boots from my father's childless cousin, the fur merchant Benzion Fixler. I was named after Benzion's father, and for this reason enjoyed the merchant's beneficence. I was usually given my pair of boots around

September, and they lasted until the weather was mellow enough to go barefoot. By then the boots needed new soles, but there was never the money to repair them. During winter I loved to slide on the ice. This was the main cause of the soles being ruined. It was no good telling me not to do it; other children did it, so why couldn't I? I did not catch on to the fact that other children's parents were better off and could afford the repairs.

In autumn 1932 Mr Fixler seemed to have forgotten about my need for boots. By the beginning of October the soil was already frozen solid in the mornings, and still I went barefoot. Mother nagged Father to speak to his cousin about the boots, but my father would not budge. At last Mother went to see him on her own and came home with a pair. Perhaps Mr Fixler's reluctance to fulfil his yearly act of charity towards his relatives had something to do with the general economic downturn; Chust was not exempt from the Great Depression, and Mr Fixler hadn't sold many furs that year. Or perhaps he had merely heard of my escapades and decided I was not worthy of his patronage.

Things were no easier in the playground than they were at home. The previous summer one of the older boys in cheder decided to have some fun at my expense.

Before the bully could get a laugh out of his audience, I jumped up and slapped him in the face. The big boy laughed and said, 'Look at him — he jumps like a rooster!' From then on the other children called me 'rooster', and wherever I went I heard the rooster's crow. I hated it. The more I hated it the funnier it seemed to the children. I'd throw stones at my tormentors; I broke many a windowpane, and also two children's heads. A third boy of about twelve I even attacked with an axe; he survived by sheer chance. But still they kept calling me rooster and crowing at me in school and on the street.

I regularly received terrible beatings from the teacher's cane, until one day I looked at Reb Borech and whispered, 'This is the last time you beat me.' Reb Borech never laid a hand on me again.

4

A Chair of Gold

During the following summer I spent very little time at school or at cheder. I was busy putting on fat for the lean winter ahead. Those occasions when I did feel compelled to attend, I got no enjoyment out of the experience. Nor did some of my schoolmates, who stopped many a stone thrown by me with their heads. I became quite notorious, and not even the bigger boys dared challenge me openly. Yet from somewhere there always came a loud 'Koo-koo-rikoo'. While I looked in one direction to see who was taunting me, another 'Koo-koo-rikoo' came from the opposite way. The children had great fun and I went wild with anger and frustration. The same thing went on as I walked the streets. I'd throw stones in the direction from which the crowing seemed to come, indifferent to the destination of my missiles, in my desperate efforts to stop the hated sound.

In these circumstances my mother's appeal to me to leave home fell on fertile ground. It remained only to figure out how to go about it. I could see several problems: the biggest was my fear of loneliness, especially at night, when it was dark. As I have said, I had a tremendous fear of the dark, and believed that ghosts and all kinds of lost souls of the dead lurked there. Furthermore, all my short life I had been surrounded by people. I was a social being and, despite my problems, still had a few friends. They often came along to a football match, or on market days took part in my schemes to steal food and go on a picnic with me. One of those boys, Beni, was a particularly good friend of mine, and I began to work on him to come along with me — 'into the world', as they called it. Beni was not very keen on the idea. His parents were not rich by any means, but they were reasonably well off. There was no lack of food in their house, and he was fairly well clothed and shod. He had no good reason to leave home and naturally was very reluctant to do so.

But I had more than enough reason. There was no suggestion of 'running away'; it was a question of bowing to my parents' wishes. My father very much wanted to be rid of me, disappointment that I was to him. He had neither the energy nor the patience to try and turn me around. My mother believed me capable of finding a better life for myself away from the family, knowing she had no hope of providing it for me or any of the other children.

As my situation at home, school and even the town I lived in worsened, I kept pressing Beni to come with me, promising him he would find all he was wishing for out there in the world. But the winter set in before I could persuade him, and now there could be no question of either of us leaving. Not before spring arrived, anyway.

It was a very harsh winter — the harshest I could remember in every way. There was even less food than usual in the house. The cold was terrible, Mother hardly earned anything and the family hungered. Even I, with my enterprising outlook, could find few ways to relieve the constant rumbling in my empty stomach.

And things were getting worse with my father. As my notoriety spread, he would come home from beit hamidrash angry and frustrated by what he heard of his son's latest mischief and misdeeds. Only Mother's pleading saved me from the worst of the terrible beatings Father intended, cane in hand. Despite not being very strong, Father did quite a job with a cane, though he could not keep it up for very long before running out of breath and energy — something I had many occasions to be thankful for.

One evening Mother came home late. She had been working all day in the laundry of a well-to-do family. As usual we children ran towards her when we heard her coughing. We grabbed her nearly-frozen hands, massaging them as they brought her into the house. After a few minutes' rest, Mother unwrapped a parcel of food — a meal she had been given by the woman she worked for — revealing a hard-boiled egg, a few slices of bread and a peeled onion. At that moment Moshe came in from the prayer house and, without even saying the prescribed blessing, grabbed the egg and a slice of bread and began stuffing it down. Had I not seen it with my own eyes, I'd not have believed it. Here was my father, so strictly religious, putting food into his mouth without first washing his hands, as ritual required, and without saying the proper prayer. In front of my very eyes, the eyes of my mother and those of the little children!

Mother looked at him open-mouthed and was so astonished she could not utter a word for a considerable length of time. Then she said in a low, quivering voice, 'Moshe! The children!'

'I am hungry,' Moshe replied tersely. And then he broke down crying.

That was a bad winter indeed.

★ ★ ★

Slowly the snow began to disappear and the ice covering the soil started to thaw. Spring was in the air. Somehow we had survived another winter.

I felt life slowly returning within as well as in the world around me. When the weather became mild enough for me to be able to go barefoot again, I made up my mind not to endure another winter like the one just gone. Certainly not in this place. I resumed working on Beni with more enthusiasm than the previous year; I still couldn't see myself leaving on my own. I was desperate for a partner, and the only candidate was my friend. Eventually Beni gave in and promised to go with me — as much to stop my nagging as anything else, I imagine. We decided to leave on the coming Wednesday.

Early Wednesday morning I was up as soon as my father went to mikvah around five in the morning. The rest of the family was still asleep as I put on my rags, cut a big slice of maize bread off the last loaf prepared for that week, and left the house. It never occurred to me to say goodbye, even to my mother. Beni was waiting for me on the corner of the street with a sizeable parcel under his arm.

We soon found the walking not only

32

tedious but tiring. We had hardly travelled a few kilometres when we became hungry and sat down to eat some of the food we had brought with us. While I had only the maize bread, Beni had appetising brown bread and plenty of it. My mouth watered as he produced hard-boiled eggs, a chicken leg and various vegetables. My meagre rations only lasted two rest stops, and I watched hungrily as Beni tucked into his supply throughout the rest of the day. It did not occur to him to offer some of his food to me, and I was too shy to ask for any.

After walking for nearly ten hours in brilliant sunshine, we arrived in Sevlush around four in the afternoon. It turned out that Wednesday was market day there, and as we had no idea where to go or who to turn to there, we ventured into the market. By then we were both very tired and hungry (even Beni), and desperate. So when a peasant who used to grind his grain at Beni's father's mill recognised Beni and offered to take us back home in his cart, we were quite happy to accept his offer and return to Chust. Even I. On the way back the peasant fed us brown bread, onions and a piece of bacon each, which Beni only ate when he saw me wolfing mine down. It was a wonderfully rich meal, a great deal more than I could have expected at home.

It was late in the evening when I finally returned home. Mother, who had apparently seen me going in the morning, seemed surprised to see me back. But she said nothing. The next day was market day, and I was busy getting food one way or another. I told the boys who were with me of my adventure the previous day. One of them expressed surprise that the gendarmes hadn't picked us up, since they were known to patrol the highways. This was valuable information to me, as I intended to leave home again soon. But this time it would be alone. This was my first lesson from the affair with Beni: you can only rely on yourself.

★   ★   ★

I was full of self-pity, even though my situation was somewhat better than that of my three younger brothers and sister, and even better than that of my parents. Already at that tender age I was becoming hardened, unemotional. Whatever feelings I had were mostly all for myself. I had a little sympathy for my brothers and sisters at home, but as for those siblings who did not live with us, I hardly gave them any thought. To me they did not really exist.

My older sister Leah had been contracted out as a serving maid to a wealthy Jewish family outside Chust. The agreement was for a period of six months and could be renewed if both sides desired it. Leah slaved away for a pittance. Mother used her earnings to feed the family, the little distance that they went. Leah often not only worked very long hours but was given meagre nourishment. Sometimes she was even beaten into the bargain. And yet she could see no hope of ever freeing herself from these conditions; she would never have gathered enough for a decent dowry, even had Mother been able to save her earnings for her. And without a dowry a Jewish girl in that area had no chance of getting married, even if she was as beautiful as a film star. By the same token, a girl with a good dowry could not avoid marriage, no matter how ugly she was. As it was, our mother, struggling as she did to keep the family's body and soul together, had no choice but to use the money Leah earned to buy food, when there was no other money for it.

The eldest girl, Chava, the first born of our parents, was a beautiful young woman: well-formed yet slender, with a lovely round face and beautiful long brown hair. Having no dowry she was destined to remain a spinster, looking after her Aunt Golda's house. As soon as the weather turned bad, Aunt Golda returned home, spending the cold winter months in her warm house and living with her niece on the coins she had collected during the warmer seasons. My aunt had all the traits that her brother Moshe lacked: energy, courage and audacity. The two women never went hungry.

And yet, no-one should have gone hungry at that time. The Depression was still on, and there was great unemployment, but the Czech government, to alleviate the situation, initiated road-building projects. For ten koruna a day, every head of family could work five days a week.

We could have lived like kings on fifty koruna a week. Mother had tried, the previous summer, to convince Father to accept a job in that scheme, but Father refused, saying he didn't have the energy for it. 'But you had the energy to make all those children for whom you refuse to find food,' Mother protested.

As soon as she said it she was sorry. My parents had a profound respect for one another. There was never any shouting or yelling in our house, unless it was Mother yelling at the children and cursing us in her own original style. But to each other our parents always spoke with the greatest gentleness.

Father took his prayer shawl bag, put a couple of pairs of underpants in it and left the house. He was only gone a few minutes when Mother called the children in to run after our father and bring him back. We caught up with him opposite Ackerman's grocery. When he saw his children running behind him, father grinned and turned back. Where he had intended to go, no-one had any idea.

On rare occasions Chava came to visit her family, usually on her way to the nearby hospital. There, she, like our parents, had to be checked periodically for the tuberculosis she suffered from. I too was under medical supervision for years, and spent several weeks in a sanitarium for tuberculosis sufferers. My second-eldest brother had to have half his lung cut out as a result of the disease. I could hardly remember Baruch; I was too young when he left home. Once a letter arrived from Prague, and in it was a photograph of a young man lying in a hospital bed. His face was very pale, almost as pale as the sheets he lay between. I didn't even bother to take a good look at the picture. The person in it was a stranger and meant nothing to me. This, apparently, was my brother.

In 1932 Gavriel finished his apprenticeship

with the local fitter-blacksmith and left for Moravia for a hachsharah, the preparation to emigrate to Palestine, as a pioneer with the Hashomer Hatzair, a left-wing Zionist youth organisation. Gavriel's departure hardly registered at the Miller household. He was considered a 'kofer baeekar', a denier of God, having taken up with that godless mob of Zionists. So far as Father was concerned, he might as well be dead.

As it turned out, Baruch, who left home several years earlier, had become a communist activist. Both he and Gavriel were virulent atheists. And now my father was watching his third son steering in the same direction. He was sure that as soon as I was out of sight I would cut off my sidelocks, let my hair grow and eat whatever came my way. Father could only sigh and feel bitter that the good Lord had not seen fit to guide his children in the ways of His holy Torah and mitzvoth, as he hoped He would.

There were three girls born between Baruch and me, two of whom died of malnutrition in infancy. The third, Leah, survived to endure a life of servitude and misery. Following me in age was Bassia, who at the age of seven had to step into Leah's shoes, doing the chores that she had done. Bassia was a shy but good-natured little girl.

Though skinny and underdeveloped because of the poor diet she received, one could see in her the seeds of a very pretty girl. She tried her best to do what she was told, and was fairly good at looking after her little brothers, her main responsibility during the day while both parents were out of the house.

Father must have been a magician to sire so many children, particularly the last three children, in the circumstances we lived in. There were two beds in the room that served as bedroom, living-room, kitchen and bathroom, though no-one ever bathed there. In one bed slept Mum with her two daughters, while Father and I slept in the other. How he managed it, without disturbing me or the two girls who slept in mother's single bed, will remain a mystery.

One night, not long before I left home, I woke up hearing my parents whispering. Father was trying to talk Mother into something, and she was saying, 'No, Moshe, let me be. I cannot feed those already here. I have had enough. More than enough!'

'But Dvorah,' whispered my father insistently, 'the Torah commands us specifically to 'proo orvoo', to be fruitful and multiply.'

'I have done my share, bearing eleven children,' my mother replied. 'I have no more energy left.'

Father continued: 'Dvorah, you know that every daughter of Israel who bears twelve children gets a golden chair near the shkhinah. Wouldn't you like to sit there among those others in a glorious golden chair?'

'I'll make do with what I get for eleven. Now let me sleep. I am very tired.'

★ ★ ★

There was a great deal of jealousy amongst the children of our family, especially the younger ones, who competed for the little food and even scantier attention available. But while there was no real hostility between us, there was little love lost amongst the lot of us. Our own individual needs were so huge and so unfulfilled that we could hardly expect to find much sympathy for a brother or sister while we all shared such a great need.

Some time after his refusal to join the public works scheme, my father tried to make amends. In a half-hearted effort to provide for his family he took up with some people who made a living smuggling goods, mainly spirits, from Romania where it was relatively cheap. The Romanian border was only some 50 kilometres or so from Chust, so it was a handy proposition. Father went out one day and came home the next grinning. It looked like he was going to earn a crust for his family at long last. Unfortunately, however, the gendarmes turned up the next day and took him away. Nobody knew what really happened. It's likely that one of his partners was caught selling the contraband and implicated my father. He came home six months later, his facial hair missing along with his sidelocks. For about three months Father went around with his face carefully covered, ashamed to show his bare face in public.

So ended Moshe's last endeavour to earn a living.

My dearest Esther,

Here are a few pages of my humble begin-
nings. I don't know if you'll be able to
believe the terrible misery I was brought up
in. Today, when I sit down to a meal your
savta serves up, I can scarcely believe that
this isn't the normal thing and that it wasn't
like this at my parents' place. Or, looking
into the cupboards full of clothing, some of
which I hardly ever wear — dozens of shirts,
socks, underpants, at least a dozen pairs of
shoes, several pairs of gloves — I can hardly
accept that there was a time when I didn't
even know of the existence of some of these
items, let alone own them. And yet I know
that that's how it was.

I can never forget the hunger and the cold
which were so much part of my childhood
— like the toys and the affection that other
children recall of theirs. When I hear people
recall beautiful moments from that period of
their lives, I can't share their recollections.
All I can remember is misery.

I hope you're doing well in the army and
will come through your national service
with a lot of useful experiences and nice
memories.

Your loving Sabah,
Alex

5

A Professional Beggar

Following my aborted attempt to seek greener pastures with Beni, and after a fortnight of vacillation, I rose one morning and went westward — resolved, to the extent a nine-year-old can be, never to return. By nightfall I arrived at a small village and searched for a Jewish house. Any Jewish home, even a non-religious one, can be recognised by the mezuzah, a small, boxed scroll with a blessing inscribed in Hebrew affixed to the right side of the doorpost. I knocked on the door of one such house and a woman opened it. She was in her mid-thirties, well built and with a dark complexion.

'Excuse me,' I said, mustering my courage. 'Would I be able to sleep tonight under your roof? I have come from Chust and I have nowhere to sleep.'

She looked at me for some time in silence, then called her husband.

Imagine if you will a little boy not yet ten years old, but so underdeveloped as to have the body of a six-year-old, dressed in unwashed rags, barefooted and with a grimy little face framed by long brown sidelocks. I bowed my head in shame.

'The child asks to sleep here,' the woman said to her husband.

'Come on in, boy,' the husband said. He towered above me, a blond beard and moustache framing a round, plain face. He brought me water and a washbasin and told me to wash my hands, then invited me to sit at the table where a large bowl of vegetable soup and a thick slice of brown bread was put in front of me. I ate hungrily. It was my first food for the day. My hosts watched me in silence until I had polished off this feast. Then they questioned me.

'Where are you from, boy?'

'Chust,' I replied.

'And how old are you?'

'Nearly ten.'

The couple looked at each other. 'And do your parents know you left home?'

'I think so,' I said. 'They told me to.'

The woman burst out: 'Parents like that should be doused in petrol and burned alive!'

I answered the string of questions about my family, my home life and the nature of my poverty as truthfully as I could, but as I grew more and more embarrassed I made a promise to myself that I would in future claim from the outset to be an orphan.

★　★　★

For several weeks I walked from one village to another, careful to avoid patrolling gendarmes along the roads. I felt too self-conscious to beg for food during the day; I only gathered the courage to approach a place and ask for food and shelter at night.

Often enough even that was refused by some, and I had to ask again and again until finally someone would allow me to spend the night in their cowshed or barn. Usually, those who offered shelter would give me a feed as well. But it happened on some occasions that I was compelled to sleep on an empty stomach.

Gradually I overcame my fear of being alone in the dark, so that rather than having to beg for a place to sleep, I slept in haystacks in the fields. During summer I found plenty of apples, pears and cherries which had fallen from trees along the roadways. I also helped myself to vegetables, when I found them, so long as nobody was around. Thus I did not starve. I was not fussy about what I ate, but now and again, when I became desperate for a slice of bread or a bowl of soup, I'd overcome my bashfulness and approach a Jewish house. On most occasions, a concerned woman would invite me inside and put a bowl of soup and some bread in front of me. But if I was unlucky enough to strike a less compassionate soul, she would tell me to get lost, and when this happened it would take me some time to recover my courage and have another try. There were not many who didn't take pity on me.

Friday nights and Saturdays were the best times in my week, for on the Sabbath I did not have to ask for a meal. All I had to do was find a synagogue, pretend to do a good job of praying, and the good Lord provided. One of the men attending would come up to me and ask me to be his guest for the Sabbath. Sometimes more than one approached me, and I had to explain that I'd been spoken for. It is considered an important act of piety to provide for the wanderer and the poor on the Sabbath. Even when I had been at home we always had a lot more food on the Sabbath than on weekdays. Our relatives, and others who knew of our hardships, gave my mother the leftover parts of the fowl they slaughtered for the day of rest. And Mother would prepare a wonderful meal from those parts, guaranteeing some meat for each of us on Friday night.

As I went further and further westward, the land seemed richer and the people better off. The houses in the villages I passed were larger and more attractive. There were many houses that even had running water. Water pumps could be seen in almost every yard — a great improvement on the open well, where one had to work hard to bring up a bucket of water. Few houses lacked electricity, and many had small flower gardens around them. There were few children around, but those that could be seen were well fed and comfortably dressed.

The people seemed kinder and more charitable. Here and there I would be given an old shirt, some underwear or a pair of socks — things I had never before owned. I was even given a pair of used shoes. Being used to going barefoot, however, it was only on Friday evenings before going to the synagogue that I would wash my feet in one of the many creeks that flowed in that area, put on a pair of socks and my shoes. Somewhere along the way I was given a rucksack, which I slowly filled with useful articles.

I was still quite shy and would not go begging for money. But sometimes, after feeding me, people would give me a coin, so I ended up with a few coins jingling in my pocket. I had become prosperous. I was quite satisfied with my lot as it was, and did not for one minute regret leaving home. Despite the long marches and constant search for adequate food, I had managed to put a little meat on my small frame. I looked and felt a lot stronger than I had at home.

After many weeks on the road I reached the first of the larger towns, Kosice, with a population of around 100,000. I had never seen so large a town. Tramways crisscrossed its wide streets, motorcars roared down its roads — it was a bewildering sight for me. The main street was lined with shops selling everything from nails to perfume, as well as a variety of foodstuffs and sweets such that I had never seen before. I wandered around, fascinated by what I saw, and marvelled that these people had built their shops so close to one another. The towering buildings and general hurry-scurry made me dizzy.

Not far from the main street I found the synagogue and, next to it, a smaller, more unassuming building, the beit hamidrash. Here, a young man told me that the community kept a house especially for wandering beggars such as myself. I would be able to find lodgings there for a few days for a fee of fifty haller a night. But the man looked concerned and added, 'I really don't think a

48

young boy like you should be wandering around alone. You can't be more than nine.'

'I am ten and an orphan,' I replied. 'Both my parents fell into the River Tissa last winter.' (This was a story I borrowed from a real tragedy which befell our neighbours in Chust.) The man looked at me pityingly, murmuring, 'I am sorry.'

I found the guesthouse and secured a bed for the night. I left my rucksack with the couple who looked after the place and paid the fee for one night's lodging. By late afternoon I was back at the beit hamidrash. The same young man who had spoken to me earlier in the day sat studying at a long table at the lower end of the hall. He motioned me to come over.

'What do you intend to do with yourself, young man?' he asked me. 'And by the way, what is your name?'

'My name is Alexander,' I replied, 'and I don't know what I can do.'

The man looked at me in silence for some minutes, and I began feeling uncomfortable under his gaze. Then he said, 'Would you like to study, in cheder, and later maybe in the yeshiva? Who knows, maybe you could become a rabbi if you study hard enough.'

'Oh, I certainly would like to!' I said with an enthusiasm that wasn't altogether candid.

I was in need of an anchor in this city, and in my wandering life, but I wasn't sure that this was the solution I was after. 'But how could I?'

'I could probably help you, if you really want to study the Torah,' replied the young man. 'We could arrange assistance for you, find you a place to sleep, and the rest would be up to you. I am sure that if you sincerely want to become a decent Jew, even if not a rabbi, you would find our community very helpful. Think about it.'

This was indeed an offer I wanted to consider very carefully. In the past weeks I had learned the value of the freedom I now possessed. I could do as I pleased, all day, every day. But that also meant I could go hungry for most of the day. I had slept in haystacks and barns and had walked aimlessly from place to place, in constant fear of gendarme patrols. I had no idea where I was going, or with what purpose. My wanderlust, if ever I had any, was long gone. Now here was a chance to find myself a place to stay and maybe live a life like most children did. It was an offer too good to pass up.

My mentor, Reb Benjomin, arranged everything for me. I was put up with a poor family who had six children of their own, ranging from two to fifteen years old. I slept with Ezra, a boy of eight. Every day during the first week, Reb Benjomin came and took me to the family with whom I was to eat that day's two meals. This was an old tradition: a community would share the days of a poor student to enable him to study. Usually I received a cooked lunch and a light dinner consisting of two slices of bread with jam and tea or coffee. On Saturdays I ate three meals at a doctor's place.

Among the twenty-odd children in the class I was put into, there were three others like myself: students who lived on the charity of this religious community. In cheder and yeshiva together there were about fifteen such boys. They soon explained the ropes to me. 'We are free from study on Fridays,' I was told. 'On that day we go begging, mainly from shop to shop and factory to factory. At some places they give you a card with your name on it. This card entitles you to a weekly sum of between 50 to 150 haller. But everywhere you will get a few haller. Most of us make ten to fifteen koruna on Friday.' What the boys collected on Friday was sufficient to buy a little extra food during the week. If one was careful, they advised me, and saved a little each week, one would be able to buy a pair of shoes, a shirt or a pair of pants now and then.

So on Friday I joined the numerous beggars going from shop to shop collecting alms. I had the feeling that the shops did no business on that day other than hand out alms to the many poor.

Kosice had three different Jewish communities: the ultra-orthodox, which was both the largest and the least well off; a middle-class group, which was made up of the town's professionals; and a wealthy sector. Each community had its own synagogue and rabbi, and one community would have nothing to do with the others' religious ways. However, they were all very charitable people. In the course of time I ventured into homes belonging to the rich Jews, and came away with some used but still very serviceable clothing. Some of the clothes even fitted me, more or less. By the time winter came I had two pairs of fairly good shoes, a pair of boots and a brand-new pair of galoshes.

In these circumstances, I didn't mind going to school regularly and learning the weekly portion of the Torah. I only had to study the relevant portion of the five books of Moses, plus Rashi's commentary thereof. I found that pretty easy and did not have to study in the evenings in order to pass the weekend exams, which in any case were held for me and the other poor boys on Thursdays, to allow us to be free to go alms-collecting the following day. Overall, I was fairly content with my life in Kosice.

Having nothing better to do most evenings, and having lost some of my bashfulness, I started begging outside a hotel. This was a tip from one of the younger boys, who told me that he often accosted people coming out of a hotel at night, with much success. I picked a nice hotel not far from the synagogue and tried my luck. I'd approach men going in or coming out, mumbling something and putting out my hand in an unmistakable gesture. Some people ignored me, others rudely pushed me aside. I did not make much at the beginning, but slowly I became bolder and approached my prey in a more appropriate manner. Most obliged me, some giving me as much as a koruna. Although by then I had put a bit of flesh on my bones, I still projected a pitiful sight, and most people who bothered to take a look took pity on me. On a good night I made as much in two to three hours as I did throughout the whole of Friday. In winter, when the temperature was several degrees below zero, I'd spend no more than an hour in front of this hotel and yet make as much as in two or three hours on milder nights. Apparently people thought I must be very desperate to stand there in that weather and so were even more charitable than usual.

And so I prospered. I opened an account with the Postal Saving Bank and regularly deposited ten or twenty koruna. When I had over 200 koruna in my account, I sent half of that amount to my mother. Mum was quick to acknowledge this gift from heaven. She asked a neighbour to write me a letter, in which she expressed her joy that I was so well off that I could even help her, especially in these hard times. Thanking me profusely for my help, she had the letter signed: your unfaithful mother.

For two years I lived this life in Kosice. I looked well, dressed reasonably well and wanted for nothing — except, maybe, some parental love and attention. I was still only eleven. Having seen parents cuddling and kissing their children, talking to them and helping them with their schoolwork, I realised I was missing out on something. I became restless.

Since leaving Chust I had learned that the grass really *was* greener over the horizon, but now it occurred to me that maybe it was greener still over the next horizon. I lost interest in my studies and consequently did badly at the weekly exams. My teachers became impatient with me, and that resulted in further loss of interest on my part. I started missing classes and gradually ceased attending altogether. My mentor wrote me off as a bad investment. He had made a half-hearted effort to steer me back to the straight and narrow, but had given up when he saw that I was unmoved.

I was forced to leave my lodgings and I lost all of my 'days' except Saturdays, because the doctor had no connection with the community that had adopted me. The doctor kept feeding me on Saturdays, and feeding me well. For a while I sang (for a small fee) in the choir of the middle-class synagogue on Friday nights, but after a while I stopped going to that synagogue too.

In the meantime, winter turned into spring and spring into summer; it was time to go. And so I took off once more, heading in a westerly direction. This time I was well prepared. Not only did I have a reasonably good idea of what I could expect, and how to go about the business of a wandering beggar, I also had a tidy sum of money to fall back on. I walked from village to village and town to town, stopping for a day or two in the larger towns. I was in no hurry to get anywhere and had no particular goal in mind. I ate well and slept well; I was no longer ashamed to ask for a meal or a place to spend the night. People in general seemed a lot better off than those I saw on my way to Kosice. That meant they were also more generous. The money in my pocket increased and I had to make deposits into various post offices en route.

I had become a professional in my field, and I was happier than I ever had been.

Dear Sabah,

I have just finished an officer's course, at the end of which I was exhausted. The first two days of my leave I slept most of thetime. Now it's the fourth day and I am perfectly rested, glad to be at home. Sabah, I don't want you to write about it to my parents, but I met a very nice boy at the officer's course, whom I like very much. We haven't spoken yet about anything impor- tant — we just talked about things in general. But we seem to have similar views on a lot of things. He comes from a family like mine in the way he was brought up. Like myself, he is a bit shy but very decent. He is a parachutist, and his unit is due to go to South Lebanon. I hope, when his unit returns from there, he'll come to visit me at home so I can introduce him to my parents. Then we could meet more often, and openly.

I have read the few pages you sent me. Sabah, I am not prone to crying, but read- ing about your childhood I shed a few tears. Please send me the rest of your story; I am very curious to find out how you managed.

All my love to you and Savta,
Your loving Esther

6

The Reed Stands Up

Somewhere on my way from Poprad to Kezmarok I met an adult beggar who was going in the same direction as me. He was about twenty-five, slim-built but wiry, with sidelocks, a sparse brown beard, shifty light-blue eyes and a smooth tongue. By now I had developed some sort of a sixth sense about people. I could smell a con-man from a mile off, and this character seemed a very slimy specimen — insincere and treacherous. Try as I may to lose him, I could not shake the man. He insisted on accompanying me, saying with a false smile, 'A child like you needs someone to protect him.'

I didn't consider myself in need of protection, and certainly not the protection of this man. But I did not dare say so. When he offered to be my partner I flatly refused, yet I could not avoid him walking alongside me, and I had to listen to his unsavoury stories as we travelled from one place to another.

At that time I had no real idea about sex. What I knew was what most children my age knew — the basic crudities and mechanics. I knew nothing of homosexuals or men who liked children. However, I did know that certain men repulsed me, and this man was one of those. When I'd sit down to rest at the side of the road he would sit down close to me, and often play with his own penis. Sometimes he tried to grab mine. I would move away.

I had to endure the company of the man for several days. With every day that passed I liked him less. I did learn something from my unwanted companion, though: he taught me to masturbate. And I liked it.

Once he told me a story that puzzled me very much. Years back, he said, when he was fifteen, he lived in a big city where he studied in a yeshiva. After some time he abandoned his studies and lost his 'days' and lodgings. With no savings to fall back on, he soon found himself destitute. Hungry and homeless, he was sitting on a park bench one evening when a middle-aged man came and sat beside him. The man started asking him all kinds of questions — where was he from, what was he doing there? Eventually the man talked him into following him to a secluded part of the park, and there he told the boy to pull down his trousers. He then tried to enter him through his anus. But the boy was so scared and shocked that the man was unable to accomplish his act. He was told to put on his pants. Then the man made two fists and told the boy to pick one. He picked the left hand. The man uncurled his fingers and revealed a ten-koruna piece, which he gave the boy. Being curious, the boy asked what was in the other hand. He opened it, and there lay a very small pistol. 'I wonder,' the older beggar said to me, 'do you think he would have shot me, had I picked the other hand?' I didn't answer him. The whole story sounded most improbable, but what perplexed me more than anything was why a man would want to perform that act with another male.

When, at long last, we arrived at Kezmarok, I heaved a sigh of relief. Now I'd be able to rid myself of him, I thought. I managed to, but not in the way I imagined. I found the house the Jewish community kept for wandering beggars and secured a bed, then went into town to collect alms and to look around. I was quite happy to have lost my sex teacher, and hoped never to see him again. After a few hours' walking around I went into a synagogue and there, to my horror, I met the man again.

'So you don't want to be my partner, boy?' he asked me.

'No, I don't,' I replied. 'And that is my last word on the subject.'

The man smiled his slimy smile and said, 'Oh well.' That was it.

Next morning I was woken by a policeman and taken into custody: a wandering child in need of protection. The low-life bastard had denounced me to the police!

I was terrified that they would send me back to my parents — back to the squalor, hunger and misery. I was filled with rage. For the first time I understood why a religious Jew prays every morning with the words, '*Oolemalsheeneem lo tihye tiquah*' — 'Informers shall have no hope'.

After spending several days in a prison cell among adult offenders, my worst dream came true: I was sent back to Chust with a police escort.

Moshe was not very happy to see his prodigal son back home, especially as that son did not seem one bit repentant for having strayed from the narrow path of the faith. On the contrary, to my father I did not even look like a Jewish boy. Not only had I discarded my sidelocks, I had let my hair grow on top of my head — an even greater sin, in his eyes. I kept my cap on my head in deference to and fear of my father. Still, there was a bitter smile on his face as he signed for his son at the police station and remarked to no-one in particular, 'Every horse has hair on his head.' Formalities finished, my father turned and left, with me trailing at his heels. During the fifteen-minute walk home, not one word was spoken. My father had no desire to speak to me, and I didn't dare to address him.

My mother, on the other hand, embraced and kissed me many times. She was a mother, and she was my mother. 'You look wonderful, my child!' she said. 'And you have grown so much. Blessed be the Lord for looking after you.' Then she added, in a voice not intended for my father's ears, 'When we received notice that you were coming home, I didn't know whether to be glad or sad. But I am glad to see you, son. I only wish that we could keep you at home and look after you like normal people do. But you can see that nothing has changed around here. If anything, it's worse than it ever was. If it weren't for the money you sent us we would have starved.' While her mouth was smiling, her eyes were crying and the tears were running down the lines of her face. She looked old, but she couldn't have been more than forty.

All the children, meanwhile, had gathered around us, fascinated by this spectacle and by the presence of their older brother. I looked around — my younger sister Bassia, a

62

ten-year-old Jewish beauty with black hair, dark eyes and long dark eyelashes; the three little boys aged five to eight, grimy in unwashed rags, their bones showing through their skins, staring at me with saucer eyes. I hardly recognised any of them. They had grown considerably but they all looked small for their ages. The youngest, Yosef, watched me with bewildered eyes from his hiding spot behind his sister's skirt. I looked around and saw the misery and abject poverty of this place: the dirty earthen floor, the timber bed, the benches that served as the makeshift bed where I used to sleep with my father. Nothing had changed. Now that I had seen and experienced better, the sight depressed me.

I looked at my mother, whose eyes seemed to be pleading. For some minutes I did not understand. Then it hit me. I put my hand in my pocket, took out all I had on me — some twenty-odd koruna — and handed it to her. My mother took the money and bowed her scarf-covered head. She asked Bassia to go with her to Ackerman's to buy a few things and help her carry the shopping home. My father pretended not to see the scene. Although normally at this time of day he would have lain down for a couple of hours before going back to beit hamidrash, now he turned and left. He did not return until after the evening prayers were over. When he finally re-entered the house, the whole family was waiting hungrily so that everyone could sit down to share a rare meal provided by my money. My father smiled his wry smile, sighed deeply, washed his hands and sat down to the table. It had been some time since he had eaten such a good meal, and he beamed with pleasure — until he remembered by whose generosity this meal was provided. Then he became sullen and his face soured as he looked around him, observing his family enjoying their feast.

I put aside my depression and resigned myself to the situation I had been thrown back into. It was my misfortune to have been brought back to this travesty of a home, into the hands of a father who was no father at all. But I decided to sit tight for a while. I had learned a lot in those two and a half years away, including the lesson that people can only hurt you if you let them. I was stronger now. When some youngster called me 'rooster', I simply ignored him. I also ignored those who tried crowing after me. After several failed attempts to upset me, the children saw no point in continuing the practice, and it died a natural death. I gained a certain status and respect in the eyes of my peers. I was the boy who had been 'out in the world' and returned looking better, stronger and more prosperous.

I bided my time. I went back to cheder and state school. In the few months I had attended school in Kosice I had picked up Slovakian. I had also become fluent in Hungarian, the language of most of the population of Kosice. And in the short time I sang at the synagogue, where I was surrounded by German-speaking Jews, I picked up some German. I had discovered that new languages came easily to me. So now, back in my school in Chust, it was no great struggle for me to resume lessons in Russian. But my basic schooling was poor, and I felt humiliated: although twelve years old, I was only in Grade 2, with seven-year-olds as my companions. I returned to my old habits of truancy and unruliness.

In the state school it was the practice of the Ruthenian kids to beat up Jewish kids during the breaks. When I found myself surrounded by three Ruthenian boys, I didn't wait for them to attack me: I kicked the one closest to me in the shin and ran for my life. At the next break I took my little bag, filled it with books, and when the same trio turned up intent on giving me the beating they hadn't managed earlier, I again attacked first, this time wielding my bag and hitting out left and right at their heads. Two of them fell and the third ran off. The Jewish children who had witnessed this scene whispered amongst themselves excitedly. From that point on I organised the Jewish kids to stay together for safety in numbers. Several of us held our bags in readiness. But the Ruthenian ruffians learned their lesson, and since they only attacked when they were sure the Jewish kids would let them have their fun without resisting, they gave up their game.

My new-found reputation came to my father's attention. Some of the Jewish fathers whose children had regularly come home bruised and bloodied by the little Ruthenian cowards thought my action was just what was needed. But others, my father included, were afraid that I might be inciting the wrath of the Ruthenian population on the whole community. So my father came to me one night, having hardly spoken to me since my return, and tried to reason with me. 'We are in exile here,' he said. 'It is our destiny to suffer at the hands of these people, on whose soil we live the punishment for our own and our forefathers' sins, until the coming of the Messiah. If we try to defend ourselves, we only get punished more, because we are so few and they so many. Our only chance to survive is to imitate the reed, which, when the wind is strong, bows with it. Some strong, proud trees, which resist the wind, break when the storm strikes. The reed lies low in times of storm and, when the bad weather has passed, straightens out again and is no worse for wear.'

I sat and listened to my father, eyes cast down, my face a mask. My father looked at me and heaved a deep sigh. I am sure he felt that he had not got through to me. But he *did* get through. I heard him, and stored away the information for a time when I could use it. In the not-so-distant future I was to understand that my father spoke of the strategy by which Jews had survived for nearly 2000 years. Taking every humiliation and cruelty that their non-Jewish neighbours cared to dole out, they lay down and hoped, often in vain, to come through it alive. In spite of their faith in God and a hereafter, Jews clung to life tenaciously. In this way, Judaism seemed to me a very pragmatic religion.

But at twelve, I could neither perceive nor comprehend this. I could only see the horror and the hardship resulting from the way of life my father advocated. I had already seen that there were better ways to live, even as a Jew. And for now, all I knew was that taking a beating without a fight only invited another beating; fighting back made your enemy think twice before attacking you.

My father's disappointment must have had some effect on me, however, because I soon stopped going to cheder. It wasn't long before I gave up on school as well. I was bored. One day towards the end of summer I was sitting near an open window in class, looking out into the schoolyard instead of listening to what the elderly teacher was saying. There was not much to see outside the window, except butterflies and the occasional bird. Even these sights were more interesting to me than what the teacher had to say. She noticed that I was not listening to her and asked me to repeat what she had just said. Naturally I had no idea, and just sat there staring at her. The teacher raised her cane to hit me, but I moved out of her way and when the cane came down on the desk in front of me, I grabbed it, pulled it out of her hand, broke it in two and threw it out of the open window, jumping out after it. That was the last time I was seen in school.

I decided to concentrate all my energies into the business of survival on better terms. I had spent a little of my savings on helping my mother make ends meet. But I was determined to keep at least a one-hundred koruna note for an emergency, which I felt might soon arise. I took a job selling

newspapers and delivering them to sub-
scribers. The pay was a pittance, but I made
up for that by stealing a few of the papers I
was supposed to deliver and selling these
privately.

I intentionally muddled things up so that
even though people complained that they had
not received their papers, and there were
others missing, I was able to carry on my
scheme for several weeks. When eventually
the owner of the newsagency, a skinny,
cross-eyed Hungarian, found out what was
happening, I knew it was time for the
disappearing act.

The day before taking off, I took the
precaution of not sleeping at home. So when
the police came in the morning to arrest me,
my parents could honestly tell them that they
didn't know my whereabouts.

My dear Esther,

*I am very glad to hear your news. I will say
nothing on the subject of your new friend,
other than that I hope with all my heart that
things go just as you should wish them to.*

*I have been diligent, as you can see from
the accompanying pages. Mind you, I
could've and should've managed more than
I have. Though I do spend the time, I find
the going pretty hard. Not only are there
many distractions but I have problems with
the language. As you know, I am fairly conversant in five languages, but, like the jack-
of-all-trades, I'm master of none. I have
acquired a reasonable vocabulary in English,
yet I find that it's not enough for the task I
took on. I am often frustrated, unable to
pull out the proper word or expression.*

*Most of all, I have struggled to find the
words to describe the misery we lived in at
home. Even today, from the distance of so
many years, the memory of what I had to
call home depresses me. These days you see
on TV shanty towns in Africa, South
America or India where people live in
abject poverty, but you don't associate such
conditions with Jews. However, that's how it
was.*

For many years I was angry with my

father, blaming him for all the woes our family endured, but I changed my mind quite some years back. Firstly because I realised that he was a sick man and was simply unable to do more than the little he did in terms of looking after his family.

Later on I came to another exonerating conclusion, and that was that we are all creatures of conditioning. We are conditioned by our genes, our parents, their attitude towards us, their wisdom or lack of it. And the environment in which we live — the conditions, economic and spiritual, we grew up in. All these elements combine to create what we are and how we shall live. My poor father was simply acting the way he had been conditioned to act. His only alternative would have been to try and swim against the stream (and he didn't have the physical strength for that) and live a life of frustration. Life was frustrating enough as it was.

It is the same for the rest of us. If we try to act contrary to the way we are conditioned, we only frustrate ourselves. The best way to go through life is to swim with the stream — carefully, so as not to be hurt by others or inflict injury on others. For by hurting others we inevitably hurt ourselves too.

I hope to hear from you soon. In the meantime, I'll go on writing, if time and situation will allow it.

> *All our love from Savta and myself,*
> *Alex*

7

Seeing the Light

Early in the morning I took the train to Kosice, arriving there in the evening. This time I knew where to go to secure a bed for the night, and went straight to the house the community kept for my kind.

The next day was beggars' day. I set out to visit my 'customers', some of whom used to give me a koruna or more a week. They were surprised to see me, but kindly accepted me again with good grace. But times were tough, and it wasn't so easy for me to carry on where I had left off nearly a year earlier. The Depression was biting; business had never been worse. Every week there were more beggars. Some shops went broke and closed down, and even those which were still open didn't do too well. Many shops simply stopped handing out coins on Fridays. Those who used to give half a koruna or more to selected 'customers' halved that hand-out, and if one of the regulars dropped out they would not take on another beggar as once they might have done.

My income shrank. I no longer had the benefits of cheder: the lodgings and the meals that I had received while studying. Even the Saturday I had had at the doctor's was lost to me. Now I had to provide my own food and accommodation. What little money I made during the week hardly covered my basic expenses. Now and again I had to dip into my savings; my money was slowly running out. The winter was setting in and I needed warm clothes, but people in those days were reluctant to part with their old clothes if they could still be worn. I had outgrown my clothes and had nothing to replace them with; I looked like a scarecrow. Finally I was forced to spend all of what was left of my savings on an overcoat and a pair of boots. After that there was nothing to fall back on. I could ill afford to buy food whenever I was hungry, which was most of the time.

That winter I was cold and miserable. It was almost like being at home.

But somehow I survived. As soon as the nights became milder, I and another boy my age, a runaway from Solotvina, found a hayloft above a stable of horses where we could sleep for free. This way I could spend more on food. But there was a drawback: there were no washing facilities and I had to sleep in my clothes. I was infested with lice in no time.

I was no stranger to lice; I had known them since birth. My mother was unable to create conditions to avoid them. But she used to keep them under control by occasionally boiling the clothes and trying to eradicate the insects from the bedding, killing every louse and destroying the eggs along the seams where they usually lined up. In the last three years I had learned that one could live without lice; all it took was to keep clean and change one's clothes periodically. I learned to wash frequently and boil my underwear, and to iron my shirts and trousers. So long as I slept in a clean bed, I was free of lice.

In my new circumstances, however, I was in no position to keep clean, and so I once more became a victim of those little parasites. This time was worse than ever, since I wasn't even able to keep them under any degree of control. At times I would go into the toilet by the synagogue, take off my clothes and massacre as many of my little tormentors as I could. The effect was minimal: I was constantly itching and scratching myself. I scratched and scratched until I was covered in infected sores. I went to see the old doctor who used to feed me on Saturdays and he gave me some lotion to put on my sores. It wasn't much help.

As spring passed and summer came and went, my condition deteriorated. Late in autumn most of my body was covered with sores and I presented both a pitiful and repulsive sight. I was emaciated, wild-looking in the ragged clothes I had outgrown, and I stank.

One night I accosted a man coming out of the hotel where I begged for coins. The man grabbed my arm and, after looking me over, told me he was an officer of the Department for the Protection of Children and that I would have to go with him. I was both bewildered and relieved. I had slipped so far down, any change could only be an improvement, I thought. The officer took me to a city orphanage where they removed my clothes and burned them. They cleaned me up, attended to my sores, fed me and put me to bed between clean sheets. It was a long time since I had slept so well.

I woke up next morning in a dormitory housing some twenty or so other children. The room was clean and tidy. A small set of shelves beside each bed held each child's belongings. A middle-aged woman came into the room and clapped her hands. 'Up, boys, time to get up. Up, up, up!' The children started to rise and dress. I found some used but clean clothes on my shelves, put them on and followed the other children to a washroom where we had a perfunctory wash of hands and face, then marched into a large dining room. We sat at rows of long tables, waiting for the signal to eat. There was bread, jam and white coffee for each child. When I finished my breakfast I was taken to the surgery. 'Nothing basically wrong with this boy,' said the doctor who looked me over. 'He needs a bit of fattening up and to be kept clean.'

Next I was taken to an office where a young woman took down my particulars. She asked me many questions about my family background. Omitting only to tell her how I had had to leave home to avoid arrest, I drew a truthful picture of conditions at home. The young woman wrote everything down. When I finished she asked, 'Why did you pick Kosice of all places to settle down?'

'I don't know. It seemed a nice place, and I thought I might be able to live here.'

'But you don't have any relations or friends here.'

'No,' I replied.

'How were you able to live on your own, with no-one looking after you?'

'I learned to look after myself.'

'Well, you didn't do a very good job of that.

I was told you looked terrible when they picked you up — unwashed and full of lice.'

I did not respond to that.

'What would you do if we let you go?'

'I don't know. Probably carry on as I did before I was picked up.'

'You wouldn't go home?'

'I have nothing to go home to. There is no room for me at home, and no food or clothing. Nothing.'

The woman looked at me pityingly. 'I see.'

After checking through what she had written, she looked up. 'Could you wait outside, please? I may call you in later.' I went out and sat on a bench in the corridor opposite her office. I looked around me, at all the order and cleanliness. Everything was done quietly. It wouldn't be bad for me to stay here for a while, I thought. It seems a decent place, despite the regimentation and the restrictions. But then, I reasoned to myself, what good to me is the freedom to roam the streets, hungry and unkempt, eaten up by lice? I'd rather stay here, where meals are provided and I can sleep in a clean bed.

But it wasn't to be.

I watched the young woman go into an office next door to her own, and caught most of an argument that ensued between her and a man, apparently her superior. 'We can't look after our own poor!' I heard the man say. 'We can't afford to take on every wandering child from all over the country. He is the government's responsibility, not ours.'

'Would one child make such a difference?' she pleaded.

'We have our locals to consider. He is not a local, he doesn't belong here. Let the government look after him.' When the woman tried to interrupt, he said, 'I know everything, I read your report. But in the circumstances we cannot keep him here. And that's final. He is clearly a child in need of protection, but since he does not belong to our city it is up to the state to look after him — in the area where he belongs.'

I was tired. It made no difference to me where I was to be sent. Since I was not able to stay in Kosice, I was prepared to be taken wheresoever these people desired.

I was ushered into a sort of a waiting room. After sitting there for a couple of hours, a gendarme arrived and I was delivered into his hands. From the orphanage I was taken to the railway station where we boarded a train going east. After a ride of several hours we alighted at Mukacevo. Here the gendarme took me to the door of a huge building surrounded by a high, whitewashed stone wall. The entrance was nearly overgrown by a creeper. The gendarme knocked on the door, but there was no response. He knocked again and again with the same result. Then he noticed a bell handle, hidden by the vine, and pulled it.

The sound of a bell reverberated from far inside the building. A short time later the door was opened by an elderly nun. The gendarme handed her the papers without saying a word. The nun glanced at them, signed the receipt and returned it to the gendarme, who saluted and left. The nun stepped aside and opened the door wide. 'Come on in, my son,' she said in Czech.

I just stood there, riveted to the spot. Here before me stood a nun, inviting me into a place which was the very embodiment of Christianity. The nun, a large, obviously good-natured woman, looked down at me and smiled. 'Don't fret, little fellow. This is not such a bad place at all. Come on in, we can't stand here all day.' She took my hand and gently pulled me in. I followed, full of fear and suspicion. I had received my mistrust of Christianity with my mother's milk, just as most Christian children had received their mistrust of the Jew. No matter what one later experienced in life, one was incapable of shaking off these deep-rooted emotions.

After a short check-up by a nurse, the

decision was made to isolate me on suspicion of having scabies. I was put in a small, bright cell where the only furniture was a bed, a table and a chair. 'You will have to stay here for a week,' the young nurse told me. 'If your sores heal by then, you will be brought in among the other children.' She closed the door, which could only be opened from the outside, and left. She came back a few minutes later, saying, 'If you need something or want to go to the toilet, just knock on the door. Someone will come and attend to you.'

For some time I tried to ignore my unpleasant surroundings by daydreaming. Although I hated being on my own, I could tolerate it by this method, and the days passed reasonably. Nights, however, were a different matter altogether, especially that first night. As soon as it became dark, a small electric globe was switched on from the outside. While the light was on, everything remained tolerable. But at eight o'clock the light was switched off and I was told to sleep. My terrible fear of the dark kept me alert. There was a little window in the door, and if I stood on my tiptoes and put out my hand, I could reach the switch. In this way I switched it back on, and after a while managed to fall asleep. But I woke during the night to find myself in total darkness again. I lay there in fear, not daring to move, listening and trying to pierce the darkness with my eyes. The silence and the darkness were total. In my imagination there were noises, frightening noises, and even more terrifying sights. I let out a fearsome cry, which brought a sleepy young nun running to my cell.

'What is wrong with you, you little devil?' the nun yelled at me. 'Have you gone mad or something?' I stared at her, still under the influence of my night-terrors, half-blinded by the sudden light. She then began beating me with her little fists, shouting, 'I will teach you to disturb people in the middle of night, you little devil!' I pulled my head in and raised my arms to protect my face. The nun's fists, colliding with my bony arms, must have hurt her, for she stopped hitting me, saying, 'Ugh, you damned Jew! You'd better be quiet for the rest of the night.' With that, she left my cell and switched off the light.

But she left the light on in the corridor, which sent enough light into my cell through the small window in the door to prevent total darkness from taking over. I managed to fall asleep, despite my fear of the cruel nun, which had almost displaced my fear of the dark. The next day passed in peace, and for the rest of the week they left the corridor light on after putting out the light in my cell. This was enough to drive off any creature of horror lurking in the darkness, and I slept in relative peace through the nights, only occasionally disturbed by nightmares of one kind or another.

It was a long and miserable week spent in isolation, but eventually it passed, as all things do. At the end of it a doctor came to check me over and found me fit to join the other children in the orphanage. I was taken to a large room where some twenty children, all boys aged between ten and fifteen, sat cross-legged on the floor or on chairs around small tables. They were in total silence. A young horse-faced nun was teaching religion. A crucifix and several religious pictures adorned the walls of the room, which was bright and warmed by a large oven. I felt a shiver, despite the warmth of the room.

The nun looked me over, appraising me for several seconds, then told me to sit at the rear. I sat there, head bowed, deep in thought. The nun's words hardly entered my ears. Having lost all interest in my own religion, I certainly had no interest in Christianity. But I pricked up my ears when she started talking about loving Jesus, and how he had taught that a Christian must love even his enemy. I laughed involuntarily: I had experienced Christian love at the hands of the

Ruthenians at school. I could do without that sort of love!

'What is so funny?' the stony-faced nun asked. 'You, the new boy, stand up and tell me what you were laughing about.'

I stood up with my head bowed, saying nothing.

'Well? Are you dumb or have you suddenly lost your tongue?' When I did not respond, she told me to go and kneel near the oven, where I remained for the rest of the lesson. Before she left the room, the nun gave me a malevolent look, saying, 'I'll deal with you later. Now go back to where you sat before.' My feet were numb from kneeling. I stood with difficulty and returned to my place.

It soon became clear that although all the children were harshly treated or cruelly punished for the slightest transgression, I was to be singled out for even harsher treatment than the rest. I learned the Christian's daily prayer: 'Forgive us our trespasses as we forgive those who trespass against us.' What forgiveness? Those nuns never forgave anything, and they seemed to enjoy meting out punishment.

I made up my mind to be as inconspicuous as possible to avoid notice and consequently punishment, but that was impossible. The nuns seemed to be watching constantly, and pounced on me at the slightest provocation. Showing no interest in what they taught was reason enough for severe punishment. And they did not miss the opportunity: I was frequently beaten with bamboo canes and made to kneel for long periods of time. I was also, at times, forced to kneel on kernels of corn.

Now, persecution was nothing new to me, and I usually suffered in silence until one day, whilst kneeling beside the oven, one of the nuns passing me said, 'You accursed Jew,' and kicked me in the kidneys. For a second I was stunned by the pain of this unexpected blow. I looked up at the nun with murder in my eyes, then looked at the red hot poker in front of me. The nun must have seen my thoughts in my eyes, because she let out a cry and fled.

Some ten minutes later a burly man appeared, grabbed me by the arm and took me to the isolation cell where I had spent the first week of my stay at the orphanage. I was left there for the rest of the day, without food or drink. Early the next morning I was woken by a man and told to dress. I was given breakfast and then taken to the railway station, where we boarded a train. After about an hour's ride we arrived at Sevlush, the destination of my first failed attempt to leave Chust with my friend Beni. There I was instructed by my escort to alight, and together we walked to the Institute of Correction for Children. I was delivered to the man at the gate.

The institute was situated at the edge of town in a huge building that must have been the mansion of some noble family in earlier times. There was a sizeable farm attached to it, complete with milking cows, chickens and other fowl, vegetable gardens and flower beds, all contained within the high fence surrounding the institute.

It was still early in the morning when I arrived, and the inmates were all at breakfast. The huge building was ominously silent as I was led in through heavy doors to an office, where I was told to sit and wait. Though it was only the end of February, the weather was mild, the snow already gone. Looking through the window I could see that some of the trees were coming into blossom. I wondered what kind of place I had been brought to. Had I been able to read the sign on the gate, I would have known that I had been brought to the worst possible place a youngster could be brought to. This sort of institute was well known for its harsh regimes and cruel masters. It was an institute for young offenders.

After a short time a large woman arrived.

She sat down at the desk, hardly giving me a glance. Upon reading the papers accompanying me, she looked up and said, 'So you misbehaved at the orphanage, did you? I am sure you won't make the same mistake here. Stand up.' She inspected me. 'You're a bit small for your age, aren't you? You will go to Group B — first floor, look for Master Probic. Tell him you are the new boy from Mukacevo.'

With that I was dismissed. I soon found out where my misfortune had placed me.

Dear Sabah,

I am most surprised that you are able to look back at those horrible times with such composure and, at times, lack of emotion. I sometimes dream about you, seeing you shivering from cold in the winter, hungry and miserable. Then I wake up and can't fall asleep again for thinking about the conditions under which you lived. It is very depressing. And yet, I wouldn't want you to stop telling me about it.

I have been given a most interesting job on a new base not far from home, and I often go home for a night. Mum is delighted to see me. Naturally I return the compliment and am happy to see my parents, and my younger sisters and brothers, the youngest of whom is still in nappies. On Saturday I am always home, unless I am the duty officer for the weekend, which only comes around about once every two months. I am impatiently waiting for my friend (boyfriend?) to return from Lebanon.

> *All my love to both of you,*
> *Esther*

8

Exodus

Master Probic turned out to be a vicious-looking man in his late forties: stocky, balding, with small, deep-set eyes. He gave me a malevolent look as I presented myself. I was shown my bunk and told to be down in the yard in five minutes. I did not linger. The yard was full of children aged between ten and sixteen, mostly boys, all dressed in jeans. There were a few girls, similarly dressed in denim, but in skirts.

I stood there, lost, not knowing which group to join. Finally I approached one of the older boys.

'Could you please tell me where Group B is?' I asked. This tall, swarthy youngster bent down to me. 'We are arranged in alphabetical order. The first group nearest the gate is Group A, the next one is your group, B.'

'Thank you,' I murmured.

The boy smiled. 'Don't be afraid; relax, you'll be all right here.'

A small group of men and two women came out of the building. The children stopped talking and bickering among themselves and stood silently to attention. Each teacher went to his or her group and counted them. When the numbers tallied, about half of the children, myself among them, were sent to the classroom. The remainder were given work assignments, some in the fields outside the fence, others in the farm inside it, others again in the various workshops set up within the institute. Through all of this the children, some 250 of them, observed total silence. Every one of the teachers had a thick bamboo cane in his or her hand — apparently not for show, as I soon learned when I accidentally fell out of line as we filed into the classroom. I felt a sharp pain across my back as the master shouted, 'Get back into line!', lifting the cane to strike again.

The children in my class were between eleven and thirteen years of age, but their learning material was that of Grade 4, allowing for the poor schooling most of them had received. Even so, I was in trouble, as this was a Czech school teaching in that language and using the Roman alphabet. The very little I had learned was in the Russian language using the Cyrillic alphabet.

As soon as instruction began, the teacher wanted to know what the new boy's standard of knowledge was. I was called to the board and told to write what the teacher dictated. I just stood there, looking dumb, fingering the piece of chalk. Before I had a chance to explain, the teacher, enraged by my slowness and what he must have perceived as impertinence, gave me a mighty whack with his cane. He yelled, 'Do you think you are the only pupil in this class?' I tried to explain, my voice quivering as I struggled with the pain: 'I don't know the Roman alphabet.' The second blow was not so unexpected and I only winced as it struck my shoulder. I was sent back to my seat.

That was the beginning of my schooling in the institute. From then on the teacher took no notice of me, and I was glad to be left alone. I learned very little there, if anything at all. Neither I nor the teacher cared much. What I did learn was what I knew already: that the only way to avoid punishment (and there was a lot of that on offer) was to avoid notice. And I tried my best to do just that.

School ran from eight o'clock in the morning till three in the afternoon, with one small break in the morning and a longer one for lunch. From three till six, the children worked in their appointed places of work. I was detailed to the cabinet-maker's work-shop, ostensibly to learn the trade. But the only thing I learned during my time there was to clean the workshop and replace the master's tools in their allotted places. If a tool was not in its proper place, I'd receive five blows with the cane on my left palm, after which my left hand would be useless for days. I was always the last to leave the workshop to see that none of the tools were out of place before locking up and going to the evening meal. Even so, it happened twice during my stay there that a tool was missing from its proper spot, and I received my fiver. If I arrived late for the evening meal I received at least two whacks from the masters overseeing the dining room. Lingering was frowned upon.

The evening meal lasted for about an hour, until seven o'clock. After that, if the weather permitted, we were allowed to play in the yard for another hour until it was time for showers and bed. By nine o'clock the lights were turned off and we had to sleep, or pretend to.

The dormitory was a large hall filled with beds lining the walls. There was a small chest of drawers next to each bed for any personal belongings. Not many had any. On one side of my bed was Pongo, a gypsy boy of my age and size.

The two of us took a liking to each other the minute we met. After lights out, we often whispered to each other about our life experiences, which, though short, were pretty colourful. As Pongo had come to the institute nearly a year earlier, he knew the ropes and helped me avoid trouble, where possible.

Though fairly lean, Pongo was strong and agile and full of courage. Some of the bullies who terrorised the weaker children had tried their tricks on him. But only once. Although he seemed very placid, Pongo could be wild and vicious when roused.

I was very appreciative of Pongo's friendship and often talked to him about escape. Pongo argued against it: 'It would be easy enough to escape, but you would not get far before they caught up with you. They have well-trained tracker dogs to lead them to you. Of course, if you had money, maybe you'd have a chance. If you could get to the railway station before they realised you were gone, and take a train ride to some place . . . Even so, they'd soon find out you were on the train and send the gendarmerie to intercept you. Without money, you don't have a prayer. And you'd better remember that.'

I wasn't to be so easily dissuaded. 'But Pongo, couldn't we ride the train anyway? Even without a ticket? We could hide from the conductor, maybe even travel on top of a carriage.'

Pongo looked at me for a few moments. 'That possibility never occurred to me,' he said. 'But let's say we managed to get to some town 100 kilometres or more from here; what then? You know how bad the situation is outside. People aren't willing to help as they used to. We would starve or be caught by the police and returned here quick smart. You can't imagine what would await us here then! I don't even want to talk about it.'

Yet I could think of nothing else. How to arrange an escape was my preoccupation. And the more I thought about it, the more discouraged I became. Slowly I came to realise that only a miracle could get me out of the institute.

Then one day a miracle appeared, in the form of my father.

It so happened that my parents were notified that their son Alexander had been placed in the institute. They were told that they could visit me once a month, and that they could also apply for permission to take me home for certain holidays. As neither my father nor my mother could read Czech, they asked a Jewish neighbour to read the letter to them. Had my father been able to read the letter, it would never have come to my mother's notice. He would have destroyed it and forgotten about it. But my mother could not forget me, no matter how much shame I brought upon them. Somehow she persuaded my father to have me home for the coming Passover. Passover was the best time for our family because, for the eight days of the holiday, we were assured of the unleavened bread eaten throughout the festival, given by a charity called Meaot Chitin. Relatives and others gave potatoes, which were the main food during those days, so the family had more food than at other times of the year.

Of course, I knew nothing of this at the time. And so one April morning I had been in class hardly ten minutes when I was called to the office: someone was here to see me. I was amazed to see my father at the gate of the institute. I was told I could go home for the Passover holiday, but to make sure I returned the day after the end of the holiday. I was given a new pair of jeans and a shirt and was sent on my way.

Once out of the gates, I vowed never to return.

Dear Grandchild of mine,

I am deeply sorry that your friend was killed. You say it could have been you, that pure chance spared you. Life is nothing but a series of chances. If you are lucky, you make the right choice when a choice is presented to you. No more. And a choice is never between the good and the better but rather between the bad and the worse. Those who choose the bad and not the worse are either wise or simply lucky.

My own life is a perfect example. Certainly I wanted to leave home, but I had to be pushed along by my fear of the consequences of my misdeeds at the newsagency. The officer from the Department for the Protection of Children happened to be at that hotel at that particular time. Not all nuns were anti-Semites, but I was placed into the hands of those at the Mukacevo orphanage who were. And I would never have expected my father to be the one to help me escape that terrible institute in Sevlush. Yet it was he who blind fate sent along to bring me out. Chance and blind choices, all of them. Who knows where I would be if not for them?

There is nothing like a little luck. A very rich man was once asked how he got to be so rich. His answer was: 'Ninety per cent luck and ten per cent brains, but I'd gladly exchange the ten per cent brains for five per cent luck.'

I hope your courage has not been shaken by the death of your friend. Be well, and please keep writing. Your letters bring me strength.

Your loving Sabah

The distance from Sevlush to Chust was a mere 20 kilometres. My father and I walked at a leisurely pace for most of the day, resting every few kilometres. Not a word passed between us all day. I would have loved to talk to him, but I could sense his bitterness as he watched me out of the corner of his eye.

There is a Jewish prayer recited on Saturday nights: *'Hamesheev lev avot lebonim, valev bonim el avotam'* — 'The one who turns the hearts of fathers to their children and the children's hearts to their fathers'. Along the road to Chust my father chanted that prayer several times, emphasising the second part. He chanted it with great feeling. But like all his other prayers, this one wasn't answered either. One by one his sons had turned away from Judaism. I had betrayed him, just as my older brothers had.

When we arrived in Chust it was late in the afternoon — time to go to the evening prayers. My father went straight to the beit hamidrash to fulfil the mitzvah of praying with the community. I went with him, reluctantly.

Home was the same hovel I remembered, only now it seemed smaller and more crowded, not to mention shabbier, dirtier and more miserable, than ever it had looked. My younger siblings looked in awe at their big brother, not daring to speak to me. The poverty should have neither shocked nor surprised me, yet it did both. I remembered that when I returned the last time I had had some money to give to my mother. The need was always great in this house; now, before Passover, it was even greater. But I did not have a penny to contribute. I was there only to take from what was already insufficient for these poor souls. I felt terrible. Despite the conditions at the institute, I wished I was back there. Even that harsh prison was better than my home.

That night I slept badly. As soon as it was light, I got up and went into town to look around and see if there was any way I could earn a few haller. My father was gone. He always rose very early to go to the mikvah before going to the beit hamidrash to pray and study a chapter of Gemara, the latter part of the two portions of the Talmud.

The town looked just as I remembered it; nothing had changed here, either. The same shops on the main street, the same market place, now deserted, surrounded by the same small buildings. I remembered the railway station: maybe I'd find someone whose bags I could carry into town for half a koruna or more? Now I was stronger and able to carry even a good-sized suitcase into town.

It was a fairly long walk to the station, but the weather was mild, the sun was shining and there was hope. Hope to earn a meal, and maybe even more than that. There were several horse-drawn carriages waiting in front of the station; this told me a train was due shortly. I sat on a bench to wait. There were few other people waiting, as it was the day before Passover, and very few Jews travelled during this holiday time. In this region, Jews were the vast majority of travellers.

After some twenty minutes of waiting the train arrived. Only a handful of people got off, but amongst the ones that did I spied a middle-aged woman carrying a suitcase. The lady was well dressed and good looking, and her suitcase didn't seem too heavy, since she carried it with ease.

I approached her in Hungarian: 'Lady, may I carry your suitcase? I could carry it into town for one koruna.'

The woman stopped, put down her suitcase and smiled, asking, 'Isn't it a bit too far to walk into town?'

'No, not too far. I mean, it is a little, but not that much.'

The lady laughed. 'And you would carry the suitcase all that way for one koruna?'

'Yes, oh yes,' I replied eagerly.

'You must be desperate for a koruna. What

do you intend to do with the money?' she asked.

'I would buy some bread and marmalade. I haven't had anything to eat yet today.'

'I see.' The woman looked at me for a few seconds, contemplating something, then said, 'Okay, let's go.' Leading the way, she went straight to a waiting carriage. 'Put the suitcase in,' she told me. Seeing my disappointment, she hastened to add, 'You get in too, and don't worry — you'll get your koruna, and a meal too.'

I climbed into the carriage, bewildered and unhappy. But I half overcame my reluctance by reasoning that I had nothing to lose. At least I wouldn't have to walk all the way back into town. Another train wasn't due for hours, and by then it would probably be too late, as it was Passover eve.

The cab driver cracked his whip and called 'Dio', and the carriage was on its way. The woman watched my face and saw the anxiety and confusion I was feeling. She smiled and put a hand on my shoulder. 'Don't look so worried,' she said. 'Nothing bad is going to happen to you, my boy. We will go to a hotel, I will put my suitcase in my room, and then I'll take you into the restaurant to have a good meal. After that you can show me the town. All right?' I looked up into her smiling face and, encouraged by her kindness, relaxed a little.

The carriage stopped at the Hotel Central, which was the better of the two hotels in town. The lady paid off the cab and I carried the suitcase inside. 'You wait here,' she told me. 'I'll be back in a few minutes, and then we can dine.' And she went up with the bellboy.

Two years earlier I would have been worried that someone might see me enter a non-kosher restaurant. Now I could not care less. I made up my mind not to worry whether the food I could get was kosher or not. Besides, I had been fed pork ever since I was caught in Kosice the previous year, and even before that I hadn't been very fussy about what I ate. For the first time in a long time, I ate my fill. The woman watched me wolf down everything that was put in front of me. My spirits rose with my stomach filled to bursting. The depression I had felt since stepping into my parents' home almost disappeared. I smiled and thanked my generous host.

'You are welcome,' she said, smiling back at me. 'You don't smile very often, do you?'

I thought for a while before replying. 'I have very little to smile about,' I said finally. I felt uneasy. This was the first time in my life that I had sat in such a luxurious restaurant, and I felt out of place.

The lady must have recognised this, for she suddenly got up and said, 'All right, now our stomachs are full, let's go and explore the town.'

As we were leaving the restaurant I said, 'By the way, my name is Alexander. That's Sandor in Hungarian.'

The lady smiled and offered her hand. 'And I am Esther.'

'Are you Jewish?' I asked.

'No,' Esther replied. 'Are you?'

'Yes. Only by chance.'

'You don't look it, Alexander.'

'What should a Jew look like?' I asked.

'Well, in this area a Jew looks quite different from a non-Jew. He dresses differently. In most cases, a young man like you would have sidelocks and no hair on top of his head. You dress like a young worker, a non-Jew.'

'I have been away from here for several years,' I said. Then, as an afterthought, 'I don't look at myself often.'

'No, I don't suppose you do,' Esther replied.

We walked the length of the main street, and since the weather was mild we continued to the fortress hill at the northern end of town. At the bottom of the hill we stopped and drank from a well — pure, sweet water. Esther shook her head in amazement. 'I never tasted such wonderful water as this!'

'Neither have I, and I have tasted the water of many places, from here to the Tatra Mountains.'

We sat in the shade of a tall pine tree. Esther turned to me. 'I am an author, I write books,' she explained. 'I have come here to rest for a few weeks and maybe write something about the people around this place. I would be willing to pay you a good wage if you were willing to help me.'

'Whatever it is I can help you with, I'd be more than willing to do,' I said. 'But I'm afraid that I can only stay here for eight days.'

'How is that?'

'Well, I am on leave for the Passover holiday from the youth correction centre in Sevlush. Actually,' I confided, 'I am not going back, but I can't stay here where the gendarmerie can find me.'

'I see. And what do you intend to do?'

'Maybe I'll go to Hungary.'

Esther laughed softly. 'Why there? And how do you intend to get there? I don't suppose you have a passport? And if you do get there, what do you intend to do in Hungary? How will you live?'

'As I did in Slovakia, where I spent nearly three years without anyone looking after me.'

Esther frowned. 'How old are you?'

'Fifteen.'

Esther's face turned grave. Under her gentle questioning, I slowly unravelled my past — the poverty, the cruelty of the orphanage, my father's rejection. As she listened, in her eyes I saw her sadness and astonishment deepen. Coming from a well-to-do family, she could hardly believe that such misery existed. Especially among Jews. Like most gentiles, she believed Jews to be at least well off, if not rich.

By the time I finished my story it was late in the afternoon. I got up and said, 'I have to go home. Tonight is the eve of one of our most important holy days, called Pesach, or Passover. I'd better get home.'

'Will I see you tomorrow?'

'Only in the afternoon,' I replied. 'In the morning I have to go to the prayer house with my father. I don't really feel like it, but for the sake of peace between us I have to go. I could be at your hotel by about two o'clock.'

Esther flagged down a passing horse and carriage. 'All right,' she said. 'If I am not outside the hotel when you arrive, go in. The receptionist will have a message for you.' She paid the driver to take her to her hotel, and me to my parents' home. Before we parted she gave me two ten-koruna coins, saying, 'This is for you. I'll wait for you tomorrow at two.'

I couldn't believe my eyes. Twenty koruna! A fortune for the few hours we had spent together.

When I arrived home, the whole family stared as I alighted from the carriage. I went to my mother and handed her a ten-koruna coin. She took it, amazed. 'Where did you get this?' This was more than she made in two days, if she *had* two good days.

'Don't worry, Mother, I didn't steal it. I earned it.'

'Ten koruna in one day? What did you have to do for it?' she asked nervously.

'Take a lady around the town, showing her places and telling her about it,' I said, then added, 'a rich Hungarian lady.'

My father looked up from where he stood preparing the table for the Seder, the ceremonial meal ushering in the Passover. He said nothing. After a little while he called my two little brothers, Chayim and Yosef. 'Are you ready to come to beit hamidrash?'

'Yes Father,' they answered in unison. Dressed in their best clean rags, they set out together.

My mother turned to me. 'Have a good

quick wash, Alex, and go after them.' Once again, to keep the peace I obeyed.

The Seder meal and ceremony were always a sombre affair in the Miller home. My father carried it out according to custom and tradition, reciting the prescribed readings of the Haggadah. It took nearly two hours to get to the best part of the evening — the meal, prepared by my mother and my sister Bassia, who was now eleven. On these holy occasions there was always nearly enough food, even at our poor table. But on this occasion we ate our fill and more. My mother piled my plate high, ignoring my father's questioning glance.

★ ★ ★

The following afternoon I found the lady waiting for me outside the hotel, a hansom at the ready.

'Lady,' I said to her, 'I can't possibly climb into this hansom with you.'

'But why not?' she asked, surprised.

'Because this is a strictly religious community, and everybody knows everyone. Within minutes my parents will be told about their son riding in a hansom on the holy day, which is strictly forbidden. I have caused them more than enough shame and embarrassment.'

Esther reluctantly dismissed the carriage, and we set off on foot. I led the way to the other side of our town. Again she encouraged me to talk about my life and the local Jewish community. When it came to the question of my planned escape to Hungary, she pleaded with me to reconsider. 'Hungary is not the answer,' she said. 'You can't make a move there without the police knowing about it. In Hungary you have to register with the police if you stay in one place for more than one night. And no-one will accommodate you without your police registration.'

'I will manage somehow,' I replied. 'As long as I am out of reach of that institute's claws.'

'I'm telling you that the situation there is considerably worse than here. Especially for Jews. And it's going to get worse. There is stricter control over the population; there are more police and gendarmes. And the Hungarian gendarmes are famous for their cruelty. You are more likely to get caught in Hungary than in this country.'

I did not want to show it, but her remarks made me fearful. She scribbled something on a piece of paper. 'If you ever get to Budapest, here is my address. Look me up, I may be able to help you. I have several Jewish friends who are very active in various Jewish charities. I am sure they would help you, if I asked them to.'

On the last day of Passover I said goodbye to Esther, knowing that the next day I had to disappear. Esther again cautioned me against going to Hungary, and gave me an extra five pengo — Hungarian money the equivalent of thirty-five koruna. 'In case you do go there I want you to have some money in Hungarian currency. And for God's sake, be careful, and may God bless you.' With this, she quickly turned away.

The next morning I woke early, but waited for my father to leave before getting out of bed and dressing quickly. I was about to leave when my mother called me. 'Senderl,' she said, addressing me by my pet name. Her voice was quivering. 'Won't you say goodbye to your mother?' I embraced her, then she kissed me on both cheeks and recited the old Hebrew prayer: '*Yevoreheha hashem veyishmereha*' — 'May the Lord bless you and watch over you'. By this point in my life I had become pretty hardened: I never cried. But now, as I left my home for what I believed would be the last time, I felt very much like crying.

I did not go to Hungary. Instead I bought a train ticket to Poprad in Slovakia, where I spent two days. From there I went to Lucinec, where I stayed three days, then on to Zvolen. In Zvolen the head of the Jewish community took pity on me. He suggested I learn a trade and offered to find a family to take me in. The idea appealed to me. So the man took me to a mechanic who had a small car-repair shop in town. The mechanic, a man of about forty, lived in a small house next door to his workshop. He took me to his wife and told her that I would stay with them and learn his trade.

I stayed with the mechanic for three months, working six days a week, from seven in the morning to six in the evening. I never got a penny, but they fed me reasonably well. I slept in a bed with two boys aged five and seven. They protested and made it quite clear to me that I was unwelcome, pinching and kicking me at times. When I returned their kicks and pinches, they'd cry out and complain to their mother. Their father, hearing my explanation, tended to take my side on these occasions, but his wife would come over and give me a few whacks with whatever came to hand. After several such incidents I decided that there was no future in that house for me, and I left.

Banska Bistrica was my next port of call. There I stayed with a shoemaker for four months. As with my previous apprenticeship, I was taught nothing of the trade. It was customary for a boy beginner to be used only as a messenger and cleaner for the first year. If a boy was very keen, he'd learn a little by watching the master or an assistant, and sometimes by offering to do things he knew he was able to do. Often a boy would get a terrible hiding from his master if what he did wasn't good enough. If, however, the master approved of what he'd done, he'd be given another chance when it came around to performing some simple task, all the while not neglecting his cleaning duties and other jobs he was given.

As I only stayed a few months at any place I was apprenticed to, I never learned anything of the trade. I was always kept busy doing messages, cleaning the tools and the workshop, and sometimes helping the mistress clean the house. Sometimes she would take me along shopping, to carry the baskets for her.

I was growing increasingly tired of wandering aimlessly. I had never been a good beggar. I had nursed what money I had most carefully, but the precious little I had to supplement the help I got from kind people was starting to run out.

Dear Sabah,

As I told you over the phone, the boy I think I loved, the first I ever did, fell in Lebanon, together with several of his men on patrol. Ambushed by Chizbulla murderers. I am still devastated. Like most Israelis, I also grieve for the others who fell with Arnon. This tragedy going on in Lebanon is a terrible burden on us all. But what can we do? Leave the area and let the various terrorist groups return and better terrorise our border settlements? Also, there are several thousand Christians who have allied themselves with us. We can't possibly desert them now without making some arrangements to ensure their safety with the Lebanese authorities. We are in the unfortunate situation where we can't win, whatever way we turn. We shouldn't stay, and we can't leave. Not in the present circumstances, while the Lebanese are unwilling to talk to us about a reasonable arrangement for our security and that of our Christian allies.

It turned out that Dad knows Arnon's father, who is also in the building trade, and he went to the funeral and the prayer meeting at their house. I couldn't go to the funeral, as I was the duty officer that day, and anyway, I don't think I'd have had the strength to stand there without betraying my feelings.

Reading about your unhappy childhood helps me put my own unhappiness in perspective. So send more on fast.

All my love to you and Savta,
Esther

9

Margaretta

I felt the need to settle down and attempt to satisfy an increasing itch for knowledge. Knowledge, I knew, was stowed away in the many books I could not read. I could read Hebrew and a little Yiddish, but I was not proficient in either language. I had a flair for languages, and had picked up Hungarian and Slovakian effortlessly. But I was unable to read in either language. If I settled down in a reasonable place, I figured, I might have an opportunity to learn to read and write properly.

After leaving the shoemaker I found work on a farm. I chopped wood for cooking and heating, cleaned the stables and fed the cows and the geese. The farm was owned by a Jewish couple: the man a robust fellow in his early thirties, and his wife a pretty, fragile-looking woman in her early twenties.

The farm covered 1000 hectares or more, some half of it rolling hills — good grazing ground for the many cattle and sheep. They also grew wheat, barley and hay. Nearly a dozen people worked on the property, among them two women of note: one young, about my age, and the other about forty. The latter was a round, hard-faced woman who took a dislike to me immediately. She warned the young girl to keep away from me, saying that I had shifty eyes. But I sensed that this young girl liked me, and decided to ask her to help me learn to read and write.

It took several weeks before I gathered the courage to ask her. It was nearing the end of summer, the days were still long and the evenings were bright. I walked around the farm seeking an opportunity to meet the girl after she finished her work in the big house. Sometimes, I knew, she would go home to her parents in the nearby village.

On one of these occasions I waited for her, hiding behind a tree. As she passed, I caught her sleeve, startling her. 'Hi. My name is Alex. What's yours?'

For a moment the girl just stood there. Then, looking down at her shoes, she said softly, 'Margaretta.'

'Margaretta,' I repeated. 'My name is Alexander. As I told you already . . . ' I was fumbling for words.

'I know your name and you know mine, too.'

'Yes,' I said, my cheeks flushing. 'I just

didn't know what to say first. I'd like to talk to you.'

Margaretta looked up at me for a second, then lowered her gaze back to her shoes, waiting to hear what I wanted to talk to her about. 'How old are you, Margaretta?' I asked.

'Sixteen,' she replied. 'Why do you ask?'

'I just wondered if you were younger or older than I am. I am only fifteen. Did you go to school, Margaretta?'

'Yes. I only left two years ago.'

'I never went to school much, and anyway it was a Russian school. I didn't learn much there. But I'd like to learn to read and write. And I wondered if you would be willing to help me?'

Margaretta stood there silently, eyes to the ground, twisting her foot for a while. Then she looked up, regarding me seriously. She seemed to be trying to make her mind up about something. Next thing, she turned to continue on her way home, as if I had never even spoken. I grabbed hold of her wrist.

'Please wait,' I pleaded. 'You don't have to help me if you don't want to. But would you just talk to me sometimes when you are free?'

At this she stopped and, looking me straight in the face, with a hint of a smile, said, 'I don't mind helping you to learn to read and write. And I will also talk to you when I am free. If you promise to keep it a secret.'

'Oh yes!' I exclaimed. 'I won't tell a living soul.'

'All right then. Let's go over to that clump of trees. We can sit under one of them and talk a little if you want to.' I followed her, charged with excitement.

We met three or four times a week, if the weather permitted. I brought along my exercise book and showed her the letters I copied line after line until I thought I had them right. Margaretta checked my work and commented on it briefly, saying it was good or not so good, or occasionally writing words and short sentences for me to copy. We sat and talked about our lives, sometimes for hours. Margaretta was surprised to learn that I was a Jew and yet came from such an impoverished family. 'I always thought that Jews were rich,' she told me. 'Some extremely rich. I certainly never saw a really poor Jew. All the Jews in this area are well off, you know. The owner of this farm is also a Jew.'

'I know, Margaretta, I know. I have heard this story many times from many people. Some people don't believe me when I tell them about my family, about how poor we are. And there are many families living in similar circumstances in the area I come from. But my family has the distinction of being the poorest of the poor. I met people who thought I only pretended to be Jewish. God only knows why anyone in his right mind would pretend to be a Jew! But then, maybe they thought I was not in my right mind.'

'You know, Alex, I believe you are telling me the truth, but many people wouldn't credit this story. Even the way you talk, you don't sound like any fifteen-year-old I have known.'

'I don't think many fifteen-year-olds have lived the life I have.'

We sat quietly for a while, contemplating each other. Suddenly Margaretta laughed.

'What's so funny?' I asked.

'I don't really know,' Margaretta replied. 'But it seemed terribly funny to me, the two of us sitting here looking at each other, not knowing what to say.' She began laughing again.

Soon both of us were laughing uproariously, without reason or care. After a while I stopped and said, 'You know, Margaretta, you are a beautiful girl, especially when you laugh.'

She stopped laughing and looked soberly at me. 'Why did you say that?'

'I don't know. No reason, except maybe because it's true.'

'I think you are only making fun of me. I'm not beautiful at all. I know I am not ugly, but nobody ever said that I am beautiful.'

'Well, you are still young. You will be told many times, by many men.'

'Now you are talking like a fortune-teller.'

'I am no fortune-teller, Margaretta. I just have eyes, and I can see you in a few years developing into an even greater beauty than you are now.'

'Oh but you are a big flatterer!' She smiled and hit me lightly on the arm.

Over the next two weeks I went in vain to our secret meeting place. Margaretta did not show up. Over the following fortnight the weather was unfavourable for outdoor meetings. I tried to stave off sadness by using my free time to practise my writing skills, which I considered of the utmost importance. I would write a certain letter or word fifty times or more, until I thought it was right.

I might have made greater progress had Margaretta helped me, even if only by meeting with me. I missed her company and the sympathy I felt she had for me.

The men I worked with mostly ignored me as soon as they found out I was a Jew. Slovak nationalism was on the rise throughout the land, influenced by the vile wind blowing from Nazi Germany, and with it came the grit of anti-Semitism. Slovak politicians, probably in German pay, proposed the dismembering of the Czechoslovakian republic and the establishment of an independent Slovakia. A sizeable German minority living in what used to be Bohemia were demanding what they called sudeten gebiet, the transfer into German hands of the territory in which most of this German minority lived. At the same time, in what used to be Pod Karpatska Russ, agitators, no doubt also in German pay, were trying to rouse the Ruthenian population to declare themselves Ukrainians and demand to secede from the Czechoslovakian republic. While their various agents inside Czechoslovakia worked hard to undermine the integrity of the state from within, Nazi Germany massed troops on the border to threaten and intimidate from without.

This was the situation in Czechoslovakia at the time I was considering my future at the farm. Having seemingly lost the only friend I had in the place, I found myself once again contemplating moving on — to where, I had no idea. Margaretta kept out of my way and sight for reasons I could not fathom. I thought and rethought every word I had said to her at our last meeting but could not find in them any grounds for her avoiding me. I had not insulted her, nor tried to seduce her; I would not have known how, anyway. So why was she avoiding me? No matter how much I thought it through, I could not come up with a plausible answer to the riddle.

While I pondered my future, Hitler decided it for me. The German army invaded Czechoslovakia, occupying Czechia and Moravia while leaving the Slovaks in charge of Slovakia. One morning the owner of the farm called me into his office and said to me, 'I would have liked to keep you here as long as you wanted to stay. But you must have heard what has happened. In the circumstances, my wife and I are thinking of leaving. It is only a question of where to.' He pulled out his wallet and counted out 500 koruna, a tidy sum at any time. 'Here — take this and leave as soon as you can. Your best bet would be Hungary. The Hungarians have occupied the part of the country you come from, so you won't have any problem entering Hungary. We may try to go there ourselves.' We shook hands and wished each other luck.

It didn't take me long to gather my belongings and head for the railway station in the neighbouring village. As I was about to exit the farm gate I heard Margaretta calling after me. She looked excited and anxious.

'I'm very sorry you are leaving,' she said breathlessly. 'I wish you were a Catholic, then you could have stayed and maybe we could have been married. I would have liked to marry you, you know. But my parents made me swear by the cross that I would not meet you again. They said you could have gotten me into trouble and would not have married me. And anyway, I could never have married you because you are a Jew. I know all that isn't as my parents told me, but they are my parents and I must obey them. I had to tell you this before you left. I wouldn't want you to be angry at me.' With this, she said goodbye, turned and ran off back towards the house.

I stood for some time, leaning on the gate. I wasn't exactly shocked. I could imagine her parents, though I had never seen them, and understood their concern for their daughter. The prejudice wasn't unexpected. But her confession touched a nerve: the tears came streaming down my face. I had never so much as kissed her cheek! How I would have loved to embrace and kiss her. But it was not to be. Slowly I collected myself, wiped my face and set off to the railway station.

My dearest Esther,

I am now at the end of an era in my story. I didn't realise it then, but that was the end of the Czechoslovakia republic, and the end of the good days (if ever there were any) of its Jewish citizens. From here on their situation slowly but surely deteriorated. My own situation changed little at the beginning, though I sensed more than comprehended the harshness and authoritarian nature of the Hungarian regime.

I could probably have written a bit more than this, but I recently had a bit of a health scare: my lungs suddenly filled with fluid one night. I drove to the hospital, hardly able to breathe. Within a couple of hours they drained close to 5 litres of fluid out of me. After that I felt much better. I still had to stay in hospital for a week, however. Poor Savta was terribly worried, and hardly left my bedside.

Now, two weeks later, I still have a bit of a problem with my breathing, but I am slowly coming good. At times I manage to take a deep breath, which is very satisfying. You'd be surprised to learn what can make a person happy! I didn't tell your parents about all this — I didn't want to worry them. You don't have to tell them either; let this be our little secret.

As soon as I feel well enough I'll get on with my writing and send you some more of my escapades. In the meantime, be well, and look after yourself. Savta and I send you our heartfelt love.

Your loving Sabah

10

Food and Friendship

Overnight, I transformed myself from a Czechoslovakian into a Hungarian. But I remained a Jew, just as I had always been. The only difference was that in Czechoslovakia I had been a '*zatraceni zid*' — a 'damned Jew'; now, in Hungary, I became a '*budos zsido*' — a 'stinking Jew'. It was hard to judge the benefit of the distinction.

Since 1936, Hungarian legislation forbade Jews from holding government office, excluded them from various business activities and kept them out of higher education. Thus the Hungarians enshrined their anti-Semitism in laws. For the Czechs, on the other hand, anti-Semitism was a folk tradition, reinforced by the Church. And as the Czechs were economically better off than the Hungarians, their hatred of the Jew was a lot milder.

All over the world, it seemed, the degree of anti-Semitism demonstrated by a community was relative to the economic standing of the people. Where a populace was worse off, anti-Semitism was more virulent.

But these problems did not matter much to me. What I had to worry about when I came to Hungary was the law of vagrancy, which was a great deal harsher and more rigidly enforced there than it had been in Czechoslovakia. I had to keep my eyes well open, so as not to be surprised by the regular patrols of gendarmes on bicycles. As soon as I saw a gendarme in the distance, I ran for cover. To make things more difficult, people in Hungary were not very keen to offer a vagrant a place to sleep, and would often notify the authorities.

I was quickly forced to change my mode of operation. I gave up walking from village to village and instead travelled by train from town to town. Even that was not absolutely safe. Officers would sometimes patrol the trains, checking the identification papers which every citizen over the age of sixteen had to carry when leaving home.

Upon arriving in a town, the first thing I did was look for the synagogue. There was at least one in every Hungarian town of any size. There I'd find people who would inform me as to who would be likely to contribute to my wellbeing, and where they could be found. According to Hungarian law, a person staying away from home for more than one night had to go to a police station and fill out a form stating where he was staying. Because of this I could not stay in any place more than twenty-four hours.

I kept moving from place to place, town to town, arriving one day at a little town called Tata-Tovaros. Here the local Jewish baker offered me an apprenticeship. By this stage I was fairly tired of playing hide and seek with the gendarmerie, so after considering the offer for a few minutes, I accepted it.

Tata-Tovaros was situated between Gyor, a fair-sized industrial town, and Budapest, the capital of Hungary. In the beginning, Tata and Tovaros were two townships, Tata down in the valley, and Tovaros up on top of a hill, which got its name from the lake situated on the plateau. The united township had about 6000 inhabitants, among them about a hundred Jews, mainly tradesmen and small merchants. Of these Jews, perhaps half a dozen were landowners. But they only managed to hold on to their property by employing a 'good Christian' who officially bought it off them, against certain securities, and managed the property, paying the proceeds to the Jewish owner for a good return. According to the 'Jew laws', a Jew could not own land except what he could cultivate himself.

There was a veritable industry of such arrangements, since not only was ownership of land forbidden to Jews but they were also excluded from many industries, and even from selling certain merchandise over which the government held a monopoly. In order to be able to trade in articles like alcohol, tobacco and matches, a Jew had to have a partner whose Christian roots went back at least three generations. Thus those businesses too small to carry a partner were forced to find someone willing to act as a front man.

Most of the trades were still open to Jews, however. The baker who supplied bread for most of the little township of Tata-Tovaros was fairly secure in his position, for the time being. For whatever reason, though, he had been unable to find an apprentice, and was therefore willing to take a chance on a young vagrant. This way, he also appeared a good Jew, providing another Jew with a job at a time when jobs were hard to come by.

I accepted the offer of an apprenticeship to the baker on a trial basis — I had some misgivings on account of the hard work I imagined it to be. I knew I had a rather weak constitution as a result of having been malnourished for most of my life, and I wasn't sure that I would be able to do the job adequately.

We settled into a routine. The baker would wake me at half past two every morning and I would work, with short breaks, until about two in the afternoon. My master went to bed for a half-hour rest at four o'clock in the morning, but I had to stay awake and watch the fire in the oven. This was for six days a week. On Sundays I was free and, having nothing better to do, and little energy to do it, I rested that day. The food was good and sufficient in quantity — one great plus. Not since leaving the farm in Slovakia had I had such quantities of tasty and nourishing food, and I savoured it.

I might have stayed on there and become a baker had it not been for the baker's wife. She was twenty-eight, tall and attractive. He, on the other hand, was a heavy-set forty-year-old, short and balding, and not what could be called handsome. There were plenty of young men who fancied the baker's wife, and she had a tendency to give in to her admirers. She was apparently not satisfied with what her husband had to offer.

Every time the baker found out that his wife had had a fling with another man, it was I who suffered for it. Not daring to punish his wife, the baker hurled all the abuse at me. Sometimes he even slapped my face for no good reason. I was not amused.

I persevered for nearly a year. Then, in May 1940, I was notified by the local Jewish community that I would get one of the two places reserved for their community's poor children to go on a four-week holiday on the shores of Lake Balaton.

I was elated! I had never had a holiday in my life, and the prospect of one filled me with joyous anticipation. I was nearly sixteen years old, and the good food I had regularly been receiving had filled me out. I looked healthier and stronger than I had ever been.

A week before I was due to take the holiday, a woman came to see me with her son, a lad of about twelve. He too had been selected to go on the camp. The woman asked me to look after her little boy, who had never been away from her before. I looked at the little boy and his mother. Both were reasonably well-dressed — better than I had ever been — and both seemed well-fed. Were these the poor people here? I promised the lady that I would look after her boy, though I thought the request unusual.

Although I didn't even know this boy's name, I resented him. As soon as we were on the train, travelling to Budapest where we would link up with children coming from all over Hungary, I ignored the little fellow. If he tried to speak, I scowled at him. At the

Budapest railway station we were met by officials from the Jewish Welfare Society, who took us to the carriage where other Jewish children were already settled. I looked with contempt at the little boy who had been placed in my care, sitting there full of fear and incomprehension, wiping the occasional tear from his face. I felt no pity for him and made no attempt to reassure him in any way. *I* had suffered when I was cast from my home and my family; who had *I* been able to turn to for comfort?

The more this sad boy sought my sympathy, the more violently I rejected him. At the camp at Balaton Boglar I did not want to have a bar of the little fellow, who was bewildered and frightened by all these strange children. Knowing no-one else, he tried to stick to me. I would frequently push him away, sometimes with a punch or a kick. It was a rare sense of superiority that I enjoyed.

I made friends with two boys from Budapest, both about my age, and both named Bandi. One, a rather large, flabby boy, was Fodor Bandi; the other, a red-haired gangly youngster, was aptly named Veres (meaning 'red') Bandi. The fathers of both Bandis were clerks and so were considered poor. I was most confused seeing these 'poor' boys: they were well fed and nicely dressed, and both attended high school. Where I had come from, poor meant being dressed in rags, being half-starved and having hardly any education. Children looking as these children did were considered well-off where I came from. Despite my many years of wandering among these people, I had little idea of their lives and standards of living. And I did not understand the relativity of poverty.

The two Bandis, who had been friends for years, once came upon the scene as I was beating my little protégé. At first they felt embarrassed, but then Fodor asked, 'How would you like being beaten by a bigger fellow?' I felt ashamed and, not wanting to upset my relationship with the two Bandis, tried to make a joke of it. But the Bandis would not buy that. They made me promise to be kind to the poor defenceless child. They also promised to look after the little fellow, and henceforth took him under their wing.

This turn of events immediately changed my attitude to little Feri. I began treating him the way the two Bandis expected me to. Poor Feri was happy as a lark! Once he started to enjoy himself he proved to be a very pleasant, well-mannered and intelligent boy. I began to like him. A few days after this turn-around in our relationship, Feri turned to me and said, 'I will never tell my parents what happened at the beginning. I will only tell them how nice it was after.' I could not help smiling, and embraced the boy who clung to me long after I was ready to let go.

I had a ball. It had been a long time since I had had the opportunity to act my age — in fact, I could not recall when there was ever such a time. I hardly ever had the time or energy to play as a child, being more or less hungry most of the time. My mind had been focused mainly on ways and means to satisfy the gnawing in my gut. This was the first time I could eat as much as I liked without having to worry about what the cost would be, or how I might have to pay for it. It occurred to me that there probably wasn't another kid in the camp who was able to appreciate so well what they were being given here. When I tried to talk about it to the two Bandis, they looked at me in puzzlement.

Another delightful experience for me was my new friendships. For a long time now I hadn't had anyone to confide in. Suddenly, here were two friends who were happy to share thoughts and feelings with me, even if they couldn't always understand the way my mind worked or the values I held.

All too soon the four weeks were up and we had to return home. The group travelled together to Budapest, and from there each was put on the train that would take him or her home. I had difficulty holding back the tears as I parted from my newly found friends, promising to seek them out one day.

Feri and I were very quiet during the train ride to Tata-Tovaros. We arrived early in the afternoon and I escorted little Feri home before going back to the bakery. By then I had decided to leave for Budapest as soon as possible. I had had enough of the exhausting labour of the bakery and more than enough of the baker's deflected anger and frustration.

It was Friday when I returned, and I was afraid to tell the baker of my decision to leave straightaway, fearing he might turn me out immediately. On Sunday night as we worked preparing the dough for the bake, I told the baker that I wanted to leave. He wasn't surprised. All he said was, 'I thought you might come back with something like that. I won't even ask you why. Only when.'

'As soon as possible.'

'Do you mean today, tomorrow, next week?'

'If it would suit you, sir, I'd like to work this week through and leave next Monday.'

'All right. If that's what you want. Now let's get on with the job.'

That week dragged on endlessly, but it did give me time to contemplate my immediate future. I remembered Esther and the address she had given me in Chust nearly two years previously. Perhaps she would be able to help me find a reasonable job and a place to live? I had managed to save most of my weekly pay, about one pengo per week, and now had about forty pengo. I figured that that would be enough to live on for at least a month.

With my week nearly up, I went into the town for the last time. Suddenly I found myself standing in front of young Feri's mother.

'I was just on my way to the bakery to see you,' said the fragile little woman. 'I haven't had the opportunity to thank you for looking after my Feri.'

I was embarrassed, remembering how I had first treated her son. I murmured something about not having done anything to deserve thanks, but the little woman insisted that she was very grateful. 'He came back looking better than he ever has,' she said. 'And he said he had a wonderful time, in part thanks to you. Here is a little something, a small token of our appreciation.' With this, she pulled out of her bag a neatly wrapped shirt. 'Wear it in good health.' She smiled, and left me standing there with my guilt.

On my last night at Tata-Tovaros I hardly slept a wink. I heard the baker starting a couple of hours earlier than usual, to do the jobs both of us had done together. He made plenty of noise. I could hear him yelling and cursing his bad luck. Eventually the sun came up and I got up, washed at the tap in the yard, collected my few belongings and left, without saying goodbye.

I caught the early train to Budapest and arrived at the western railway station before ten in the morning. It was the biggest town I had ever been to. The traffic was tremendous, on streets wider than I had encountered before. Trams, buses, vans and motorcars rushed by. Now and again a huge dray drawn by powerful horses carried beer barrels along the street. I could not take my eyes off the commotion — people in their hundreds rushing around the wide footpaths in every direction.

I looked around bewildered, wondering how I would find my way in this huge metropolis. I had Esther's phone number, but I had no idea how to use a phone. I looked up the addresses of the two Bandis and saw that Veres Bandi lived at Podmanicky Street, which, as fortune would have it, was the very street corner I was standing on. Number 49 was only a few minutes' walk from where I stood.

I went up to the second floor and rang the

bell of the flat. I heard young Bandi's voice saying, 'Coming!'

Bandi could not have been more surprised. 'You are lucky to have caught me at home. I was just preparing to go to Fodor's place. You want to come along?' Then something occurred to him: 'Have you had something to eat yet?' I hesitated to reply, and Bandi got the message. He made a big salami sandwich and we headed off.

The tram ride from Veres' place to Fodor's was only a few minutes long — time enough for me to scoff my sandwich. Fodor was no less surprised to see me than his friend. I told the pair all about the baker and my decision to come to Budapest. The two looked at each other, puzzled and a little embarrassed. In retrospect, I doubt they ever expected me to make good the offer to visit them, let alone show up so soon looking for a new home.

'What will you do, now you are here?' they pressed me. 'Where are you going to live?'

I showed them the money I had saved, and told them about Esther, who I hoped would help me find work. They snapped into action. Fodor led me to his phone to call Esther.

Bandi dialled the number I had been given, and as the phone started to ring he handed me the receiver. I took it hesitantly. I had no idea what to say or how to say it, but I was granted no time to consider these things for a voice said, 'Hello?' It was a young female. She repeated, 'Hello? Who is this?'

Startled out of my fear, I answered, 'My name is Alexander. I would like to speak to Mrs Endrey.'

'I am sorry,' the same voice returned, 'my mother is not at home. She is away for the week. If you ring next week at this time, you may find her here.'

I felt dejected as I replaced the receiver on the phone. I had been counting on Esther's help. My two friends looked uncomfortable, watching me, sensing my feelings, wondering how they could help. My problems were to some extent incomprehensible to them. They had no idea how one went about finding a place to sleep. As for a job, it was not yet on their agenda. Besides, when the time came, their parents would find something for them. But they still had two years of schooling before that problem arose.

'I wonder if you boys know someone who lets rooms?' I asked. They looked at each other blankly. This was another problem they had never encountered. The boys shook their heads once more.

'Do either of you know anyone who could tell us?'

Fodor suddenly brightened up. 'Let's ask

the caretaker!' he said.

Down we went to the ground floor flat belonging to the caretaker, but before we had even raised our fists to knock on his door, out he came and looked critically at us. The two Bandis were familiar to him, but I was a complete stranger. It was his duty to be aware of everyone who visited the block of flats, which comprised some twenty-five units. If the police asked, he had to give an account not only of the people living in the building, but also of who their friends were, who visited them and how often.

Looking hard at me, he asked, 'What can I do for you, young sirs?'

'Our friend here has just arrived from the country and he is looking for a room to rent,' said Fodor. 'But we have no idea how to find one. Maybe you could help us, please?'

The caretaker scratched his balding head. 'I don't know of anyone who lets rooms, but I think if you bought a newspaper you will probably find an advertisement offering rooms to rent.'

We soon found a room in a neighbouring street, some ten minutes' walk from Fodor's place. A middle-aged couple living in a two-room flat wanted to let it for five pengo a week. Although five pengo was a lot of money, I liked the place, if only for its proximity to Fodor — a point of reference in this huge, unknown city. And the couple seemed amiable enough. I took the flat.

The rest of the day was spent being shown around the city by the boys and becoming familiarised with the area. Then we scoured the newspaper for jobs. Few were on offer, and those that were had been filled by early morning. Apparently people bought newspapers at midnight as they came off the presses. Hours before the advertisers arrived at their offices, hopefuls would wait in line to be interviewed. By the time *we* arrived at an office that advertised for unskilled workers, the people laughed at us: *now* you come?!

I was not worried; I still had great faith in Esther. I looked forward to the Monday when I would be able to see her.

One night during the week I was invited to dinner at Fodor's, where I met his older brother and his parents. The father was a stocky man with thinning hair, a small moustache and a cool disposition. He greeted me casually and then had not a word more to say to me. Fodor's brother showed even less interest in his younger brother's protégé: he didn't even want to be introduced. By contrast to the two men, Fodor's mother greeted me warmly and inquired with real interest about my situation.

Dinner was a fairly formal affair. The table was set elegantly, the cutlery and dishes were beautiful, and I was served a variety of foods, some of which I had never before seen or tasted. If the Bandis were the poor people of Budapest, what were the rich like, I wondered? I felt ill at ease and made up my mind never to accept such invitations again. This was far from my own family's table, where the only utensils we had to eat with were spoons. I had to watch how my tablemates used their cutlery and tried awkwardly to imitate them. If they noticed, they didn't show it — all except Fodor's brother, who seemed to enjoy my discomfort. Fodor's mother tried to make me comfortable by a word or two now and again, and by piling my dish high with fine food. She seemed to have a lot of sympathy for me.

That night I slept badly. I tossed and turned in my bed for a long time, trying to make sense of my experience with the Bandis. My father had said that only goyim (non-Jews) ate with knives. But here was a Jewish family who ate with knives and forks. What did this mean? Despite the coolness of Fodor's brother and father, I sensed that these were good, decent people. Fodor's father was formal and detached, but he created no tension like my father had in my household. This old man seemed tired after his day's work, but not forbidding, like my father, who was always tired and tense though he never did a day's work in his life. Another thing that made me restless in my bed was my memory of Fodor's mother. I had noticed her glancing with pride at her sons as they spoke, smiling at them and watching them eat. She must also have been tired, having done her domestic chores on top of her day's work at the office, but she showed no sign of it, and was cheerful throughout the meal and after it. I was reminded of my own mother and the love and care and energy she always found.

I sighed. What luck, to be born into a family such as this! How nice it would have been, had I been so lucky. I imagined myself going off to school in the morning, nicely dressed, with a nourishing sandwich in my bag, and coming home to a warm house and a good meal. Maybe from now on I would be lucky and never feel hunger again. Maybe, I dreamed, I could start a new life: a life without hiding from police or gendarmerie, a life with money and a job and the experiences of normal people.

Unfortunately, this was not to be. In the days and years to come, life for everybody changed. What had been accepted as normal became little more than a fond memory.

My dearest Sabah,

I dearly hope these lines find you in good health and you don't have any health problems in the future.

One secret deserves another, and here is mine: I am going out with a boy, a Yemenite boy, my own age. He is only a sergeant in the military police, but he is a nice, quiet fellow and I like him. After a couple of weeks of knowing each other he asked me to marry him. Of course I couldn't give him an answer. For one thing, I'd first have to introduce him to my parents and ask their permission. (This is how I was brought up. I'd do nothing behind their backs.) For another thing, I haven't forgotten Arnon. His death is a wound that won't heal too quickly.

I am otherwise well. I like the job I am doing (I won't tell you what it is). I still have some fourteen months to serve, including the extra year I have to serve as an officer. I am a full lieutenant now; if you were here and served in the Reserve, you'd have to salute me!

Please, not a word to my parents about my new friend. For the time being I am still thinking how and when to invite him home.

All my love to you and Savta,
Esther

11

To God's Ears

In the beginning it looked like my dream was going to come true. Esther received me in her palatial home on the Monday. She was as kind and gracious as she had been the first time I met her. She rang several people on my behalf, and arranged for me to meet a certain Mrs Revesz the next morning.

Mrs Revesz was a beautiful middle-aged woman, grey-haired but with a kind, youthful face. She listened to my life story without interrupting. When I had finished she told me that her organisation was in the process of setting up a home for Jewish apprentices. It was due to open within the next ten days, and she assured me that there would be a place for me in that home. With the help of the organisation I would be matched with a trade which suited me, and apprenticed.

I was elated. My faith had paid off. I ran to tell the two Bandis of my good fortune, and they shared my delight.

A week later I received a telegram ordering me to present myself at a given address where this home for apprentices was set up. On arrival I was received by a large man in a grey suit who introduced himself as the manager of the home. I was taken to a room where there were six beds arranged on two sides of the room, shown my bed and a small chest of drawers for personal belongings, and introduced to the rules of conduct and a schedule of the home's routine. There was a long list explaining what one was allowed to do and what was forbidden in one's free time.

I was the first to arrive, but by midday most of the boys had settled into the home. There were boys both younger and older than me. One of the older boys, an apprentice to a dental technician, considered himself already a man and showed his contempt for the younger kids in every way possible. His name was Tibor Gelber and he came from a small town in eastern Hungary. For some reason I wanted to be friends with him. Tibor looked down his nose at this scrawny little fellow that I was and shooed me off unceremoniously. But I would not give up so easily. One day I asked him why he refused to be my friend. He ignored me. But after I had repeated the question several times he said to me, 'Because I don't like you, you are not my type.'

'I don't understand,' I insisted. 'Why?'

145

'Because you are a primitive little bastard and I can't stand you. End of discussion.'

I didn't try to be friends with Tibor Gelber after that.

During the first week I was sent to an institute to assess my suitability for a trade. It was suggested I learn shoemaking, tailoring or fitting. I was sent first to a Jewish shoemaker in the fifth district, a well-to-do area of Budapest. The shoemaker was a kindly man and was quite willing to teach me the trade. But it soon became apparent that I was not made to be a shoemaker. Mr Schwartz liked me but could not overlook the fact that I had no inclination to learn the trade. He told me, 'We are wasting each other's time. You had better look for another trade, this one is not for you.'

Next they found me a tailor's apprentice-ship. This lasted no longer than the shoemaking.

Several weeks passed before a fitter's workshop was found for me. Again it was a Jewish firm, headed by an elderly gentleman named Sipos. His son, a tall, good-looking man of thirty, was managing the workshop. When I presented myself to him, he looked at me dubiously.

'You sure you want to learn this trade, young man?' he asked. I nodded. Fitting appealed to me more than the other trades I had tried.

'All right then. Be here at seven tomorrow morning.' With that I was dismissed.

I went gladly every morning, and did what I was told by the senior tradesmen. I did my duties promptly and efficiently to the extent I was able to, and I befriended the two older apprentices. Everything pointed to the fact that I had found my niche. The younger Mr Sipos talked to his father about me, commending my keenness. My future seemed secure.

But when Mr Sipos went to register me with the Apprenticeship Commission and book me in to the proper school, it turned out that for a boy to be legally apprenticed he had to present a certificate showing he had attended at least four years of school and had a reasonable ability to read and write Hungarian. I could only show a certificate from Grade 2, and even that was incomplete. It showed that I had failed all subjects except singing. On this basis I could not be awarded an apprenticeship, and my application was refused.

I was told I could study for a year or two, privately. If I passed an examination of the subjects taught in Grade 4, I could apply again for an apprenticeship. But in two years I would be eighteen, and at that age I would not be eligible for an apprenticeship. For several months Mrs Revesz, the Jewish Welfare Society and the manager of the home of apprentices tried everything possible to enable me to learn the trade I chose. But there was no legal way to do it. And no self-respecting Hungarian Jew would do anything illegal.

Thus I was compelled to leave the home for apprentices and find myself a place to live. Old Mr Sipos promised to keep me on as an assistant tradesman, however. In this manner I could learn the trade and maybe even pass the necessary exams to become a tradesman.

When I was forced to leave the apprentices' home, much of the light went out of my life. But, like a cat, I landed on my feet and moved on. I busied myself studying to read and write Hungarian. In this, the two Bandis, who shared my disappointment, were of great help. They supplied me with books and checked my work, correcting my mistakes. I managed to reoccupy the room I had first rented with the Bandis' help, and was glad for the little familiarity with which my landlords received me.

I tried to settle down to begin a new chapter of my life, yet again, only this time under vastly better conditions. I had a nice sum of money saved, plus a sum that was given to me by the Jewish Welfare Society to allow me to equip myself with the basic necessities after leaving the home. I had a more or less secure job which I liked. And I had the friendship of the two Bandis.

At times, the differences in culture and upbringing between the two Bandis and myself seemed huge. The two boys, like most other Hungarian Jewish youngsters, saw themselves as Hungarians first and Jews second. I, on the other hand, saw myself as nothing but a Jew. I sought to strengthen my Jewish roots by joining the Zionist youth movement Hashomer Hatzair. The 'Hashy', as it was called, was officially banned in Hungary, but it was still active unofficially. The two Bandis would have nothing to do with this movement. Not only did it seek to awaken their Jewish identity at the expense of their Hungarian nationality, it was also an extreme left-wing movement. They, like most Jewish boys in Hungary, were members of the Levente, a patriotic Hungarian youth move-ment which taught military skills and had right-wing leanings. They tried to convince me to join their group, but like them with the Hashy, I would not have a bar of it.

I was unable to understand how it was that Hungarian Jews were able to show such patriotism when they were blatantly treated as an inferior, alien group. Since 1936, Jews had not been allowed to play any part in the country's political life, and by stages their role in cultural and commercial spheres had become more and more restricted. Angry clouds were gathering around, boding ill for Hungarian Jews, and yet they stuck to their belief and tried to prove their devotion to the Hungarian nation in every possible (and at times impossible) way. Hungarian Jews only spoke Hungarian. Some of the best Hungarian poetry was written by Hungarian Jewish poets. However, such acts of patriotism were largely spurned by most Hungarians and their leadership. Yet the Jews ignored the signs, and, carrying on as usual, placed their faith in a better future ahead. They could not have been more misguided.

The shoemaker who had tried, unsuccessfully, to teach me his trade, had a son around my age, and we struck up a friendship. Michael Schwartz was a clever high school student who, like his father, was a most patriotic Hungarian. He had great faith in the country and its people, despite the vicious anti-Semitic policies of the time. Any tale of Jewish nationalism, or Zionism, cut no ice with him.

In spite of this difference of opinion, I liked

to go to the Schwartz home to soak up the warmth of a loving family atmosphere. At times I could not help making comparisons: any free time Michael's parents had, they spent with him and his sister. Here were parents endowed with understanding, devotion and patience. I could hardly believe that such a household really existed. At the time I failed to realise that a father earning good money and providing for only two children could afford to put so much time and energy into creating a happy family. All I felt was my own acute misfortune.

By that time World War II was well in progress. The Germans had their huge successes in Eastern and Western Europe; all of Western Europe was in their hands. In the East the two dictatorships of Russia and Germany had divided Poland between them, and within days of the German occupation of their part of Poland, terrible stories of the persecution of Jews started to circulate in Hungary. Some Jews managed to escape into Hungary, and they told tales of horror. German soldiers had beaten, robbed and humiliated Jews in the streets and in their homes, and sometimes even murdered them. The Hungarian Jewish establishment tried to suppress these tales, which they could not believe and did not wish to. But the rumours could not be stopped and they spread rapidly across the country.

One evening while visiting the Schwartz household, Paul, the father, suddenly turned to me and said, 'You've made me curious about your idea of Zionism. Tell me what you know about it — its aim, its politics.'

'I can try, though it's not easy to explain to a fellow Jew with such a different background as yours.' (The shoemaker was not a religious Jew, yet I didn't want to offend him by saying that he was Jewish only by birth.) 'Zionism starts with the premise that Judaism isn't only a religion, it's a nationality. It is unique in the sense that it is the only nationality which is so closely tied to a religion. You can be a Hungarian or a German or a Pole and belong to any one of the Christian religions. But you cannot be a Jew and belong to a different religion, even though you can be one and not belong to any religion at all.' I saw that Paul was smiling, and hastened to add, 'That is, in the eyes of the Zionist Jews.'

'And who is this Herzl we hear about?' asked Paul.

'Herzl started the Zionist movement just before the turn of the century. He was a Hungarian but lived in Vienna, working as a correspondent for a Viennese newspaper at the time of the famous, or rather infamous,

152

trial of a French Jew, Captain Dreyfus. In a rigged trial, Dreyfus was found guilty of spying for the Germans and was sentenced to life imprisonment on Devil's Island. If it hadn't been for the efforts of a dedicated group of French intellectuals, lead by Emile Zola, Dreyfus would have died there. But what Herzl saw was that it was Dreyfus's Jewishness which was on trial. He became convinced that the only solution to this timeless problem was Zionism.'

'But it sounds like Zionism is all about ideas,' interjected Paul. 'What do Zionists think Jews should *do*?'

'Well, Zionism begins with what our enemies call the Jewish problem, and it offers a solution: to recall the Jewish people to their ancient home, which we call Eretz Yisrael and others call Palestine, and there rebuild our national identity.

'Zionists have shown that in most nations normal social and economic structures have a broad base of peasantry and unskilled workers, a smaller proportion of tradesmen, then upwards to groups such as merchants and traders, with a small section of intellectuals at the top. Herzl pointed out that the Jewish people had almost the reverse of this structure, with a large body of merchants and intellectuals, and only a small body of tradesmen or peasantry. He said that in order to become a normal nation again, as we were 2000 years ago, we must reshape our national structure and resettle our land. We must become the workers of our land again.'

The Schwartz family listened to all this with bewilderment and fascination. When I was finished, they remained quiet for a fair length of time. Eventually Paul said, 'I must confess, I had no idea about Dreyfus, or Herzl. You have given me a lot of food for thought. Something that needs some time to digest.'

Young Michael turned to me with a new respect and said, 'Where did you get all that stuff from?' Before I could answer he asked another question: 'Why do you think the Jewish social structure turned out the way it did?'

I paused for a moment before answering. 'For two main reasons, I think. The first is that Jews have been persecuted in most countries for almost 2000 years. Until fairly recently, Jews had to pay special taxes, sometimes for the very air they breathed. In order to pay those taxes they needed money, which could not be had from tilling the soil. The other reason was the fact that in most Christian countries Jews were not allowed to own land and were excluded from the various trade unions. Only in the last hundred years or so have Jews been allowed into commerce in Europe. Money-lending was one of the very few opportunities left to them, since this was forbidden to Christians, so a large number of Jews became bankers, or usurers as they were more often called.'

'And how do you know all of this?' Michael asked again.

'This is what they teach us at our youth movement.'

Paul had been silent some minutes, pondering what I had been saying, but now he came at me anew. 'You know, Jews may have been a single nation in our early history, but for many centuries they have ceased to be one. Judaism has become a religion only. We are members of the nations we live amongst. What do I have in common with a Russian Jew? Or a Turkish one, for that matter? But I have a lot in common with Hungarians, whose language I speak. I share in the culture of this country, and have no other. I feel I am a Hungarian, just like any other.'

'You are right, Mr Schwartz, you have nothing in common with Jews of another country. But that is because you do not practise your Judaism. Nonetheless, you have been pronounced a Jew by those who hate Jews, on the basis that your parents were also

Jewish. Had you been educated as a Jew you would have plenty in common with your brothers in other countries: a past history, a common culture and even a common language.'

I was flattered by their silence. I felt I had made an impression.

However, in time I realised that what I had said did not change anything for the Schwartz family. Paul stuck to his beliefs and went on acting as he had before. The children, in particular Michael, might have harboured some doubts about their father's views on the subject, but they loved and respected him too much to bring their concerns to voice.

* * *

As time passed I improved rapidly with my reading and writing. I spent a lot of my free time reading books and pamphlets which my madrich (instructor) from the Zionist movement had given me, on the subject of Jewish history and the teachings of the socialist Zionist scholars. I seldom saw the Bandis, who were also busy with their studies.

By 1941, a year after my arrival in Budapest, and two years after the start of war, I became increasingly restless. Somehow I felt I should be a part of the fight against the Nazis. I did not feel safe in Hungary, seeing how the Germans were killing off the Jews under their jurisdiction in other parts of Europe. New tales of Nazi atrocities against Jews kept filtering through the Zionist movement, and I wondered for how long Hungarian Jews would be safe.

At any rate, I made up my mind not to wait my turn. At a meeting of the youth movement I got to know a boy of my own age, by the name of Gaby. He shared similar views to my own. We decided to flee Hungary and try to reach Palestine via Yugoslavia, Greece and Turkey. Once we reached Palestine we would join the British army to fight the Nazis.

At the end of May I quit my job and began preparations to depart. Gaby and I spoke to our madrich, who tried to dissuade us, but when he saw that we were determined to try our luck he gave us two addresses, one in Zagreb and the other in Belgrade, where we might find help to continue our journey.

It was the beginning of June when Gaby and I set off by train to Nagy-Kanizsa, a town close to the Yugoslav border. That night, we attempted to cross the border into Yugoslavia. It was dark and silent as we quietly made our way, the rucksacks on our backs laden with all our earthly possessions. Suddenly, two gendarmes materialised. I managed to eat the piece of paper on which the Yugoslav addresses were written before being led off to the gendarmerie station. That same night we were transferred to a military prison in Nagy-Kanizsa, where we were separated. I never saw Gaby again.

I was thrown into a dark cell where I remained for four weeks. During that time I never knew whether it was day or night. Once in every twenty-four hours I received half a litre of soup and 250 grams of bread. Most of the tiny cell was taken up by a wooden bunk, and I had to lie down much of the time, since there was no room to move. By the time I finally left the cell, the skin on my hips was as hard and coarse as that of an animal's.

I was taken to an office where an army officer questioned me as to why I was found on the border and where I had been intending to go. I played the idiot and gave silly answers. I must have been convincing, because from that office I was led to another cell where I could see the light of day. It was a larger cell containing six bunks. My companions were five Yugoslav granichars (border guards) who had committed various misdemeanours. During the three weeks I spent with the granichars, who only spoke Serb, I learned some of their language.

Even though the army intelligence authorities did not consider me a danger to Hungarian security, they were not going to take any chances. At around that time, the Hungarian authorities were rounding up Jews in the territories that they had taken from Czechoslovakia, Rumania and Yugoslavia. Those who could not prove Hungarian citizenship were, I had heard, taken over the border into Poland, where they were shot and buried in mass graves. My fate, I feared, was going to be the same. I was taken to Chust and delivered into the hands of gendarmes guarding a group of Jews waiting to be deported to Poland.

We were held in the yard of the Jewish community centre. It was surrounded by a high iron fence on one side and a three-storey building on the other.

I kept to myself and waited. It seemed that we were to be kept in this yard overnight. Looking around, I saw that there were only a handful of gendarmes guarding the perimeter, and I figured that it would not be too hard to get over the fence if the night was dark enough. I prayed that there would be no moon.

My luck was in — as night took hold, there was not only no moon but clouds gathered early in the night, threatening rain. For those around me, especially those families with tiny children, their night on the ground would be miserable. My heart went out to them. But I knew I had only a slight chance to help myself and none at all to help these poor people.

Before midnight it began to rain, lightly at first, then harder and harder, thundering down. People tried to find a little shelter, at least for their little ones, hugging the wall of the building. I slipped away quietly in the opposite direction, quickly climbing the fence and making good my escape. I knew I could not go to my parents' place, as that would be the first place they would look for me if my absence was noticed, and I did not want to involve them in my problems anyway. A hayshed stood not far from the railway station. I went there and won a good night's rest.

I still had my rucksack containing the few belongings I had been captured with on the Yugoslav border. Even the little money I had had on me was returned at the time of my release from the military prison. There was just enough for a train fare to Budapest. I was convinced the big city was the best place to hide.

I decided not to go by my real name any more, though what that was was a confused matter anyway. My father's name was Miller, and I had spent my childhood bearing that name, but it had become apparent in more recent years that although my parents went through a Jewish wedding ceremony they had not bothered to notify the authorities. For this reason I couldn't legally carry my father's name. But neither could I carry my mother's family name. Her parents had made the same mistake when they married, and so she carried her mother's name, which was Stauber.

I doubted whether the gendarmes would notice my absence, or, if they did, whether they would risk losing face by admitting I had escaped. After all, I was not a dangerous criminal, only an undesirable. I figured also that if they were deporting all these people to Poland they might not even bother to check the numbers. All the same, I thought it best to play it safe and change my name. For my first name I chose the Hungarian equivalent of Alexander, which is Sandor, and for my family name I decided, for no reason in particular, to use Sovari.

I arrived in Budapest the next morning. I was then nearly eighteen years old, but looked perhaps fifteen, and at that age I did not have to carry an identification card. Unfortunately, though, my starved looks made me conspicuous. Before anything else, I needed to put on some weight.

I decided to seek Esther's help again. I rang her, and she told me to come over to her house. As she opened the door, her face turned ashen. 'What on earth happened to you?' She led me into the kitchen and made me a nourishing breakfast, which I ate ravenously. After breakfast I told her of my recent misadventures, including my escape. She listened with amazement.

'You are one very lucky fellow. I have heard some disturbing news about those deportations; I'm glad you escaped. But you can't walk around looking the way you do — you will be picked up in no time. You must be fattened up a little.' While I waited, she changed her clothes and packed a bag. 'You will stay with my mother for a few weeks until you look human again,' she said.

Esther's mother, Erzsi Neni, lived on a farm some 70 kilometres outside of Budapest. As she drove me, Esther warned me not to reveal my true identity, nor that I was a Jew. 'My mother is a very decent sort,' she explained, 'but what she doesn't know can't hurt her. I will tell her you are the son of a family I met in Kassa, and that you have fallen on hard times. You will be safe at my mother's place.'

* ★ ★

I spent six weeks on that farm before the old lady would permit me to leave. While there, I made myself useful; my time on the farm in Slovakia had given me a reasonable know-ledge of what needed to be done on a farm and how to go about it.

Before I was driven back to Budapest, the old lady told me I had not only earned my keep but was entitled to some pay for my work. She gave me twenty pengo, plus a pair of new pants and a shirt which she had specially bought.

'What do you intend to do now?' Esther asked as she drove me back to Budapest.

'I will find a job. There seem to be plenty around, now that Hungary is at war.'

'I hope you are not going to get into more trouble,' she pressed me.

'Not if I can help it. I think I've had enough trouble to last me for a while.'

At this, she smiled. I thanked her profusely for her help and we said goodbye.

I had no problem finding accommodation on the west side of the River Danube, where I shared a house with a childless couple. My room was on the high street, only a few minutes' walk from the banks of the Danube. I found a job on the same street, working for

Hungary's greatest expert on healing herbs: Dr Varro Aladar Bela.

The good doctor had the job of mixing and packaging certain spices for the armed forces. He also made various tea concoctions that would heal many ailments. My job was to mix, pack and occasionally deliver them.

The Varros were a well-to-do Hungarian Jewish family, very proper and correct, but generous of spirit. I felt good about working for them. The one apprehension I had was about the young Hungarian woman, Miss Barna, who acted as the doctor's secretary. She often looked at me as if appraising me and was very cool towards me. She was fiercely loyal to the good doctor, who induced loyalty without trying, simply by his kind and dignified personality. Miss Barna probably suspected that I was not who I said I was, and she sometimes asked me embarrassing questions about my origins which I found hard to answer. Eventually I refused to answer her questions, and told her, not in so many words, to mind her own business.

I liked to work at the herbarium and learned a lot about herbs. My lack of a sense of smell (a condition I was born with) was a bit of a disadvantage in this business, and I had one unpleasant experience because of it. Miss Barna told me to bring some liquid ammonia from the store above the shop. She told me that it was in a big glass container. 'You will smell it,' she said. Knowing no better, I uncorked the container and stuck my nose in. It knocked the breath out of me, and I fell. Miss Barna and the others ran up to find me lying on the floor, struggling for breath.

'What happened?' they all asked.

'I tried to smell it,' I gasped. 'But I have no sense of smell.'

In spite of their sympathy for me, they burst into laughter.

I would have been happy with my lodgings, too, as they were conveniently located, clean, relatively quiet and not too expensive. There were two hitches, however. One was that the man with whom I lived, a small, sick-looking fellow of about forty-five, was a devout member of the Nyilas kereszt Party, the Hungarian equivalent of the Nazi Party. He tried hard to recruit me, promising to introduce me to the Führer, one Szalasi Ferenc. For obvious reasons, I was not very keen on the idea of joining the party. I said that at fifteen I was too young for politics.

The second and even bigger problem was his wife. She was at least ten years younger than her husband, fairly good-looking and healthy. She had taken a fancy to me, and whenever her husband wasn't home made it clear that she liked me. Now it wasn't that I was a prude or in any way disinclined to respond to her advances, but I knew that if I let my pants down I would blow my cover and she would see that I was a Jew. In Hungary, only Jews were circumcised.

On Saturdays, the man would go to the race track and usually lose what was left of his wages. He used to try to coax me to go with him, but I always declined. I had no money to lose on the horses. At the same time, staying at home meant giving his wife an opportunity to seduce me. It was becoming harder and harder to avoid the woman's attention, and in particular to resist her advances. It got to the stage where I couldn't trust myself to stay alone with her in the flat. Yet I did not like to go out in the street unnecessarily, for fear of being picked up by the police. One Saturday, in desperation, I joined her husband at the races.

He asked me to pick two numbers from a list he gave me. I did as he said, and put one pengo on the quinella. It came in and paid fifteen to one. I grabbed my winnings and left the track. When I got home in the evening, the man was already back, and though he had won a lot of money on the first race with me, he eventually lost it all during the rest of the program.

One day I came home at lunchtime and the woman informed me that a policeman had come to see me. Since I wasn't home, he had requested that I go to the police station — to clear something up. This set off alarm bells in my head. Naturally I wouldn't dare go to a police station where I might be scrutinised about the details in my registration form. I packed my belongings into my rucksack and took it to the flat the Varro family kept as a storeroom.

All afternoon I considered my situation. It was clear that I couldn't stay in the area, where I might be seen by my fascist landlord. He would no doubt guess at my true identity and denounce me to the police. The question was only whether I could trust my employers with my secret or whether I should just disappear. Vanishing without a word would mean the loss of what I had earned that month, and it was close to the end of the month; something I could ill afford.

I decided to trust the Varros. That evening I went to their home and there confessed who I was, and what had happened to me since I had tried to flee Hungary. By then it was common knowledge what had happened to the poor Jews who were 'deported'. The Varros were very sympathetic. Yet the old man, despite his age, was a little naïve. He offered to keep me on, regardless of what had occurred.

'I would love to stay on, sir,' I told the good doctor. 'You have all been very kind to me. I don't know how to thank you for what you have done, but I must move on.' They paid me what I was owed, and added an extra twenty pengo, wishing me the best of luck.

I spent that night in a cemetery. When dawn broke, I looked around and found I wasn't alone. A few graves away lay another body, stirring in the early rays of the sun. I went closer and saw it was a young man of twenty-odd years, fairly ragged, unshaven and thin. The man opened his eyes and, seeing me, said, 'Maybe you have some food in your rucksack? I haven't eaten for two days.'

'I am sorry,' I replied, 'there is no food in my bag. But I have a few pengo on me. As soon as the shops open I'll buy bread and marmalade and share it with you.'

The man stretched, scratched himself and rose to his feet. 'That is the best news I've heard in two days. But do you have food coupons?'

I assured him that I did. How long they would last I did not know, but I would cross that bridge when I came to it.

We exited the cemetery, introduced ourselves (each giving false names, of course), and told stories to explain our presence in the cemetery where we had met. We were justifiably suspicious of each other. My companion looked in considerably worse shape than me, yet he seemed to know the ropes; I concluded that he had been surviving thus for some time. He told me that there was a place some ten minutes' walk away where we could have a hot shower and have our clothes disinfected. Concerned for the money I was carrying, I declined the shower, but said I would wait for him.

We filled our walk to the delousing station with trivial conversation, but beneath our babble, each was scrutinising his partner suspiciously, asking the same question — can I trust him? It took about twenty minutes for the man, who introduced himself as Nagy Janos, to emerge from the station, and when he spotted me still waiting for him, he grinned from ear to ear. 'Frankly,' he said, 'I did not expect to find you here. I thought I might have frightened you, and that you were only waiting for me to go in before running off.'

'No,' I replied, 'you don't frighten me. It wasn't long ago that I looked very much like you. Only I had someone I could turn to at that time. Now I am ashamed to turn to that person again. I will have to find a solution to my problem by myself.'

We found a bench in a park, where we sat down to scoff the food I had bought. We washed down our meal with water from a public fountain. Our suspicions were fading with each minute that passed. 'Listen,' the man burst out, 'my name is not Nagy Janos. I am Gross Bela, and I am a Jew. You may as well know it. And if you don't like Jews, we'd better go our separate ways.'

I smiled. Offering my hand I said, 'Meet a friend. My real name is Alexander Stauber and I am not exactly pure Aryan either.'

'What do you know!' Bela exclaimed. 'I had an aunt who used to say everyone you meet is either a Jew, or at least from your home town. I am from Beregszasz. My family has been deported. I wasn't at home when the gendarmes turned up and took them away — five months ago now. For a couple of months some relatives on a farm gave me shelter. Then they got scared, fearing they might be deported too if I was caught on their property. They asked me to find another place to hide.' Then, as if he read my mind, he justified their actions. 'I can understand them. I don't know if I would have acted any differently had I been in their shoes.' Bela went on to tell me about how his parents had been well off, and how, if they had had an inkling of what was brewing, they would have been able to buy themselves out of trouble by bribing the right officials. Unfortunately, they weren't given the time. 'I think someone was after my father's business,' continued Bela, 'and that that was the only way to get it. I don't really know what happened and why, but I don't dare show my face in Beregszasz, for fear of being deported and you know what.'

I shared my story with him, and wondered aloud about the haste with which I had abandoned my comfort this time. 'The problem is, my identity papers would not stand up to scrutiny. And I can't take the chance of being checked until I can somehow establish an identity with more credibility.'

We discussed our predicament. Where could we hide and shelter? The cemetery would only do for a night or two, and even then only provided it didn't rain. We also needed money. The few pengo I had was not going to last very long — certainly not more than a few weeks. 'I don't know if there is any real chance,' I surmised, 'but the Jewish Welfare Society might help us. These people are so careful and law-abiding, they may refuse to help people like us. But it certainly can't hurt to try.'

This was a line of pursuit which had not occurred to Bela. I gave him directions and a pengo for the tram fare and we parted. Being seen together increased our vulnerability. We re-met at the offices of the Jewish Welfare Society. As we sat waiting to be admitted to an office, I told him, 'There is no point endangering each other by being together. From here on you'll have to find your own way.'

Bela sighed. 'I suppose you're right. But you are just the redeemer I have been praying for. It's funny; I am so much older than you, and yet you are guiding me. I had almost given up hope when you turned up.'

I assured him that I possessed nothing that he lacked, except more bad experiences.

I was called into an office where a young woman listened to my story — of how I had escaped from a group destined for deportation, and how I had managed to get to Budapest and find work and lodgings and live normally until the police called. She didn't seem to believe my tale, and asked me if I had any papers which identified me as a Jew, or where I came from.

'I have no papers at all. What I had, I destroyed when I decided to take another identity,' I explained. 'But I can prove my

Jewishness before a man who knows something about Judaism.'

The young official decided to take my case to her superior and asked me to wait outside the office. My first instinct was to get up and run for my life. I was afraid that the woman would deliver me to the authorities. Certainly, in earlier days, the appearance of a person such as myself would have sent them phoning for the police. But something had changed. Even these law-abiding Hungarians had begun to feel that the ground under their feet wasn't as solid as they had believed it to be, and that they might owe rather more loyalty to their own people than to the authorities. I stood my ground. I thought, even if they won't dare to help, they surely won't turn me over to the police.

I sat there for quite some time before the woman returned. 'There seems to be another man here with a similar story,' she said. 'Do you know him?'

'In a way I do,' I replied. 'I spent last night beside him in the cemetery.'

The woman looked at me in astonishment. 'In the cemetery?' Then, with a matter-of-factness that was not devoid of sympathy, she said, 'I wish we could do more for you but unfortunately we can't. We are a legitimate organisation and we can't afford to risk our standing by participating in illegal activities — like helping people who are sought after by the authorities to avoid capture. All we can do — and even this isn't strictly legal — is give you some money and advise you to avoid this place, as the police do come around here for random checks. Here is a voucher for fifty pengo; please go to the cashier, he'll cash it for you. Goodbye and good luck.'

With that, I left. The money, I figured, would be enough to feed me for a month, and with what I had on me it would last perhaps for two or three months. The only immediate problem remaining was where to spend the night. I dared not register again and find myself lodgings for fear of being picked up by the police.

That night I found myself a bench in a deserted market. There, I was fairly protected against the elements. The night was dark, and rain threatened; the cemetery would have been miserable. I had been asleep for perhaps three hours when I was woken by a policeman. Beside him was a little fellow telling the policeman that he had just happened to be passing by when he heard snoring. The policeman looked me over. He saw he was dealing with a youth who had probably run away from home to seek a better life in the big city. He didn't seem too happy to have to drag me along to the station at the end of his shift. It would mean another hour or two of work for him: paperwork plus a trip to the delousing station. But he couldn't be seen to neglect his duty by a civilian.

On our way to the police station we passed a pub where a drunken soldier was just being ejected, having been beaten by some Nazi sympathisers, probably for speaking out against the war in the east. The policeman stopped and questioned the man's attackers. While he was busy with them, I took off and quickly disappeared into a side street. I think the policeman would have been glad to be rid of me.

The rest of the night I spent walking the streets. In the morning, as soon as the all-day cinema opened, I bought a ticket, sat down in a corner and slept for several hours.

The next night it rained. Fortunately, I managed to get into a Salvation Army shelter for the homeless, winning a good night's sleep on a mattress on the floor, my rucksack under my head and a couple of clean blankets over me for warmth. If I could have enjoyed such accommodation every night I would have been happy, but one was not permitted to spend more than a single night in these places. I knew I could get another night if I went to one of the other shelters spread around the city, provided I got there before it was full. I learned that if one arrived there early enough to take part in the evening prayer session, one got an evening meal — a big bowl of nourishing soup and a nice big slice of bread. The trouble was, there were only five such shelters, and if a person turned up again after a matter of days, he or she would be recognised and denied entry. One had to let at least ten days pass before turning up at the same place again, and even then make sure to be as inconspicuous as possible.

The winter arrived early that year, and with it the snow. Sometimes I managed to get a few nights' work clearing snow from the main streets. On those days when I had only caught three or four hours' sleep in a cinema, it wasn't easy to shovel snow all night. But the few pengo I earned were a godsend. Another bonus was that all the while I was working I was safe from the police.

But more often than not I missed out on the snow-clearing job. I didn't always dare to queue up early in front of the hiring office for fear of the police check, which often happened at that time in the evening. On nights like that, when I had no work and no bed, I had to walk the streets in the bitter cold. Now and again I'd slip into a public toilet, even if only for a short while, to escape the biting-cold wind blowing outside. On such nights I dreamed of warm rooms, of a mattress and blankets, of a fireplace. Once or twice I managed to hide myself in a synagogue and sleep the night there. It wasn't very warm, but at least I was sheltered from the wind outside. When the caretaker of the synagogue caught me hiding in the toilet one night, he turned me out, and that was the end of that sleeping place.

Then one evening my nights of wandering came to an end. As I was coming out of a public toilet I was grabbed by a policeman and asked for my identification papers. I spent a week in the tolonchaz, a sort of a remand centre for prisoners waiting to be tried or deported. Then I was transferred to a temporary concentration camp, set up in a disused synagogue in Rumbach Street. This place was a haven compared to the conditions under which I had lived for the previous months. In the hall were about fifteen beds, each provided with mattresses, sheets and blankets. The place was heated and the food very reasonable and sufficient. The only drawback was that I couldn't walk out of the camp at will.

I found that my fellow inmates were all Jews: some from Slovakia, others from

Poland, others again from Yugoslavia. There were a few Hungarian Jews there who had helped illegal Jews to hide. Among the Slovakian Jews was my ex-employer, the farmer. 'Mr Ostreicher!' I exclaimed in surprise.

'Call me Rudi. Everybody else does.' He seemed pleased to see me.

I soon discovered that two of the Slovakian Jews, very wealthy men, had paid for the food for all the inmates. This explained why the food was so good and came in such generous portions. The policemen didn't mind; they could pocket the little which the Hungarian treasury advanced for the inmates' food.

There was a roster for cleaning the hall. Having lived away from home for years, I was handy with home duties and offered to do anyone's turn for a small consideration. Soon I had enough customers to keep me busy five days a week. Noticing my work, the policeman asked me to clean his place too, and do his bed for him. He gave me five cigarettes a day for my trouble.

I was almost happy in this camp. If they had wanted to keep me there for the duration of the war I would not have complained. I was confident that the war would end with the destruction of the Nazis and their

Hungarian allies. It was only a matter of time. In the meanwhile, I was living better than I had in a long time and had even managed to save some money.

I turned my curiosity towards my educated companions, questioning them on my many interests. I read any scrap of paper that came my way, any book I could lay my hands on. Some of these books were well beyond my comprehension, and in order to understand them I asked questions of anyone who happened to be near me at the time. Most people did their best to oblige. But there was one Hungarian Jew, a man of about forty, tall and athletic looking, a real intellectual, who was often annoyed when I asked him to explain something to me. At times he even objected when I asked someone else. One day he turned to me and said, 'I bet you ten pengo that you won't be able to keep quiet for forty-eight hours.'

I accepted the bet, to the amusement of the people around us. For the next day I held my tongue whenever anyone approached me or spoke. I wouldn't answer any question except with a shake or nod of my head.

On the second day, some of those who knew of the bet tried good-naturedly to trick me into saying something, but I held fast. Ten pengo was a lot of money, and I wanted to prove to myself that I was capable of the self-discipline.

Some ten minutes before the forty-eight hours were up, the Hungarian, Aladar, as we called him, came up to me and pulled out the pencil in my breast pocket, saying, 'What is my pencil doing in your pocket?'

This was one of my few valuables, and I burst out indignantly, 'It's not your pencil, it's mine!'

'Yes.' Aladar beamed. 'The pencil is yours, but the ten pengo is mine! You just lost your bet.'

I threw myself at him — a man capable of giving me a serious beating. My ex-employer jumped in and restrained the two of us. Looking hard at Aladar, Rudi said, 'You haven't lost your bet, Alexander. This was only a dirty trick and Aladar will now hand over the ten pengo he lost. Won't you, Aladar?'

Aladar was not a stupid man. He knew he could beat me with one arm tied behind his back, but Rudi was a different kettle of fish. At 100 kilograms, the farmer was not someone to take on. Ungraciously, Aladar pulled out a ten-pengo note and threw it at my feet. I bent down to retrieve it, but Rudi held me back, saying, 'Now that is no way for a gentleman to pay his debts, is it?' At that, Aladar bent down and picked up the note, handing it to me more reasonably. I accepted it with thanks.

This episode gave my spirit a tremendous lift. During my years of wandering I had come across many Aladars. I had also come across some very decent and generous people, but never one as fiercely honourable and with so strong a sense of justice as Rudi Ostreicher. Here was a man who was willing to physically stand up for me against a bully. And yet I had to reflect that that same bully was in prison because he had helped other Jews find a haven in his country. Aladar was a wealthy man; he hadn't done it for money. At the time it puzzled me that someone who had been unpleasant in my experience could be so generous towards others. In time I found out that human beings can be one thing at one time and its exact opposite in different circumstances.

After the episode with the ten-pengo note, Rudi and I talked freely. He told me the unfortunate circumstances by which he had found himself in this camp, and I in turn unfolded my own misadventures.

'You have a story worth telling,' he said.

'Maybe I will tell it one day — if I live long enough,' I replied.

'Oh, you'll live to be a hundred,' he said with a chuckle. 'You are a survivor!'

'From your mouth to God's ears,' I said.

12

Out of the Forest and into the Trees

The days passed almost without my notice. After completing my cleaning duties, I would read and struggle to understand whatever it was I was reading. I practised my writing, and learned to write neatly. Spring returned, the weather grew mild. I felt quite happy: most of the people liked me and I had grown fond of them. Even Aladar seemed to have softened a little towards me. Then one day, out of the blue, I was told to pack my belongings — I was to be transferred to Kistarcsa, a concentration camp in the country.

I was greatly buoyed by the expressions of sadness from the friends I was leaving behind. Even the policemen on watch said they were sorry to see me go. Rudi, to whom I was particularly attached, looked particularly despondent when I came to him to say my farewells. 'Remember what I told you: you'll be all right,' he said, then quickly turned away.

A plain-clothes policeman came to fetch me. He took me to the railway station where we boarded a rattly old train to the camp. From what I had heard, I knew my planned destination was not a pleasant one.

After some time I asked my guard to allow me to go to the toilet. He nodded and let me go unescorted, since he could see the toilet door from where he was sitting. I went in, locked the door, then quickly pulled out the small sheets of glass covering the window. I studied the scenery moving past me: all unfamiliar. I had no idea where we were. The train was pulling hard and slowing a little as it took a rise. I pulled myself through the window and jumped, fortunately landing on some vegetation which softened my fall. As the train disappeared from view I stood tentatively and checked my aching body: no bones were broken. I knew I had to move away from the railway track, and could not travel on any road where I might be seen, and so headed towards some woodland I could see about a kilometre away. I planned to hide there until dark before deciding in which direction to move on.

Because of the pain in my bruised body it took me longer than I had hoped to reach the safety of the trees. When eventually I made it, I discovered that the woods were not as thick as I had hoped; after a hundred metres or so the trees petered out. Still, it was safer than being out in the open.

From my position of relative security I surveyed the landscape. There was a road leading to a farm. The place seemed familiar; I looked hard at the farm buildings and suddenly realised that this was the property of Esther's mother, Erzsi Neni.

I slumped down at the base of a huge tree, out of sight, letting the sunshine calm me. Should I try to throw myself at the mercy of the old lady, and if she agreed to help me, would it be fair to involve her in the danger I had created? For the moment I didn't have to make any decision. For as long as it remained light I would have to stay hidden. By now my escort would have realised that I had escaped, and all police and gendarmes around the area would have been notified to look out for an escapee. I hadn't been photographed, and consequently they had no picture to identify me by. But on the other hand, they could describe me, especially my clothing — I had nothing I could change into. My few belongings remained in the rucksack on the seat opposite my guard. Fortunately, I did have about 300 pengo on me, enough to see me through many days.

The only traffic I saw for the rest of the day was the occasional peasant cart pulled by a snorting bullock. The hours dragged on and I grew thirsty and hungry, but I didn't dare leave my hiding place to look for water. A peasant might have caught me and delivered me into the hands of the gendarmes. People in the country were very patriotic, I knew, and were likely to regard any suspicious stranger as a spy.

At long last the sun set and all traffic ceased on the road. Farm hands had long left the fields and lights had begun to glimmer like stars in the distant windows of the farmhouse when finally I turned my thoughts to the future.

Erzsi Neni, the occupant of the nearby farmhouse, was a large, grey-haired, kind-hearted lady. I knew her to be the widow of a high-ranking government advisor on foreign affairs who had met a untimely death some ten years earlier. Erzsi Neni had never got used to city life. Although her husband had left her well off, after his death she chose to retire to the farm left to her by her parents. She managed the farm extremely well, with the help of whatever hands were available. Like all farms and industries during the war, Erzsi Neni's was chronically short of working hands, and my hopes lifted as I wondered whether the old lady might be grateful for another helping hand. They sank again as I considered that she, like most Hungarians, was also fiercely patriotic. I could only count on her trust in and loyalty to her daughter. But coming now, on my own, clearly a fugitive from the authorities, I had some fear that Erzsi Neni might find me too heavy a burden.

I quickly came to the conclusion that I really had no other option but to throw myself on her mercy. I could not show myself in public, looking as I did, without being seized by a gendarme or a zealous citizen. I needed time for my scratches and bruises to heal. I felt sure the old lady would take pity on me, and if she did not, I would deal with that when it came.

There was no moon as I came out of the woods and approached the farm. Darkness enveloped the area. Hunger, thirst and fear urged me on, and I soon found myself in the farmyard, where two big dogs greeted me as a remembered friend. There was a blackout order for all of Hungary, but people in the country rarely took the order seriously. Through a window I saw that the old lady was already in her bedroom, reading a book. I knocked softly at the window.

'Who is it?' she called out.

'It's me,' I whispered.

'Alexander?' came Erzsi Neni's voice after a pause. 'Come to the door.'

She switched on the light as I entered, and cried, 'My God! What happened to you?'

'May I first have a glass of water, please?' I asked. She rushed off and returned with a large mug of water, which I drank greedily.

'Sit down, sit down,' she bade me, and took a chair herself, but as I began to talk she suddenly jumped up again. 'Oh my!' she cried out, 'How inconsiderate of me! You must be starving.' Within minutes there was bread and ham on the table, and a big mug of fresh milk. Erzsi Neni watched me silently as I ate. Only once did she try to slow me down, reassuring me that there was plenty of food and that no-one would take it away from me.

At last I began my story. I felt compelled at the outset to reveal my Jewish background, which had previously been withheld from her by her daughter. I then told her of my journey since leaving her farm.

She looked at me pityingly for some minutes, deep in thought. Finally she said, 'I am glad you came here. Don't you worry about a thing — I'll help you all I can.' She took away my filthy clothes, attended to my scratches and bruises, brought me a pair of pyjamas, placed a mattress on the floor of her bedroom and made me a bed there.

'Now you sleep here. And tomorrow, don't make a noise and don't show yourself. I probably won't be here when you wake. Here is a bucket for your toilet needs. I'll also leave some food for you. Just stay put until I return.' Then, as an afterthought, she said, 'I am a little surprised that my daughter didn't confide in me. Did she think I might turn you away because you are a Jew?'

'Oh no!' I hastened to reassure her, 'She only thought you had enough worries as it was, and didn't want to add to them.'

This pleased her, and she nodded knowingly, then bade me good night.

When I woke, it was nearly midday. I found a message near my pillow, saying: 'Remember, no noise! And remain hidden. You may go into the kitchen, but quietly.' I could hear someone cleaning in the room next to mine. I waited till whoever it was had finished and left the house, then I went into the kitchen, had a wash under the pump and ate a hearty breakfast: fresh bread, pink bacon, two silken tomatoes, crisp spring onions and plenty of thick milk. A meal fit for a king.

When Erzsi Neni returned late in the afternoon she found me sitting on the floor in my pyjamas. With apologies, she went to find me some clothes. 'Here,' she said. 'I think these may fit you. They used to belong to my son, may he rest in peace. I don't know why, but I kept his things. Had he lived he would have long since outgrown them.'

The clothes fitted as though they had been made for me. Her son could not have been older than fifteen in these clothes. How he had died I dared not ask.

Later in the evening, when all hands had gone home and there was no danger of anyone overhearing us, we sat at an open window talking.

'I have been away in the village finding out a few things,' Erzsi Neni began. 'I think I may have found a solution to your problem. I had a cousin in the next village who had a son about your age. He was five years younger than my son, Feri. Some seven years ago he simply disappeared, and no sign was ever found of him. Two years later his parents left for America. A year later they both died in a train disaster. Now the boy, though I am sure he is dead, has never been declared dead. His name was also Sandor — Sandor Molnar. I could get you his birth certificate. Another cousin of mine is in charge of the registry of births and deaths in this area. I had a chat with him today: I can have the birth certificate within a couple of days. This would give you the ability to live legally anywhere for the next three years until you were due for military service. But in three years' time the war will be over and all this madness will have disappeared. I hope. So what do you say?' I didn't know what to say. This would be the greatest thing any person had ever done for me. I could hardly believe that anyone would go to such lengths to help a poor wretch like myself.

'You know, Erzsi Neni,' I said after a silence of some moments, 'I find that most, if not all, of what I have been taught at home is false. I have been fed so much rubbish about Christian-Jewish relations. You and Mrs Endrey have been kinder to me than almost any Jew has ever been. What you are offering me may very well be the answer to my prayers.' I could no longer hold back my tears. 'I am overjoyed.'

Erzsi Neni clasped me to her bosom, then lifted my chin. 'Now listen,' she said. 'We will wait until your scratches are healed. Also for any visit from the gendarmes that may or may not come within the next few days. Then you'll appear with my daughter one evening, and stay a few weeks with me, before you take off with your new identity. Tomorrow I'll phone my Esther from the post office in the village and ask her to visit me — let's say in five or six days' time. Okay?'

The next day at around midday, two gendarmes showed up. Erzsi Neni was at home. She offered them a glass of wine, which they gratefully accepted. They asked if she had seen a youth lurking around the area, and gave a fairly good description of me. Erzsi Neni told them she hadn't seen any strangers at all in the last few weeks, and they left.

'Now all we have to do is wait for your scratches to heal,' she said.

Four days later my face had healed. That same evening Mrs Endrey arrived in her car. She was not too pleased when her mother told her the circumstances which had brought me there. She confronted me. 'You had no right to come here and endangering my mother like that,' she burst out angrily. 'It was a different thing when I brought you here. At that time she knew nothing and was therefore guilty of nothing. This time, you force your way in as a fugitive, pursued by the gendarmes. What if the gendarmes came and searched the place and found you here? It would have brought disaster on my poor mother's innocent head. I won't forgive you for that.'

I stood before her, my head bowed, tears in my eyes.

Erzsi Neni rose to my defence. 'Be reasonable. What choice did he have?' She took Esther in her arms, trying to pacify her. 'I know how you care for me. But in this case the poor fellow really had no choice.'

'Oh yes he had,' Esther retorted. 'He could have bloody well gone on to Kistarcsa and waited there for the war to end.'

'Now you are unjust, my love. You know what's going on there. I wouldn't wish that place on my enemies. He did right to escape when he had the chance. And when he found himself near my place, what would you have suggested he did? Give himself up to the authorities, or let himself be caught by over-zealous peasants? They would have torn him limb from limb as a spy, you know how they are.'

'I don't care. Your welfare comes first,' said Mrs Endrey, but with less conviction than before.

'And in my place, what would you have done? Turned him away? I know you better, my daughter.'

Mrs Endrey didn't reply, and her mother hugged her again, kissing her forehead as she said, 'I understand your reaction, but it is based on emotion, not reason.'

Esther nodded, reduced to a small child in her mother's hands.

'Now,' Erzsi Neni said in a business-like tone, breaking the mood, 'I called you here so it would appear that you brought young Sandor out again to stay a few weeks and help me out a little. As you can see, he doesn't look so bad this time around. And the scratches on his face have disappeared. You should have seen what he looked like the night he got here; I hardly recognised him . . . ' The two of them began to chat and I quietly took my leave.

Esther departed the following morning, and Erzsi Neni put me to work. I was in charge of the substantial vegetable gardens around the house, and I worked them happily. I also tackled whatever chores around the house I could: I cut wood for winter heating, cleaned the house and tended the fowl yard.

When sawing the logs of wood, I had a young peasant girl to help me. She must have been nineteen or twenty, with pleasant features, a full figure, bright brown eyes and beautiful long hair which she wore braided. This girl, Anna, seemed to fancy me: she would use every opportunity to be near me; and she would touch me, as if by accident. I could not have missed her intentions, but just as I had with my previous landlady, I was afraid to be discovered a Jew. Then I thought, maybe this girl wouldn't know about circumcision, or who is and isn't circumcised?

While I was agonising about it, Anna took action. One day as I carried wood into the

194

shed behind the house and stacked it neatly inside, Anna appeared, grabbed me and kissed me fully on the mouth. It was a long, passionate kiss, and I had no strength to resist her. Then she pulled out a breast and put it in my mouth. I was spellbound. I sucked on the soft breast while the nipple grew harder and my loins stirred like nothing I had experienced before. Anna knelt slowly, taking me with her; she lifted her dress and I discovered that there was no clothing beneath it, in the way of most peasant girls. As her hand went for my fly, I pushed it away and pulled out my erect penis myself. I was inside her before I realised what I was doing. There followed a frenzied coupling. Anna cried out several times before we both fell apart, exhausted.

I stood and, turning away from the girl, wiped myself with a handkerchief. Then I turned to Anna and said, 'Anna, you are a wonderful, beautiful girl, but I never want to do that again with you, or with anyone else for that matter.'

'But why?' she asked. 'Don't you like girls?'

'I like girls well enough, but what if you fell pregnant? I couldn't marry you. I am only fifteen. And I couldn't provide for a wife and child. I have no rich parents to support me, and neither have you. You would be disgraced and nobody would want to marry you with a child. I like you very much and don't want to harm you.'

Anna said nothing, but silently left the shed.

From then on, I was careful not to find myself alone with her in a place where such a coupling could happen again. The fact was that my fears of being discovered a Jew far outweighed my concerns for her good name.

I spent six weeks with Erzsi Neni. In that time I learned all I needed to know about my 'family', the Molnars, and felt secure in the knowledge that I now had an identity which would stand up to scrutiny.

One evening I told Erzsi Neni that I was ready to go.

'I don't know how to thank you,' I said. 'I am truly very grateful. I only wish I could prove it to you some day, in some way.'

Erzsi Neni smiled. 'It's all right, my boy. You are a good lad. You did a very good job while you were here, and I was happy to help out the little I could. Now, do you have any money?'

'Yes, I have 300 pengo.'

'Well, in that case, although I would be glad to have you stay on a few more weeks or even months, I won't stop you. May God be with you.'

Erzsi Neni gave me a used suitcase containing all her late son's clothes, saying, 'I don't know why I kept these, but I am not keeping them any longer. You make good use of them.'

My beloved Grandchild,

Here ended another phase of my life. This time I left the good old lady as an almost happy, fairly confident young man. The old fears and suspicions that had kept me alert for years were gone, for the time being, buried beneath a veneer of trust in the documents Erzsi Neni had provided me with.

As you can see, I have managed to write a fair bit since my last letter to you. I am curious to know what you think of what I've written so far. Do you find it interesting? How does it read? Savta and I are both well, and we hope that you are well and enjoying the service. Please write to us soon.

All our love,
Your loving Sabah

I left early in the morning for Budapest, prepared like never before. I had my strength and health, identification papers which would withstand scrutiny, and I carried with me a suitcase full of clothing and 300 pengo. I even had Sandor Molnar's fifth-grade school certificate. By now I was proficient enough in reading and writing for a fifth-grader, so the fraud was quite plausible.

In Budapest I found myself a room in the house of a Jewish family. The man of the family had been conscripted into a labour battalion, and the woman remained the sole provider for her two children, a boy of my official age — fifteen (I was actually eighteen) — and a girl of thirteen.

The woman hated having to let the room and have a stranger in the flat, but her earnings were not sufficient to keep the family in bread and butter. The situation being what it was, she had to tolerate a lodger, and wasn't very gracious about it. But the children seemed to like me, and we got on well. The boy, Erno, was particularly friendly, especially when I was willing to share my clothes with him. He was mad about wearing ties, and I had several. The girl, Berta, took some time to get over her shyness before she accepted me. But she did, and the three of us were on the best of terms in no time at all.

Even that irked Mrs Bernstein. She believed me to be a Gentile, and in those days the relationship between Jew and Gentile in Hungary was rather edgy.

I went to Mr Sipos's factory, where I had once worked as a turner's assistant, to see if I could get my old job back. I was told that the old man had passed away and that I must see his son about a job.

Young Mr Sipos was surprised to see me. 'I didn't think I'd see you again!' he said. 'What can I do for you?'

'I am looking for a job,' I told him, 'but . . . ' I checked to see that no-one was within earshot, 'I am officially not who I was when I worked here before.' I explained my situation and Mr Sipos said he was happy to re-employ me.

Three days later I was on the job, happily working away at the Sipos factory. In the evenings I went out strolling on the banks of the Danube, or on the island of Margit. It was liberating to be able to walk around without fear that a policeman might stop me and ask for my identification papers. And yet the old, well-established anxiety of being picked up had not disappeared altogether. I felt a strange joy and a sense of daring: I was playing an old game but with new and better equipment. The odds were with me for once.

I learned to be prudent with money and never indulged myself. On weekends I read or walked around. One Sunday I decided to visit the Hashy's meeting place again, but when I arrived I found the place closed. There was no sign of what it had once been. I rang the bell of the adjacent house and was greeted by the madrich. When he recognised me he opened the door wide, saying, 'Come on in, I didn't think I'd ever see you again! We recently received word that the boy who went with you to the Yugoslav border died in a psychiatric asylum. We thought maybe the same fate had befallen you.'

Poor Gaby. I was saddened by his fate, but not surprised. I recounted to the madrich my misadventures since trying to get to Palestine. When I had finished he said earnestly, 'You are a very resourceful fellow. We need people like you. Now that you have a good set of papers you could help us help others who are in need. The question is, are you willing?'

I answered unhesitatingly, 'Without question.'

'Very well then,' he said. 'There's a trickle of our people coming in, from Poland mainly, who desperately need help. Some of the boys and girls are helping where they can to collect money, clothing and food for these people. But we are running out of hiding places for them.' He was talking to me with a quiet intensity. It began to dawn on me that there was a whole world of suffering out there quite apart from my own misery.

'Now,' he continued, 'there is a Hungarian nobleman who has large forests in the mountains of Transylvania, far from highways or railway tracks. He is willing to let a group of our people hide there en route to Romania, provided they can work at logging. This is where you could help us. We have two men who don't speak the language and they need to be escorted to the spot. Their escort would have to stay with them for a few days until they were settled in. Do you think you could be that escort?'

'What if the gendarmes came and asked for identity papers?' I asked.

'We would disguise the men as invalids and provide some papers for them.'

I was concerned about the risks, but I felt I had to try.

It took some ten days to arrange the trip. I went to see my boss and told him I would need a couple of weeks off. Mr Sipos looked at me speculatively. 'I suppose some of your relatives are ill?'

'Yes, sir,' I said, nodding.

'All right then, take two weeks off. Come and see me when you are back.'

At the appointed time I went to the address given me, where I picked up two men in their thirties, dressed in discarded army overcoats. Both looked like invalids, their faces gaunt and pallid. Only their eyes seemed alive. With the exchange of few words, I took them to the railway station. There we boarded a train to Transylvania.

Just before nightfall we arrived at a small village, having travelled on foot the 15 kilometres from the station. We found the caretaker of the nobleman's property waiting for us there. He showed us a small bungalow furnished with the minimal necessities. 'There is food for two days here,' the man said. 'Tomorrow I am going to town to do the weekly shopping. Tell me what you need, give me the money and I'll buy you what you need. Bread and bacon you can buy from the farm, most days.' Before departing he added, 'Tomorrow morning my assistant will come and show you what is expected of you in the way of work.'

There was no electricity in the bungalow, but I found a kerosene lamp nearly full. Holding it high, I inspected the house. There were two rooms and a kitchen. In each room there were four single beds with straw mattresses and blankets. In the kitchen I found a few pots and pans, some dishes and some simple cutlery. There was a built-in fireplace, a small stack of firewood, a table and some wooden chairs. By my standards, it was luxurious. On the table sat a large loaf of bread which someone had freshly baked, plus a saddle of bacon, some white cheese, onions and radishes, some ersatz coffee and a few cubes of sugar. My companions looked yearningly at the food. I hadn't seen them eat anything during the long train ride. I indicated a washstand in the corner and said in Yiddish, 'Let's wash hands and sit down to eat.' Whether they understood me or not wasn't clear, but they washed their hands as they saw me do and joined me at the table.

They sat patiently waiting for me to portion out the bread, bacon and cheese. While I lit a fire and put a kettle on to boil, I let them eat in peace. I served them coffee and then finally asked, 'Does either of you speak Yiddish?' Both shook their heads. 'German?'

'A little,' one of them replied.

'Where are you people from?'

'We come from Greece,' the same man replied.

'What language do you speak?' I asked again.

'We speak Ladino [a mixed Spanish and Hebrew dialect spoken by Jews] and Greek.'

In a rather laborious discussion, I extracted the information that they came from a small town in Greece, not far from Athens. One was a bookkeeper and the other a merchant. I told them about myself as if I was the person my papers said I was. There was no point complicating things. I advised them to pretend they were deaf mutes when working with the villagers. While they had nothing to fear, they also had no reason to trust anyone not connected with the organisation protecting them.

In the morning an elderly man came to wake us up. I told him that the men were deaf mutes and that I would interpret his instructions to them later. The old man explained that until we were able to fell our own trees, we would have to clean the ones the villagers were felling. We were to cut off the branches and put the thicker ones aside for firewood and the thinner ones in another pile to be burned later.

'Do you people have any axes?' the old man asked.

'No,' I replied.

'You should have brought them with you. What did you expect to work with?' He eyed my companions. They didn't look like they were fit for this work.

'You'll be paid according to the amount of

work you do. I can tell you that you won't make much, cleaning other people's fellings. Maybe enough to pay for your food and kero. Now come along and I'll show you where the work is done and how.'

It was only a ten-minute walk to the section of the forest where the villagers were currently logging. Twenty men were at work, some leading two pairs of horses to drag logs to a collection point for taking to the railway station. Others were felling the trees, while a few were busy cleaning them.

'Make sure you people keep away from where the trees are being felled. We don't want any accidents. Watch those people doing the cleaning and see how it's done.' I pretended to translate what the old man said into sign language. The two men nodded their heads in understanding. Later, in the bungalow, I explained what had been said, and arranged to buy them work clothes and anything else they needed. The madrich had given me several hundred pengo to cover any necessities to help them settle in.

I decided to stay with the two Greek men for at least a week to teach them how to use an axe, how to sharpen one, and generally to assist them in settling in to a lifestyle very different from that which they had known at home.

Three days after our arrival at the village another two men arrived. One of them, the escort, was Bela Gross, my friend from the cemetery. 'My god, I expected anyone but you!' I said, greeting him warmly.

'And do you think I expected to find *you* here?' Bela retorted jovially.

Like myself, Bela was having difficulty communicating with his charge, who only spoke Russian. But between us we managed to help the three men get established and find their place among the village workers. The Russian, though still weak, handled an axe well and made a great improvement to the team. Within a few days even the two Greeks managed an almost reasonable job and were capable of doing enough work to earn more or less what they had to spend for their daily needs. I decided I could return to Budapest and leave Bela to look after the trio. We said our goodbyes and I took a lift with the manager to the railway station, where I boarded a train back to Budapest.

Dearest Sabah,

You asked me my opinion on what you have written so far. Well, I might be somewhat biased, but I think it makes good reading. I find myself impatient to know what happens next . . .

I am fairly happy doing what I do serving in the army, though in my private life I am a bit unhappy. I am unlucky in my choice of boys. I had to cut my relationship with Noam, the Yemenite boy. It's just as well my father knew nothing of it. A couple of weeks ago Noam's elder brother was arrested as a member of a drug-smuggling ring. Poor Noam is devastated, not only because I broke up with him, but because he intended to make a career in the Military Police. His brother's business has ruined his chances there.

I don't think I'll make another friend in the army. Maybe I'll have more luck in civilian life. I am otherwise fine, and in no particular danger — certainly no more than any other Israeli citizen.

Love to you both,
Esther

I had been back at work only a week or so and was finishing up for the day when I was accosted by a young boy. He handed me a written message: the madrich wanted to see me that night at the Corvin warehouse at six. I looked at the time: it was five o'clock. I had no time to go home to change, just enough to grab something to eat.

I arrived early to find the madrich already there. 'I heard you did a good job at the logging site,' he said as he greeted me. 'We need you back there. We found a way to get people there without an escort, but most of them do not speak Hungarian and are not familiar with the conditions. We need a sort of administrator and interpreter. Also, someone like you who is handy with an axe and would be able to instruct them in the job at hand. You are a decent and capable young man. We would like you to go there and stay as long as is necessary. Maybe six or seven months. What do you say?'

I didn't know what to say. I had been asked to help my people: how could I refuse?

'How would I be able to contact you,' I asked, 'if a situation arose where I needed your advice?'

'A line of communication has been established through the nobleman who owns

209

the land,' replied the madrich. 'We'll be in constant touch.'

'When do you want me to go there?'

'Immediately, if possible. The weekend at the latest.'

'I couldn't leave before the weekend. I'll have to give up my job and also my room.'

'I suggest you don't give up your room. Give me the address — we'll pay your rent while you are away. We'll give some excuse for your absence. You'd do well to leave some of your belongings there too, as a sign that you are coming back. Here is some money which you may or may not need. If any instructions are needed we'll send them through the baron. Okay?'

I nodded, putting away the envelope containing the money. With that, the madrich turned and disappeared. I went back to the factory and found Mr Sipos. I told him that I would have to quit and the reasons why. I thanked him for his kindness towards me and said I would finish at the end of the week.

Mr Sipos took off his glasses and studied me carefully, rubbing his eyes before putting them back on. He sighed. 'All right. I'll have your pay made up.' He shook my hand and wished me the best of luck.

When I arrived at the logging village later that week, I found that living in the bungalow were seven men. Six of them worked at the logging site and the seventh worked in the cottage, doing the cleaning and cooking for the group. This man was a Slovakian Jew who spoke not only Slovakian but Hungarian and German as well. He introduced himself as Jeno.

Soon the working group returned, Bela grinning with delight to see me. He ignored my outstretched hand and squeezed me with a bear hug. We talked happily into the night, and he told me quietly that he and the Russian planned to depart the following week for Romania and freedom.

The next day I went out to work on the logging site. I enjoyed working beside Bela. The Greeks had improved and were using their axes slowly but efficiently.

As we returned to the cottage that evening another two men arrived, brought by the baron himself in his car. They were both Poles. We learned that at the beginning of the war they had been given permission to come to Hungary, but lately the authorities had withdrawn that permission from those who were known as Jews. Some had even been arrested. As these men had lived in Hungary for the last four years, they spoke enough Hungarian to get by. They were in good physical shape and turned out to be a valuable addition to our workforce.

I went to see the manager's assistant, who was often at the site, and spoke to him about the possibility of our group working independently of the villagers, felling our own trees and stripping them ourselves. 'I'll talk to the manager and see what he thinks about it,' the old man said.

The next morning we were given a parcel of trees on the other side of the site, separate from the villagers. Bela and I began felling trees while the rest cleaned them. Slowly we developed a rhythm to our work, and the manager was happy with our performance.

We lived like a commune. All the money we could save after paying for our basic necessities we kept aside for a time of need. The group accepted me as their treasurer and spokesman, and voted in a three-man committee to deal with any problem which arose between us. Bela and the Russian had gone by now and another three men had joined our ranks. In the evenings most of the group learned Hebrew, with the help of one of the new arrivals who had taught Hebrew in a school before the war. I already had a smattering of Hebrew from my cheder days, so I learned English instead.

The villagers amongst whom we lived were Romanians, and there wasn't one of us who spoke their language. I tried to pick up a few words here and there. There was a young girl who used to bring her father his lunch every day. She used to throw shy glances towards me, and I nodded at her whenever she passed nearby. She seemed always to choose a path near where I was working or having my lunch. While the days were long there was plenty of daylight left after we came back from work. I would sometimes take a walk from the cottage, and the girl seemed to have a similar idea. We would meet sometimes outside the village and I would ask her to teach me her language. We never spent more than ten or fifteen minutes together, and most of that time was spent laughing as I tried to pronounce certain words in Romanian. It was an innocent relationship between two teenagers.

However, one evening as I returned home from one such meeting with the girl, I was approached by the committee. 'We have to talk to you,' they said sternly.

'Talk away,' I said.

The chairman turned to me. 'Alex,' he said, 'we are grateful for your activities on our behalf, and we don't want you to misunderstand us. But we are worried about your relationship with the Romanian girl. You could bring disaster upon us.'

'What are you talking about?' I burst out indignantly. 'Do you think I would say something to the girl that could hurt us?'

'No,' the chairman replied patiently. 'What we are afraid of is that the girl may be spoken for, and if so, the youngster who feels you are taking over his girl may go to the authorities and tell them about a peculiar group of men here — men who seem to be foreigners, behaving in a peculiar manner.'

This had never crossed my mind.

'We have decided to make a roster of two men every night watching the village entrance,' continued the chairman. 'If either gendarmes or soldiers are seen coming this way, we will flee into the forest and maybe into Romania. Can you imagine the damage to our cause if this base is lost as a refuge and halfway house?'

I hadn't, and I knew I would never forgive myself if I was the cause of such a calamity. 'I am very sorry,' I said. 'I realise now the danger and promise to terminate ties with this girl.'

With this, the discussion was ended. No soldiers or gendarmes came, and the Romanian girl was never mentioned again.

13

A Horse's Prick

It was autumn 1943. The war was showing no signs of ending, although the tide seemed to be turning against the Germans. At the beginning of the year they lost the crucial battle of the Russian Front at Stalingrad. We heard how the Russians had encircled a whole German army under Von Paulus, destroying most of the troops and taking the rest prisoners.

Stories began to filter through of German retreats and defeats on all fronts. In North Africa Rommel was defeated, and the allied forces came ashore in Italy. The Americans and their Allies were gaining the initiative in the Pacific theatre and were slowly pushing back the Japanese. What's more, American munitions were beginning to make their way into Russian and British hands. Even the passive Jews were beginning to resist: in Warsaw, a handful of them — hungry, untrained, ill-equipped — managed to hold out for weeks against the SS.

However, all this was bitter-sweet news. By

1943 some three-quarters of European Jewry under German jurisdiction had been murdered. Some 90 per cent of Jews remaining in the occupied Soviet territories had likewise been slaughtered. There was little for European Jewry to look forward to.

Slowly autumn turned into winter, and at times we Jews on the logging site could not work more than three days a week, being hindered either by rain or snow. Even so, we managed to earn enough for our daily needs, which was more than could be said for the rest of Hungary. While we could have as much bread as we wanted, and unlimited quantities of bacon, ham and chicken, all at a relatively cheap price, those in Hungary were getting only 250 grams of bread per person per day, and meat and dairy products only occasionally. The only thing we loggers were really limited in was sugar, although sometimes we bought it on the black market for perhaps triple its official price.

The baron came several times to visit us and inquired about our wellbeing. He was a youngish man, and I often wondered why he was not in the army.

As 1943 turned into 1944, several of the men were taken to Romania, and others came from Budapest. It made the work harder for those who stayed behind, since the

216

newcomers had to be taught the job and it took some time before they could work efficiently.

Early in 1944 I was called back to Budapest. The madrich greeted me at the railway station. 'We have a job for you, Alex. You seem to be the only one we have who is suitable. There is a man, a Polish refugee, who managed to get to Chust and has to be brought here. He is in bad shape, but able to travel. We would like you to go to Chust and bring him to Budapest.'

The thought of returning to the town where I had spent the first several years of my life had no effect on me. I had hardly thought of my parents or siblings in recent years; I had been too busy looking after number one. I accepted the madrich's commission without sentimentality or concern, asking only that I be allowed a night's rest.

'Of course. I didn't expect you to go straight from here,' replied the madrich. 'Naturally you'll have a night's rest. But not at your place. We have arranged a place for you to sleep tonight.'

In the morning I was given instructions to meet the mazkir (secretary) of the local branch of the movement at Chust, who would take me to the Polish refugee I was to bring to Budapest. Arriving in Chust early in the evening, I went straight to the given address of the mazkir, but the man wasn't home. He had, however, left a message for me to meet him at nine o'clock that night at the Jewish Community Centre. Having a few hours to spare, I went to the Coruna Hotel and booked a room for the night. I had been told not to contact my parents.

Some minutes before nine o'clock I went up to the first-floor office of the community centre. The door was open but there was no-one there. As I looked down through the window I saw two gendarmes turning into the staircase. There was no other way out except the window. I did not hesitate long: I jumped some five metres to the yard below, falling on my feet and registering a sharp pain in my left ankle. I ran the few metres to the iron fence, well known to me from my escape two and a half years earlier, grabbed the top rail and pulled myself up and over. Now I was in the yard of the synagogue. I kept running through that yard and into the street of the market, now deserted, and hid between the empty stalls. By now the pain in my ankle was unbearable.

My mind raced. I knew I couldn't return to the hotel. Whoever had betrayed me must have given a good description of me, even if not my name. I felt terrible for the trouble my parents would have; it was likely their names and address would be passed on to the gendarmes. I pondered my situation. My ankle was badly injured and swelling visibly. I needed help — to get away, to find a place to spend the night, and then to get out of town. I decided I would have to trust someone. Just then, I saw some movement not far from me, and then heard someone whispering my Yiddish name. After a moment's hesitation I whispered back, 'Over here.'

A shadow emerged from between the stalls. It slowly came forward, and sat down beside me. I could not make out the face. 'Who are you, and what do you want?'

'Don't you recognise me?' said the voice. 'It's Beni. I used to be your best friend. We ran away to Sevlush once, don't you remember?'

I remembered. 'Beni! What are you doing here?'

'I was sent to warn you not to go to the Community Centre, but I was too late. When I arrived the gendarmes were just going in. Then when I saw them come out alone I realised you must have managed to avoid them and I went looking for you.'

Beni knew who had betrayed me, and also the mazkir of the movement, to the gendarmes. The mazkir had already left town and was on his way to Budapest. But as far as I was concerned I still had a job to do: there was still the man to escort to Budapest. 'We could not take the train from here,' I said, thinking aloud to Beni. 'We'd have to get to Sevlush, somehow, or even further away towards Budapest.' Beni was quiet for a while, then he said, 'I'll have to go and talk to some people and see what can be done. I'll be back in an hour or so.'

I stayed where I was, nursing my injured ankle. I knew I would hardly be able to walk.

Finally Beni returned with the news that he had found a solution. 'Early in the morning a friend of mine from a neighbouring village will come and collect you and the refugee. He'll then take you to Sevlush to some sort of a safe house. Our people there will give you any assistance you need. Okay?'

I nodded.

'I have a bicycle,' continued Beni. 'I'll sit you on the back-rack and get you to a place where you can spend the night. My friend will collect you from there in the morning. Just watch out for a horse-drawn carriage. The driver will pretend to fix the harness and will whistle the Hatikvah [the hymn of the Zionist movement]. Just tell him you are Beni's friend.'

I clambered onto the back of Beni's bike

and we travelled quietly through the darkness to the place where I would spend the night. I almost smiled when I saw that it was the same barn where I had slept after I escaped deportation.

I didn't sleep a wink. My ankle ached terribly and the morning could not come soon enough. I wondered if I would even be able to make it to the carriage when it arrived. Ultimately I managed by hopping. The driver, a middle-aged farmer, looked nervous and shuttled me urgently onto the carriage. The refugee was already there. Once out of town the farmer relaxed a little and offered us some food, which we gratefully accepted.

The refugee turned out to be a Belgian Jew who had managed to escape when transported from one concentration camp to another in Poland. It was nothing short of a miracle that he had reached Hungary undetected. He looked starved and unkempt. His big black eyes emphasised how pale he was. He spoke very little Yiddish or German; only French and English. What he couldn't explain in Yiddish he managed somehow to communicate in English, and thus I learnt the gist of his story.

I told him that should we be stopped and questioned he should act dumb. He looked ill, so I thought I could explain, if necessary, that I was taking him to the capital for treatment in a hospital. I had some identification papers which broadly fitted this man, but now *I* was the main problem. In the condition I was in, train travel was out of the question for the next week or so at least. I was in terrible pain and my ankle was swollen to twice its normal thickness. When we arrived at the address in Sevlush, where a young farming couple received us, we had to cut my left shoe to pieces in order to get it off my foot.

The young couple seemed happy to be of help. They fed us a simple but nourishing meal, then bade us rest. 'We will talk when you get up,' the man told us.

We stayed a week. In this time, my host found me an excellent pair of shoes and by the end of the week I was able to walk with the help of a stick. Thus, nine days after leaving Budapest, I was at the madrich's door delivering my charge. That same day I caught a train back to the logging site in Transylvania.

Shortly after my return, on a fine Sunday morning, I decided to walk to the next village. It was a large village some 10 kilometres distant. As I approached I saw that the village was full of German soldiers. They were mostly informally dressed and casual in manner, and some were without their weapons. However, I began to grow uneasy when a young German soldier approached me cordially. Looking around, he whispered in German, 'Would you like to buy my rifle?'

I smiled. 'What would I do with your rifle? And what would happen to you if they found out you sold it?'

'Oh, they'd never find out. Many of us lost our weapons when we had to turn and run from the Russians.' Realising that I didn't want his gun, he said, 'I wish I had something else to sell. I'd like to buy some cigarettes.'

The soldier continued chatting to me, telling me how he had enlisted at the age of sixteen and volunteered to fight the Bolsheviks. But as soon as he found out how desperate the situation really was, he had wanted to leave. A year later, when he was granted leave, he told his father that he was going to desert. However, his father notified the military police, who came to pick him up. The court martial had sentenced him to death, but because he was only seventeen and therefore under-age, they couldn't execute him. Instead, they sent him back to the front.

'I don't know how much more I can stand,' he told me confidentially. 'I think I'm going to desert again. And this time, if they catch me, they'll probably hang me or shoot me. But I can't stay.'

'Here,' I said, reaching into my pocket at the end of his story, 'take this. Go and buy yourself some cigarettes.'

His face changed complexion. 'What is your name?'

'Alex,' I smiled. 'Call me Alex.'

He shook my hand, saying, 'My name is Joachim.'

We wished each other luck, never expecting to cross paths again.

When I returned to my logging team, boasting of my encounter, the committee was most upset by my adventure. 'I don't think we can afford to have you around,' the chairman of the committee said. 'You undoubtedly have courage, but very little sense. You could have landed us all in trouble. Your actions have endangered us and the whole project here. We will have to ask the madrich to pull you out of here.'

I was furious. I had accepted their criticism of my liaison with the Romanian girl, but this was outrageous. I had a perfectly sound set of documents depicting me as a pure Aryan. Those papers could stand up to any inspection. I had done nothing to constitute a danger to this group, and I told them so in no uncertain terms.

However, the committee didn't agree with me and made its view plain to me. I later realised my mistake and apologised, promising not to do anything of the sort again. They took no further steps on the matter.

But things were not so satisfactory in the outside world. On the 19th of March, 1944, the German army marched in and took command of Hungary. Prior to this event, some Hungarian politicians had begun to see the writing on the wall and pondered how to escape the inevitable defeat awaiting them at the hands of the Western Allies. Most of the Hungarian army was assisting the German military machine on the Eastern Front. The new prime minister, Dr Kallay, had slowly begun withdrawing some units and made changes to the command in others. He issued orders to stop the brutal treatment of Jews in labour battalions. All of this had to be done under the nose of a very pro-German high command. But before the politicians managed to prepare the ground for a political-military turnaround, the Germans got wind of the plans and invaded Hungary, occupying it and setting up their own puppet ministry.

Now began the real tragedy for Hungarian Jewry. The Gestapo came with lists of names of those who were unfriendly to Germany. Politicians, journalists and other public figures were arrested during the first hours of the German occupation. Horthy, the old dictator of Hungary, was effectively kept under house arrest, though officially he remained the country's ruler.

Soon, Jews had to wear yellow Stars of David on their left breasts. They were thrown out of their homes and sent off into ghettos. All the Jews in the countryside — over 600,000 people who had lived in the territories controlled by Hungary — were herded into cattle wagons and transported to concentration camps, in most cases to Auschwitz. Among them, I had to assume, were my family. Even though the Russian forces were inching westward and entering Poland, the Nazi killing machinery pressed on with its methodical annihilation, racing against time to complete the so-called 'Final Solution'.

And so it was that Hungarian Jews took their turn now, like their brothers and sisters had throughout Europe, in the ghettos, in the cattle trains, in the shower blocks and in the death pits.

Ironically, Germany's occupation of Hungary made Hungary a target for Allied aerial bombing. Budapest in particular was bombed mercilessly, especially the industrial suburbs; the British operating by night and the Americans by day.

More and more people arrived at the logging village and were taken over the border to Romania the same night.

Now and again one remained with us. Among those was a Slovakian boy of eighteen years of age who had lived in Budapest for the last three years. He spoke perfect Hungarian, like most of the Slovakian Jewry. This boy had possessed a sizeable sum of money and had had no problem obtaining fake identity papers, which served him well. Later, when his money was running out, he took a job in a furniture factory belonging to a Jew. He told me a story of the way his Jewish boss had behaved. One day a new worker appeared, a boy of about his own age, whose Hungarian wasn't very good. The new boy worked alongside him, and he was sure the boy was Jewish. This new boy told the Slovak boy that he was out of money and didn't know how he would last the week. It was only Wednesday, and payday was not till Saturday. Some of the other workers suggested he ask the boss for an advance on what he had already earned, but the Slovak told the new boy that if he wanted to keep his job he must find another way to solve his problem; if he turned to the boss for help, he would be sacked.

The Slovak shared his lunch with the new

boy on that Wednesday, but he did not want to show too much sympathy towards him, for fear of bringing suspicion upon himself. The next morning the young man came in looking hungry, and when the break was on, one of the workers, seeing that he did not have any food, asked him what he had eaten. The young fellow replied, 'A horse's prick' (the Hungarian equivalent for 'bullshit'). There was a big laugh all round.

At lunchtime the new boy went in to see the boss and asked for an advance. Sure enough, the Jewish boss paid him off and sacked him. It was a typical response from a wealthy Hungarian Jew towards a struggling one. Luckily, the young fellow now had enough money to keep him alive for a week or so. And another job at that time wasn't too hard to find.

I listened to the story, typical of the insensitivity and blindness of many better-off Hungarian Jews. Their time of reckoning was fast approaching, I firmly believed, but they could not see it coming. They behaved as if everything was all right and was going to stay that way, as if their money formed some kind of protective barrier. I thought of the Schwartz family, in particular the man of the family, Paul: a most sincere and decent fellow, if ever there was one, and not unenlightened. Yet even he couldn't see the writing on the wall. He continued going about his business, blind to what was happening to Jews all over Europe.

Instructions were received at the logging site for me and another two young people to return to Budapest. The rest were to await the coming of the Russians. Since it would have been dangerous to return to Budapest together, we three who had been recalled to Budapest set out individually in different directions. I went to a large village called Nagy-Ilonda where I joined a group of Hungarian refugees from those villages which had suddenly found themselves within range of Russian rifle-fire.

Early in the afternoon a train arrived to take us to Budapest. We arrived around nine at night. The Hungarian Red Cross took us to an abandoned school and provided mattresses and blankets, even some food and hot drinks, and promised to see what could be done to help those in need of assistance.

In the morning I took my rucksack and went in search of the madrich. There was no answer when I knocked at the door where I had met him the last time. As I stood there wondering what to do, a young girl approached and asked me who I was looking for. I scrutinised the young woman, wondering what answer to give her. I couldn't possibly trust her with the truth. Before I could speak, however, the girl, checking first to see that no-one was within earshot, asked if I was looking for the madrich. Caught by surprise, I could say nothing but yes. The woman gave me an address written on a small piece of paper. 'Read it and destroy it,' she said, and left.

I had no difficulty finding the address. When I rang the bell a young woman opened the door tentatively, but when I whispered that I was looking for the madrich, she opened the door wide to let me in. She pointed to another door, saying, 'In there.' I went into the half-dark room where the madrich was sitting at a table with three young men and two girls. As I entered, he looked up with recognition and motioned for me to sit down.

'You came at the right time,' the madrich said. Then, turning to the others, he said, 'I suppose this will be all. Please leave one at a time, at five-minute intervals. Olga, you stay, please.' Then, to me, 'How was your journey, Alex? Any problems? I am sorry I dragged you here into danger, but we are very short of good people, and there has never been a greater need for them. Had you stayed behind, I suppose by now you would have been liberated and out of danger . . . '

'I had no problems,' I responded. 'I came with a group of Hungarian refugees. The Red Cross was looking after us. As for being liberated and out of danger, I don't trust the Romanians and I'm afraid of the Russians. Now I'm here I'll do my best to survive, and help others as well.'

I inquired about my old room but was told that the Jewish family had vacated the flat. The madrich was in no mood for idle talk. There was an urgency in his movements and voice. 'Olga here has a room for you,' he said. 'You and Olga will be a team. She knows what has to be done, and if there are any new instructions you will be told. Now you two may leave together. Good luck.

'And one more thing,' the madrich called after me as I stood at the door to leave. 'Never come here, unless specifically asked to.' With that, I was dismissed.

As we walked in silence towards the tram stop, I studied my partner out of the corner of my eye. She was tall for a girl, with wavy blonde hair to her shoulders, a wide mouth and big blue eyes which looked straight ahead. If she noticed me appraising her, she ignored it. I felt no trust between us and wondered how we would be able to

231

cooperate under pressure.

Not a word was exchanged during the tram ride. We entered the block of flats where Olga lived, and a foyer revealed three doors leading into different apartments. Olga unlocked the door on the left corner and, when we were in, locked it again. It was a small room furnished with a table, three chairs, a cabinet and one single bed. We sat at the table.

'Now we can talk,' Olga said. 'Do you know about the Swiss schutzpasses?'

I shook my head.

'Well, the Swedes and the Swiss give out papers to our people declaring them to be under their government's protection. Here in Budapest we have several houses under the protection of either the Swedish or the Swiss government, and some under the protection of the International Red Cross. You and I are working with the Swiss embassy. We have those papers all filled out, awaiting the names of the protected people. Our task is to go into the ghetto and bring out one or two people at a time, fill in their names on those papers and take them to the protected houses, as long as there is room there. In the meantime other members of our group are preparing more houses, furnishing them with the essentials for more people. I don't know how long we'll be able to get away with this, but as long as we can save a few of our people from the ghetto we are doing something worthwhile.'

I nodded. By this stage of the war, every Jew in Hungary between the ages of eighteen and sixty, no matter what his physical condition, had to present himself to the military authorities for service in a labour battalion. All those who had previously been excused on medical or disability grounds also had to go: no excuses or exemptions. The constant bombings had caused great devastation, and many hands were needed to clean up the debris from the roads of the capital. Other conscripts were sent to build new defence lines, this time on Hungarian soil to try and hold back the Russian onslaught. I thought of poor Paul Schwartz with his heart condition. Naturally he too would have to go.

A reign of terror had descended on Hungary, and in particular on the remaining Jews of Hungary. I learned from Olga that many Jews, women and children included, were being taken by the Hungarian Nazis to the shores of the Danube where they were shot and their bodies thrown into the river. This was a dark period of history.

The Zionist underground movement suddenly found itself with all the money it could want. Using this money effectively was another matter, however, as finding safe-havens for the persecuted was difficult. Here and there, non-Jews helped, but the vast majority could not care less. Some were even gleeful.

I thought of Mrs Endrey and her mother in the countryside and decided to visit Esther and ask her if she thought her mother would be willing to hide some people. Although Esther had originally been anxious about the risk Erzsi Neni had taken in hiding me, I believed that both she and her mother would agree to my request, even though at that time a non-Jew hiding a Jew was putting his or her life on the line just as much as any Jew. I felt I could appeal to my friends' humanity.

Two days later Mrs Endrey told me her mother could take in two to three young women, ostensibly to help around the house, and maybe two young men as farmhands. She was also willing to hide one person. These people were delivered to the farm by Mrs Endrey in her car. Arriving back in Budapest, Esther brought a message from her mother to me: 'If you are in real trouble and have nowhere else to go, come out here. I'll find a hiding place for you.'

I tracked down the Schwartz family. Paul was happy to see me. He told me that Mrs Schwartz and their daughter were already in a

Red Cross protected house. Paul had chosen to take his fifteen-year-old son with him into the military compound, believing he would be safe there. I could not resist asking him what he thought these days of the Hungarian people. 'If you mean the Nyilas kereszt,' he said, 'they are the lowest of low. But the Hungarian people are something else. I still have faith in the Hungarian people. My people.'

For the time being, Paul was being put to work in the compound to make new boots for the officers. But I had heard rumours that the labour battalions would soon be sent westward to Germany. I managed to convince Paul that the boy would be safer with the rest of the family in the Red Cross safe-house.

A few days later the labour battalion was driven westward towards Austria. Paul could not keep up with the marchers. He was shot, only a few kilometres outside of Budapest.

Dearest Esther,

*I was a bit disturbed by your phone call.
The last time you wrote you said you were
happy doing what you did, and felt good in
the service. But now you say there has been
a changeover of staff and the new people
give you trouble. It is hard to give advice
from afar, but for what it's worth I would
suggest you give some thought to my
experience and try to learn from it.*

*I was for years a vulnerable kid, as you
know from what you have read of my childhood. Many of my peers would make fun of
me. It took me years, but eventually I
learned that other people can only hurt you
if you cooperate with them. I learned to be
my own best friend, and this is something I
strongly suggest to you to do. Accept yourself for what you are, know your own value,
and never allow anyone to undervalue you.*

*I have found that other people's views of
me depend on their mood. Today they're
in a good mood, so I am a nice fellow;
tomorrow they're in a bad mood, so I am a
fool. So I say, as we say to the bee: 'Lo
meoktzecha, valo medovshecha' — 'None of
your honey and none of your sting.' I am
not impressed when people praise me, and
take no notice when they try to abuse me. I*

consider myself not ten feet tall but twenty feet tall, and my attackers don't come up to my ankles.

You, my dear grandchild, may learn, if you wish, from my experience. My philosophy is: from my point of view I am the centre of the universe. For if I am not, nothing is. On the other hand, I accept the fact that in the universal scheme of things I am less than a fart in a windstorm.

These are some of my basic philosophies. I commend them to your notice, hoping that you will accept at least some of them.

All my love. Savta also sends her love and lots of kisses.

Your loving Sabah

As the situation on the various fronts worsened and the Russians slowly but surely pushed forward towards the capital of Hungary, the Nazis became more desperate, more bloodthirsty. They went on a killing rampage. Many poor Jews perished. The Allies intensified their air attacks, raining down bombs day and night. Many innocent people, both Gentiles and Jews, died in these raids. I was reminded of an old joke about a Jew who went to do some business in a district other than his own and was caught and beaten by the men of the neighbouring nobleman. After several such incidents, the nobleman under whose protection the beaten Jew lived told his neighbour this: 'If your people beat up my Jews, my people will beat your Jews.' Whichever way you looked at it, Jews got beaten. Still, for us Jews in Budapest, the bombing was the lesser of two evils.

Soon the rumblings of far-off artillery fire could be heard in Budapest. The Jews quietly rejoiced. 'Oh God,' they prayed, 'let them come a little faster and save what's left of the house of Israel in this country.'

But God must have been busy somewhere else. Weeks passed and the sound of cannons hardly grew louder. At night we could see the flashes of light in the distance, but they never drew closer.

Budapest was by now overcrowded with refugees. People who for decades had been fed horror stories about the Bolshevik terror now fled for their lives as the Russians came close. Liberators they might have been, but there was still reason to fear the Soviet army. Although well disciplined, they were given the opportunity to plunder and pillage as they battled their way forward.

The Zionist organisation for which I worked had now gone totally underground and was in danger of being uncovered and destroyed. All of us feared for our lives. I felt as if my whole life had been a training ground for the unimaginable horrors waiting in the wings. How well my deprived and embattled youth had prepared me, only time would tell.

Dear Sabah,

Thank you for your letter. As you wrote yourself, your advice is not easy to follow, but I'll try my hardest. I have read and reread your letter several times, and I am convinced that your advice is sound.

I didn't want to tell you over the phone, but when I rang you I was extremely distressed. Noam died. He obtained a transfer from the Military Police to an elite unit fighting terrorism. What they do is put on Arab garb and mix with the Arab population to ferret out terrorists, whom they either arrest and bring in for trial, or eliminate. In one of their actions, three members of the unit were recognised and attacked by a mob of Arabs. Noam was killed in the attack. I blamed myself for his death, thinking that if I hadn't broken off with him he may have stayed with the Military Police and none of this would have happened to him. Also, although I am not superstitious, it struck me that all the boys I touch die.

The way I feel now, I'll be glad when my service is up and I can go home. What I'll do at home I have no idea.

Please give my love to Savta. Many hugs and kisses to both of you.

Your loving Esther

14

The Circle Tightens

Towards the end of November 1944, big battles were being fought some 30 – 40 kilometres east, north and south of Budapest. In and around the city, heavy military traffic growled and droned. Men and supplies headed towards various fronts, while machinery, livestock and wounded soldiers were shuttled west towards Germany. The Russians were slowly closing in on the capital.

Much of Budapest was already in ruins as a consequence of the Allied aerial bombing. The city's industrial areas had been destroyed. Now and again one of the bombs fell on residential centres, and here and there a hospital, school or church was hit — a grim warning that nothing was safe or sacred.

By now, all of Hungary, except for the capital, was *Juden rein* — clean of Jews.

All normal activities ceased, for it became dangerous to venture out into the streets. A Jew could immediately be recognised by the yellow Star of David. Failing to wear it and

241

being identified as a Jew could result in being shot.

As bad as the situation was for the Jews of Budapest, there were some for whom things were even worse. There were scores of men who had either escaped from the labour battalions or whose units had disintegrated while the front swept forward. Having nowhere to go, and nobody to turn to in the countryside, their only chance lay in the capital where there were still Jews left who might help them.

The job of our movement was to find these men before they were caught by the Hungarian Nazi guards who roamed the city, supply them with false papers, find safe hiding places for them and, in extreme cases, save them from the clutches of the 'Nyilas guard', the military arm of the Nyilas kereszt Party. For this purpose I carried a 7.65 calibre pistol. In the five weeks I had possession of it, I only used it once. Even then I was unable to do what I should have done and shoot the little Nyilas guard — a kid of sixteen, escorting a middle-aged Jew to Nazi headquarters, no doubt to be taken from there to the banks of the Danube and shot. All I could do was disarm him and, after warning him not to show his face on the streets again, send him off with a kick in the arse.

Olga and I would walk the streets looking for these poor, desperate men. We had been chosen for this job because of our Aryan looks. Olga's blonde hair and blue eyes were supposedly uncharacteristic of Jews. As for me, my undernourished youth and weather-hardened features gave me a typical Hungarian look. If one had what was considered a Jewish complexion, even the best set of false papers was useless. The Nazis knew of the traffic in fake documents and had a very effective way of finding out if a man was Jewish or not. In Europe only Jews and Muslims were circumcised, and there were hardly any Muslims in Hungary. If a man was suspected of being a Jew, he would be taken aside to have his private parts inspected, regardless of the papers he carried.

To further aid the deception, I wore the badge of a right-wing patriotic group called the Association of Veterans of the Eastern Front, and acquired a limp to go with it. Together, Olga and I presented an incon-spicuous couple walking the streets.

In real life we had become a couple, too. Our dedication to the Jewish cause had drawn us together, not to mention the fact that we had only a single bed to share. Olga and I seldom had the time or opportunity to talk about our families and the terrible suspicions we had about their fates. For the better part of our time we were surrounded by people, most of whom had to be considered potential enemies until proven otherwise. Even where we lived, under assumed identities, we had to watch our tongues. Anyway, the present was too horrible to contemplate, so when we did have a chance to talk we talked about the future — our future in Eretz Yisrael.

Although we knew very little about the Palestine of 1944, we were convinced it was the most beautiful place on earth. It was the only place where a Jew could walk tall, his head held high, being as proud of being a Jew as a German was proud of being a German. In Palestine a Jew did not have to hide his identity for fear of his life.

Through our own channels we continued to hear horrendous reports of racism and cruelty, and there were moves in our ranks, even at this late hour, to set up some form of resistance. But even some of our own people refused to believe these reports. At a meeting between the Zionist leadership and the official Jewish leaders in Budapest, it was requested that the Zionists refrain from spreading terrible rumours among the people.

What was left for us to do except dream of Israel?

For most of the day, Olga and I would walk the streets, looking through cheap cafés, restaurants, cinemas — all the places our forlorn brethren were likely to be found. If we spotted a man we thought was one of ours, we would drop a word or two in Hebrew and wait for him to approach us. If he did not respond, but we were pretty sure he was one of those we were looking for, we'd try and try again, up to three times. If he still did not respond, we would decide that either we had erred or he was too scared. Either way he would be too dangerous to approach and we would disappear from the scene as quickly as possible.

On the 26th of November I met Olga at the trade union health service centre, where there were always people waiting to see a doctor or a dentist and which was therefore a good place to meet. I felt a bit depressed, for no apparent reason, but as was my nature at times like that I put on a facade of joviality. As I spotted Olga I smiled cheerfully, and after a brief greeting I said, 'Have you heard the joke about the Jew who wanted to commit suicide?'

She frowned and said a perfunctory 'No', but I pretended not to notice and continued.

'Well, this Jew had had enough and wanted to end it all. He climbed on top of the Margit

Bridge and jumped into the Danube. A policeman jumped in after him and saved him. When he realised he had jeopardised his own life to save a Jew, the policeman got very angry and beat the hell out of the poor Jew, sending him on his way. Next the Jew tried to jump in front of an oncoming tram. But the driver stopped the tram inches before hitting him. When he saw who he'd saved the driver got terribly angry, and gave the poor Jew a beating. After trying his luck with a bus, with the same results, the Jew, now in total despair, sees a high-ranking SS officer and gives him a big kick in the arse. The SS officer turns around and, seeing the Jew, asks, 'What? The war is over?'

I laughed heartily at my own joke, but Olga could only manage a wry smile. For the next few minutes we walked in silence.

'Let's have a look at the Teleki market,' I suggested. 'We are not far from it.'

It was a cool and windy day, and consequently there were not many people at the market in Teleki Square. We walked around the rows of stalls looking for lost sheep. This was a particularly bad spot for a fugitive to be. The police often sealed off the square, raiding the place for criminals and other undesirable elements. Anybody whose papers were not in the best order, or who seemed dubious for any reason, was system-atically rounded up and taken into police custody.

So, even though we had good papers, Olga and I were always reluctant to hang around the markets for very long. One could never be sure of the strength of those papers.

On this day I was particularly keen to do our search and leave the place quickly. But Olga was taking her time, looking around at all the men, and I was getting impatient.

'Olga,' I said, 'you are making yourself conspicuous. Some of the men are getting the wrong idea.'

'Don't pester me,' she whispered back, smiling falsely, 'I am doing what I am here for. You had better keep your eyes off me and do the same.'

I smiled back, pretending she had said something funny.

As we turned into the next row of stalls I collided with a young man carrying a rucksack. Although he looked like a true Aryan, with blond hair, blue eyes, a round face and a straight nose, he was suspiciously apologetic when he noticed the badge I was wearing. Walking backwards, he apologised again and again for his clumsiness.

Olga and I looked at each other and nodded. As soon as he turned into the row we had just left, we turned back and came up behind him.

'What should I buy you for Chanukah?' I asked Olga, using the name of a Jewish holy day.

'Something to complement what you bought me for Yom Kippur,' she replied.

The young man suddenly turned to me and said, 'Excuse me, would you know by any chance where I could find Mr Shovuot?' Shovuot was another holy day in the Jewish calendar.

'Sure,' I said, 'we are just on our way to see him. Do you know him?'

'Oh yes,' the man replied, 'he is my mother's uncle.'

'Come along then. We'll take you straight to him.'

We left the square without further ado, making our way to a small café a few streets away. The owner was a sympathiser with our cause. Sitting down to a cup of coffee, we asked the young man who he was, where he had come from and where he was off to. He told us he was Peter Steiner, from Szeged in Hungary, and was twenty years old. He had been called up for military service in a labour battalion and was in Szolnok before it fell to the Russians. Most of the men from his unit defected, together with many of the soldiers

248

from the guard unit attached to them. A Hungarian army officer who saw him wandering around aimlessly told him he had better get rid of the yellow armband which identified him as a Jew, put on civilian clothes and find a place to hide, because some Nazi bastard was likely to shoot him on sight. The officer offered to take him to Budapest in his truck, saying he'd be better off there than in the countryside. So here he was.

'When did you arrive?' Olga asked.

'This morning.'

'Who told you to go to Teleki Square?'

'Nobody. That's where he put me down. I've never been here and had no idea where to go. You two are my saving angels.'

'I don't know about that,' said Olga, 'but we will try to help you as much as we can. Have you got any relatives in Budapest?'

'No. At least, not any I know of.'

'Well, right now the only place we could suggest is another labour battalion,' I said. Seeing the look on his face I hastened to add, 'Don't worry, you will be safe there — for the time being, anyway. The commanding officer is a friend of our people and there will be someone to look after you.'

'Take a taxi,' Olga suggested. Then to me she said, 'You take Peter there and meet me an hour later at the health centre, okay?'

'Okay.' When Peter and I got out of the taxi I winked at her and said, 'See you later.' But I never saw her again.

★ ★ ★

Labour battalion 301/2 was situated in a big building in Vorosmarty Street, not far from the western railway station. The guard at the entrance knew me as Peter, and as I passed through I slipped him a packet of cigarettes, as I always did when I came.

It was about three in the afternoon as I made my way down the stairs. I had put Peter into the care of our man in the unit and was now on my way out of the compound.

Coming down the last flight of stairs I saw, to my horror, a group of SS men coming in. I felt dizzy. If the railing hadn't been there to hold on to, I would have fallen down the stairs.

So that was it! — the reason for my depression. It had been a premonition, a warning, but I hadn't realised it. I calmed myself, thinking, I have managed so far, I'll be all right now. I could hear trucks stopping and soldiers jumping out of them. Within minutes the whole block was surrounded. There was no escape.

Slowly I turned around and went back

upstairs to buy some time and make sense of what was happening. As my mind focused, I quickly removed my Nazi badge and replaced it with a yellow armband.

About half an hour later the people in the labour battalion, myself now included, were ordered to collect their belongings and assemble down in the yard. It seemed we were being moved; where to, no-one had any idea. Through the crowd a buzz of guesses pulsed: would they take us to do a job for the Germans in some other part of the capital? They surely could not move us out of the city permanently — too many of us were needed to clean up after last night's bombing. Many consoled themselves with the belief that this was only a temporary move.

I listened coldly. I had a nasty suspicion that we were being shipped to Germany. If so, I would be travelling light: I had nothing with me, not even a change of underwear. However, whatever was to become of us, I figured I had the best baggage of all to serve me — a little luck, some courage, and experience of harder times than most. I remembered what Rudi had said: you will survive. I tried to believe it.

It was an anxious gathering of men that assembled in the yard. I found myself standing beside Peter, my most recent recruit to the battalion.

'Is this the safe place you brought me to?' he asked bitterly. I looked at him silently for some seconds, then said, 'Did you think for one moment that I brought you here for this? Can't you see me standing here beside you, ready to share your fate? You may not know this, but you were in the greatest of dangers where we found you. Any minute the police or the Nyilas guard might have picked you up. You might be in the Danube now.'

There was a hush in the yard. Captain Losonci, the Hungarian commander of the battalion, walked in, followed by his deputy and an SS officer. 'Don't give up, Peter,' I whispered. 'We are not done yet.'

We stood to attention — all 500 or more of us. A normal battalion had around 300 men, but any man who had arrived at the gates had been accepted into this battalion, no questions asked. Here were the flat-footed, the asthmatic, the diabetic, the overweight. This battalion had been among the last to be created. It consisted of a number of older men who had previously been rejected on the grounds of ill-health, as well as many youngsters of between eighteen and twenty years of age. All had benefited from the humanity of Captain Losonci.

The captain stepped onto a wooden crate and called, 'At ease, men. I have come to tell you that I have been relieved of my command over you. Like the rest of you, I am a soldier and have to follow the orders of my lawful superiors. My second in command, Lieutenant Thebner, has asked to stay with you. Follow his orders as you did mine. I hope God will be with you.' With that he stepped off the crate and left, accompanied by the SS officer.

We remained standing there for a long time, dazed. It was clear now what our fate would be. In truth, we had expected a hand-over such as this for a long time, but until it actually happened, nobody had wanted to believe their turn would come. Now, reality wore an SS uniform.

A strange calm descended on the battalion. We seemed to be resigned to whatever fate might level at us. In a sense, now that our worst fears had been realised it was an anticlimax.

As we were organised into columns to march three abreast to the western railway station, I wondered at the bravery of the lieutenant who was accompanying us. A 'white armbander' (he was a Christian, but both his grandparents on his mother's side were Jews), he was one of the most decorated soldiers in the Hungarian army. On account of these achievements he had been allowed to keep his rank, though he was not allowed to command Aryans.

The lieutenant could have gone with the captain had he wanted to, but apparently he preferred to share our fate. I couldn't imagine why. What he had seen during the last few years, in particular since the Nazi reign of terror, must have left him with little hope for a better future. His decision to come with us, was, in a sense, an act of suicide.

Dear Grandchild,

I am finding the going very hard. I think,
after all, that I cannot finish this project. It
is not that my memory has faded. On the
contrary, my recollection of events is as
sharp as if I was remembering what happened yesterday. It is only that I still
struggle with the language problem. I rack
my brains, searching my vocabulary for the
right words and expressions to convey my
experiences. Dictionaries only serve so far.

To be honest, I am no longer sure why I
have been struggling for so many years with
this story. I am certain that my effort is
unlikely to improve the quality of the huge
volume of material already published on the
subject. And there is no need for me to
strain myself for profit, even if such is to be
made, should this story ever be published.
Whatever I could make from this would not
change our situation. As you are aware, a
Damocles' sword is hanging over our heads.
We are in danger of losing our home to the
bank as a result of our son and daughter-in-
law having defaulted on their loan. To be
faced with the prospect of being thrown out
onto the street in our seventies, after nearly
fifty years of sweat and toil, is no picnic. It
seems our cup of sorrows is not full yet.

Now there is another obstacle, if a pleasant one, in the way of my finishing this project. Your Savta and I are currently looking after a little foster baby by the name of Debi. We adore her, and she seems to return our love. She is at our place between nine and four each weekday, and while she is here I have no time or inclination to write. Then, in the evenings, I am often exhausted and don't feel like writing. Only on the weekends do I have no excuse, and so I sit down to write a few lines.

Keep well, my grandchild.

All our love,
Sabah and Savta

15

The End of the Line

Heavily armed SS men surrounded us like an impenetrable wall as we marched to the railway station. I was flanked by two of the men I had delivered to this 'safe' unit: Jeno Schwartz and Erno Gelber. Erno had a heart ailment, and Jeno had diabetes. I glanced at them and saw that both were looking straight ahead, seeing nothing, moving mechanically. Not only were they physically sick, they were spiritually broken.

After several minutes of marching, Erno's face reddened and his breathing became heavy. He carried a heavy rucksack on his back and the effort was obviously proving too much for him. As I had nothing to carry, I asked him to let me carry his load. He reluctantly agreed, and I took the rucksack off his back and put it on mine. Now Jeno, who was carrying two side-packs, asked me if I could carry one of them for him. This I did.

The cattle wagons were open and waiting for us. About eighty men were ordered into each wagon. There was only one small window high up on each carriage. As soon as we were in, the doors were shut behind us.

Despite the cool weather outside, it quickly became hot and stuffy inside. Asthma sufferers started to struggle for breath. Those most affected we lifted up to the small window for a good intake of fresh air. With three of them suffering badly, we had to keep lifting them up every few minutes. The relief they gained only lasted a couple of minutes, and their conditions rapidly deteriorated.

By ten o'clock that night we'd been in the wagons for several hours and the train still hadn't moved an inch. There wasn't enough room for more than one or two people to sit on the floor at any one time. Anyway, nobody had the patience to sit quietly. The stronger ones were taking turns lifting the asthmatics up to the window.

At around midnight the train finally began moving. It was then that the first of the asthmatics died. We heard him moaning, desperately fighting for breath. Quickly we put down the man we were holding up to the window and hoisted up the sicker man, but our efforts were in vain. He died in our tired arms and his body took up what little floorspace there was around our feet.

For the next eighteen hours we journeyed towards an unknown destination. The train would move for an hour or two, then stop. After an hour or so sitting stationary, we would jolt into motion again, only to stop after another hour or two. This continued until the evening of the next day. During those hours, another four people died, among them Gelber and Schwartz.

The rest of us suffered terribly from thirst, though few people were hungry: the stench from so many unwashed sweating bodies, not to mention the excrement that we had no place to deposit except in our pants, was nauseating to some, although at least here I was blessed since I possessed no sense of smell.

At about six o'clock in the evening the train stopped at a small station, and wagon after wagon was opened. Under heavy-armed escort we were told to answer the call of nature and fill our water bottles. Some food was distributed, and we were allowed to unload our dead comrades. Then we were shut up again.

The next twenty-four hours were a repetition of the previous day. For most of the day the train hardly moved. Every now and again we were put on a side rail to let other more important trains pass.

In the evening we were again briefly released: this time there were no dead in our wagon. Then, for a third day, the process was repeated. Then a fourth. By the fourth night there were two more dead in our wagon. We wondered how those in other wagons were faring.

On the fifth day, late in the afternoon, our train rolled in to the village of Bruk an der Leite. We did not know whether this was just another of the countless stops, or our destination. We could hear no noise outside; nothing of the incessant artillery duels that we had heard for days. An unsettling silence descended over our train.

Suddenly the wagon's door slid open and an SA man (one of the Nazi militia) stood shouting, '*Raus verfluchte Juden. Schnell, schnell*' — 'Out, damned Jews. Quick, quick.' For the last few hours I had found a comfortable spot in a corner, sitting half-asleep on the rucksack and side-packs I had inherited from poor Erno and Jeno. As the men near the door started to alight I stood up with difficulty, dragging my luggage.

I let myself slowly onto the ground, hoisted the rucksack onto my back and put the side-pack across my shoulders. I took a step and promptly collapsed. My legs were unable to carry both me and my packs. I wondered how the hell I was going to get up, harnessed as I was to the rucksack, and, once up, how I would proceed. All at once I felt someone grab me and lift me, none too gently, to my feet. Looking up I saw two SA men, who couldn't have been more than eighteen, grinning and shouting, '*Hoch Jude!*' — 'Up, Jew!' Although my feet were trembling under me, I summoned all that was left of my physical strength and willpower and moved up to take my place in the ranks. I was among the last to get out of the wagons. Within minutes we were marched off down the gravel road.

'Well,' I thought, 'wherever they are taking us could not be as bad as the place we have just left.' Having survived the past five days I believed I could survive whatever else they might dish out. The main thing was not to lose my head, and not to lose hope. I remembered the words of Madach, the author of one of Hungary's classics, at the end of his great work *Ember Tragediaja (The Tragedy of Man)*: 'Man struggle and keep faith.'

In order to avoid thinking of the road ahead, which seemed to be unbearably long, I struggled to keep my mind busy. I felt determined to hold onto the possessions I had inherited, believing that my survival might depend on them. For one thing, there was some food in those bags which might mean the difference between life and death. Also some items of clothing, which would come in handy since I had nothing of my own with me.

When I knew that there was no energy left within me, it was probably my religious training, of which hope was a basic ingredient, that gave me the will to continue walking. I thought of my poor father, who had suffered hunger and deprivation all of his life, yet never lost hope. His favourite song was '*Aani maamin beamoonah shlaimah*' — 'I have complete faith in the coming of the Messiah'.

We kept marching, dragging one foot after the other. The load on my back and shoulders was buckling me. I tried to take my thoughts away from my pain, but all I could think of was my parents, and that gave rise to another kind of pain. My father had not spoken to me for some years. Would we ever speak again? And my mother, an angel . . . Were they dead? I pictured their frail faces, their bodies racked with tuberculosis. Surely they would have been among the first to be transported and gassed. But miracles happened. Hadn't my own survival so far been miraculous?

My pain was winning. If I dropped the gear, I reasoned, I might be able to walk some more. But how could I throw away the warm clothes and the blanket without which I would freeze now the winter was here? And what of the food in the side-pack? I had had no chance to check, but I could feel cans. I could not possibly part with them.

This war must end soon, I promised myself. The Allies are near, perhaps already on German soil. The Russians are on German soil and pushing forward. They are coming this way too . . . How long can these bastards hold out?

Delirious with exhaustion, we arrived at the gate of a big building that looked like stables. But there were no horses in sight. I could see the first rows of our people turning into a spacious yard. I woke from my daze — we had made it! What a joy, to throw off our gear and lie down on the straw! Jesus was born in a stable, I thought. I nearly laughed out loud.

It was still dark outside when we were woken with 'Raus, raus Juden!' We wandered drunkenly into a yard dimly illuminated by a few light-globes placed sparingly around the yard. I could see a tap running and several people having a wash around it. In the middle of the yard, on an open fireplace, a huge pot was boiling. A German soldier stood beside it, rubbing his hands for warmth. I was shivering. I washed my face and the freezing water cleared my head: I remembered where I was, and how I had arrived here.

The overcoat I had inherited provided excellent insulation; I blessed the soul of poor Erno for providing me with it. I shouldered the side-pack and joined the queue for whatever it was that was being dished out of the steaming pot. Then I realised that I did not have anything to eat or drink from. I ran back to the rucksack, and sure enough there was a tin cup and a mess tin. I grabbed them and ran back to the queue, greatly relieved. Again I had to bless old Erno. What would I have done had he not died?

We were all given a cup of hot ersatz coffee, a piece of dark bread and a portion of marmalade. While we were sipping the lovely hot brew, a stool was placed in the centre of the yard and the lieutenant mounted it. A hush fell over us as his voice rang out.

'Listen, men, we were brought here to do a job. If you do your work well and behave according to the rules that will be posted, you will come to no harm. So finish your breakfast quickly and line up, three abreast, ready to move out.' Before he climbed down he advised each platoon to leave one man behind to guard everybody's belongings and clean the place. The job would rotate daily.

When we lined up it turned out that there were some thirty-odd men, myself included, who did not belong to any platoon. After a short consultation with the SA officer we were dispersed among the other platoons. Peter and I were assigned to the fifth platoon.

When we moved out into the dark, the cold mist allowed us to see only a few feet ahead. I could barely make out the shape of the little houses that lined both sides of the road. Here and there a human form could be made out standing at a gate, watching us march by. Now and again something would come flying at us; as people caught these flying objects, they revealed themselves to be pieces of bread, a slice of bacon, a pair of warm socks. It was finders keepers: whoever was lucky got something. The rest of us just hoped that maybe next time we would be lucky. Provided there *was* a next time.

We marched for the best part of an hour. Our guards walked silently beside us, some holding German shepherds on short leashes. There was no need to drive us on; we were going fast, due to the cold.

The darkness gradually rolled away with the rising of the sun. Though the land was still partly veiled by mist, we saw that the gravel road we marched on was narrow and on both sides stood fields of maize, the dried-out plants still bearing ears of grain which had been almost picked clean by the birds. The same was true for large patches of sunflowers we passed. It was evident that the majority of the peasants who owned these fields were not home to look after them.

The mist lifted and at last we could see the countryside clearly. The land surrounding us was flat and arable. Ahead was a small forest on top of a slight rise. As we approached the woods I noticed several small huts between the trees. We were stopped in front of one of these huts and issued with picks and shovels before being marched through the forest and over the hill. At the bottom, we were lined up across a couple of hundred feet and put to work, digging.

Some of the men who had been in units retreating from the Eastern Front soon realised what it was we had been ordered to dig: an anti-tank trench. Curiously enough, this moved us to work harder, almost enjoying our labour, for it was clear to us that this meant the Russians were closing in and coming our way. Some of the SA guards looked bewildered at the quickening pace of our work, suspicious of our motives.

By nine o'clock the sun was shining on us, warming our bones, and my spirits began to rise. While working we didn't dare talk openly, but words still flowed all along the line of digging men. At ten o'clock we were allowed to rest for twenty minutes.

We sat in small groups, soaking in the sunshine and talking softly, choosing our words carefully: we did not know if any of the guards spoke Hungarian. Young Peter came over to me from where he had been sitting with some other men.

'What good news have you heard, Peter?' I asked by way of a greeting.

'Nothing much,' he replied. 'Only that we are about midway between Vienna and the Hungarian border, and that it is a very good sign if they need us to dig trenches here. Hopefully our ordeal will soon be over.'

'All we have to do is survive long enough,' I said.

Peter looked at me a moment, then said, 'You know, you never told me your name.'

'Alex. Friends have called me Sender.'

Peter smiled and offered his hand. 'Well, you have a friend here.'

'Friends come few and far between, Peter.'

'You know, Sender, you talk like an old man.'

'Yes, I have always been old, my friend.'

As we searched each other's faces for understanding, the order came to resume work. At noon we received some soup and a slice of bread. The soup was thick with vegetables and a few pieces of horse meat.

After starving for a week, it seemed a grand feast, and we ate slowly, drawing flavour and nourishment from each warm mouthful.

The sun began to set around five in the afternoon and we were marched off to the shed to return our tools. On our way back to the stables Peter marched beside me, and we continued in hushed voices our conversation from the morning break. Peter began to talk about his family.

'My father was a butcher,' he explained, then fell heavily silent.

'What's wrong?' I asked.

'I just realised that I am already talking about him as if he was dead.' He looked at me bewildered, perhaps hoping I would reassure him that his father was not dead. I could do no such thing.

'We are all in the same boat, Peter. All we can do is hope. If we lose that, what is there to hang on to?'

'Are you religious?' he asked. I just laughed and gave him an outline of my life over the past nine years. When I finished, Peter shook his head.

'I find it hard to believe,' he said finally.

'I suppose to someone with your background it must sound incredible. Unfortunately — or, who knows, maybe fortunately — this has been my life.'

'What Jewish family would let a child of nine leave home? I have never even heard of a Jewish family where there was not enough food for the children. If what you say is true . . . '

'Peter, whether you believe me or not means little to me. But what reason would I have to lie to you? The biggest lie I could tell is that I never lie. I have lied a lot in the past, when I found it necessary or saw some advantage in it. But I never made lying a way of life.'

Peter put out his hand, saying, 'Sender, I don't know why, but I believe you.' I shook his outstretched palm, murmuring thanks.

By this time we had arrived back at our quarters. There was a huge pot boiling over a makeshift fireplace in the yard. Many of us had a wash, and some even changed their shirts in preparation for supper, which was the same as breakfast: a slice of bread, a small portion of marmalade and a cup of instant coffee.

By quarter to seven we were ordered into the stable and off to bed — or rather, to straw. In three days we were all crawling with lice. Not since my experience in Kosice had I known lice to be so bad. There had been times in recent years when I had had no place to sleep and had spent nights in cemeteries with no access to washing facilities and no change of underwear. Sometimes these periods of homelessness had lasted for two or three weeks. But even then I would chance being caught by the authorities by going at least once a week to a government delousing station, where I could have a hot shower while my clothes were cleaned. My loathing of lice was greater than my fear of being caught and perhaps deported.

Here in Bruk an der Leite I had decided to adopt a wait-and-see attitude, putting up with the situation until such time as things improved. But the lice changed me. I decided I had to rid myself of the little parasites at all costs, and the only way to do so was to escape the camp.

16

The Good Deed

'Listen,' I said to Peter as we marched to our day's digging, 'I'm going to escape.'

He looked at me with disbelief.

'I can't stand the lice,' I explained. 'Come with me.'

'Have you gone mad? Where the hell would you go?' There's no place within a hundred miles where you could be safe!' He fell silent after these expostulations, nervous that he had drawn attention to ourselves. After a few minutes he resumed in a quieter tone. 'These people want us to do a job for them, and as long as we do it we are safe. They do not require us to work too hard and they feed us reasonably well. Right?'

'All right,' I conceded. 'But this job won't last long. What do you think will happen to us after the job is finished? Do you think for one minute that they'll let us wait here for the Russians or the Western Allies? I tell you, they won't feed us one lousy meal after the job is finished. As soon as they have no further use for us they'll dispose of us abruptly. The lice will still be here, but we won't.'

Peter looked at me as if he was seeing me for the very first time, his face contorted with anger.

'Shut up and stop your doomsday predictions! Ever since I had the misfortune to run into you I've heard not one word of hope from your mouth. All you can predict is doom and more doom.'

'Peter,' I said quietly, 'you act like you know nothing of what has befallen our parents, brothers and sisters, and many many tens of thousands of Jews like them all over Europe. Let me tell you, and I am not going to tell unsubstantiated stories. What I can tell you are confirmed facts, facts people have managed to smuggle through to our people in Eretz Yisrael. The Germans have murdered virtually all of our brethren. By mass shootings, by gassing. And then they burn them in special factories designed for efficient disposal. There are reports of — '

'Shut up,' Peter hissed, 'Shut up! I don't believe any of that. Just shut up!' To my amazement he began sobbing quietly, tears streaming down his face.

We marched silently towards our day's work.

As the days wore on, our enthusiasm for the job began to fade. Not only had our bodies begun to weaken — the food they fed us deteriorated, and portions shrank — but as the days passed we failed to hear the reassuring thunder of the big guns we had expected any day. We began to despair of being rescued soon.

And as despair ate away at our souls, so the lice fed on our bodies. Perhaps I was more conscious of them than most. Daily my desperation grew. Whenever we had a break I used the time to eliminate some of my crawling tormentors. Thousands crawled around the linings of my clothes, and vast numbers of eggs lay scattered along the seams.

As our work efforts slackened, the attitude of our guards changed. Where at the beginning they had been relaxed and relatively tolerant, now they became tense and aggressive, hitting out with their rifle butts and kicking with their heavy boots.

On the morning of our twelfth day in Bruk an der Leite I decided to escape, on my own if necessary. As we marched to work I tried once more to convince Peter to join me. He was silent for several minutes and I thought perhaps he had not heard me. As I considered whether or not to repeat the question he turned to me and nodded his head. A great feeling of relief came over me, as if I had been granted permission to escape. The thought of Peter accompanying me filled me with courage.

My plan was simple. On the way back from our day's work, as we passed the maize field where the plants were still standing we would jump in among the stalks and lie down until the battalion had marched past. When the coast was clear we would start off towards the Hungarian border, moving at night and only through the fields to avoid roads and rail tracks.

I estimated that we were only about 60 kilometres from the border, probably less, and figured we would be able to walk that distance in two nights. I explained all of this to Peter during the midday break.

'How will we find our direction at night?' he asked.

'By the stars.'

'And what if the nights are clouded?'

'Then we'll go by the direction of the wind.' He looked doubtful. 'Don't worry,' I said, 'I have a good sense of direction. You won't get lost while you are with me.'

I could sense Peter wavering. I tried hard to think of something reassuring I could say to him, but nothing came to mind. I was not too sure myself where this action of mine would lead us. I knew that the chances of finding a reasonable hiding place to last us until the Russians arrived were very slim. But I trusted my luck, which had seen me through so many perilous situations in the past.

Yet, I told myself, we surely had at least as much of a chance in Hungary as we did in the clutches of the SA. There was no future in staying with this group.

The afternoon seemed to drag on end-lessly, but eventually the day's work came to an end and we were marched off. As we began the homeward journey the sun disappeared behind an overcast sky and the smell of rain permeated the air. We reached the spot where I had intended to jump out of the column, at a bend of the road where we were out of sight of the guards both front and rear. I winked at Peter and jumped into the maize, throwing myself down in the narrow ditch between two rows of stalks. Seconds later, Peter followed my lead.

We lay there for several long minutes until the last guard had disappeared. Once his steps had faded, we rose to our feet. 'So far so good,' I whispered to my companion. Adrenaline flooded my body.

We had walked only a few hundred metres when the rain came down in sheets. The sky was thick with black clouds and we were soon wet to the bone. We found ourselves in a huge field of carrots. Like the maize field, this one had not been harvested properly and there were still many carrots left. We gathered some, washed them in the rain and ate them.

When we left the field it was pitch dark. We pressed on, hoping we were going in the right direction. After walking for three or four hours we came upon a haystack. Our strength drained, it seemed a logical place to rest, at least until the rain stopped. We began to pull out hay so that we could crawl inside and be protected. But it was hard work and we had no energy for it. We only pulled out enough to get in up to our knees; our legs remained outside, pounded by the incessant rain. We could not sleep, but rested there for a couple of hours before setting off again.

The field was awash with mud and we sank time and again up to our ankles. I checked our bearings by the wind: it was blowing south-easterly, more or less the direction we wanted to go. After a further two or three hours we came upon another haystack. We circled it to see where it would be easiest to pull out hay for a hole to crawl into. To our horror we discovered that it was the same haystack we had left hours earlier.

'So much for your sense of direction,' Peter muttered. I had no answer, but set about pulling out enough hay this time to enable me to get completely out of the rain's reach. We burrowed like tiny animals and huddled, shivering, while the rain drummed against the hay outside. Slowly our insulation held our body heat around us and exhaustion drew sleep upon us for a few hours.

When I woke up in the morning it was still pouring relentlessly. I could hear Peter stirring next to me. I didn't feel like moving out of the warm hay and into the biting rain, but I was very hungry, and anyway, we could not stay here indefinitely. The skies were dark in every direction; the rain was not going to let up. I dreaded turning to Peter to discuss our next step. How funny, I mused, that I could not do right as far as he was concerned. While trying to save him from one peril I had landed him into another, no less dangerous. I wondered whether he should try to slip back into the camp.

After a while I gathered all my willpower and dragged myself out of the relative comfort of the dry hay and into the cold rain. I stood up and shivered. The wind was colder now and the driving rain immediately pierced my clothes. I saw some buildings about a kilometre away.

'Peter,' I said, 'there are some buildings not far from here. Shall we take a chance? Maybe the people there will help us? We have very little to lose — we are lost anyway.' Peter crawled out of his hole and we started off towards the buildings without a word being said between us.

The first building was a small house with square windows, all shut, as was to be expected on a cold, rainy day. We hid in a thicket, watching the house, while I worked up the courage to run to a window and listen. When I did, I heard men's voices from inside, but could not make out the language. I had no reason to assume it was anything other than German. I ran back to Peter and told him that there might be German soldiers in the house.

We lay in the thicket for a while, uncertain. The rain and wind eased, but still we remained crouched where we were, anxious. Suddenly a man came out to urinate just a few feet from where we lay. He wore a uniform that wasn't German, but we could not decipher what army's uniform it was. His cap looked like the one the Czechoslovak army wore. Could we be in Slovakia? There would be a reasonable chance of finding a hiding place in Slovakia; I had spoken Slovak fairly well years earlier and I felt confident I could express myself adequately in that language.

Then it occurred to me, just as I was ready

to approach the house, that we couldn't be in Slovakia — the Danube was the border between Austria and Slovakia, and we certainly hadn't crossed the Danube. That meant we were still on German soil.

So who were these men in the house? That was the question which bothered us.

'Peter,' I said, 'I'm going in. These men are soldiers for sure, but not Germans. Maybe they will help us. You stay here. If I don't come out in a few minutes then something has happened to me and you had better disappear.'

Peter just nodded his head. I stood, pushing down my fear, and dashed to the door. Slowly I opened it a fraction. Inside I could see four men wearing the same uniform as the one we had seen earlier. They were seated at a table, playing cards and smoking. It struck me for the first time that they could be Ukrainian renegades — Vlassov's men, fighting for the Germans. If so they would be even less inclined to help a Jew than the Germans. Cold sweat ran down my spine as I delicately closed the door and turned.

Suddenly I found myself staring into the face of a man who was returning from the toilet.

We eyed each other silently. I was shaking with fear and cold and was sweating profusely. He spoke, and at first I did not understand what he was saying. Then he repeated himself, speaking slowly and softly: '*Kto ste we a shto ochete. Ne rozumite? Nix fershtein?*' Then it dawned on me that this man spoke Serbian. I understood a little. He was asking me who I was and what I wanted. Then he added, first in Serbian, then in broken German, 'Don't you understand?' As soon as I found my voice I told him I was a Jew and had escaped from a camp in Bruk an der Leite.

He looked quickly around, checking that there was nobody around, and motioned me to go into the house. As we entered the men looked up and, on seeing me, stopped playing cards, puzzled. Before anyone could say a word, the Serbian went up to the table where they were sitting and, in a soft voice, told them who I was. They looked at me curiously. To my great relief, there was no malice in their expressions as they examined me.

The men held a quick conversation among themselves, then one of them beckoned me to come to the table. 'You understand our language?' he asked. I nodded. 'Well, we are Yugoslav prisoners of war. You are lucky — the soldiers usually watching us are not around. Even so, there is little we can do for you. Are you alone?'

I shook my head. 'My partner is in the thicket outside. We had no idea who you were but we are desperate. Terribly hungry, lost and exhausted.'

'We can't do much for you,' the man repeated. He turned to his companions and held another conversation, then turned to me again. 'We have little in the way of food. We are not overfed ourselves. We will give you a little bread and some cheese — Red Cross rations. Do you smoke?' I nodded. He pulled out a packet of American Camel cigarettes and handed me two. In the meantime, his mates produced a large portion of bread, a small piece of cheese, twelve cubes of sugar, and two cigarettes each. All these riches, except for one cigarette which they lit for me, they neatly wrapped into a clean piece of white cotton and handed to me. 'Now where do you want to go?' they asked.

'To Hungary.'

'All right,' said the spokesman. 'The border is only about 10 kilometres from here.' He beckoned me over to the window, which he opened a little. 'You see over there a small cluster of houses? That is the village midway to the Hungarian border. You had better stay hidden somewhere for the rest of the day. Unfortunately you cannot stay here, because our guards may show up any time.' He pointed to a small elevation several hundred metres away. 'Behind that hill there are some haystacks. You could hide there during the day, but you had better be quick about it. And good luck,' he added.

I thanked them for their kindness and turned to leave, but at the door a thought struck me.

'May I ask you a question?' I asked. They nodded. 'You don't seem to be watched very closely,' I commented. 'Why don't you escape?'

Astonished silence greeted my question. Finally, one of the group, apparently their senior man, replied. I could feel the indignation and resentment in his voice as he said, 'They are holding our families hostage. If one of us escapes, a member of his family will be shot.' I felt humbled and I murmured an apology, saying I had no idea. The man waved his hand, saying, 'It's all right. Go with God.'

All this time, Peter was watching the door for a sign as to what was going on inside. When he saw me emerge from the house with a package in my arms, he came eagerly towards me. I hurried to meet him. 'Let's get away from here. There are haystacks not far away where we can hide. I will tell you everything there.'

We took off as fast as we could through the muddy field. It took us the best part of an hour to get there. With great effort we managed to climb into the haystack, and after settling down in relative comfort we divided the food between us, eating slowly, making it last. 'I don't suppose we can smoke in a haystack,' I mused.

I told Peter about the Yugoslavs, and he listened without saying a word. His silence was beginning to trouble me. He was not responding, no matter what I said. It began to dawn on me that something was very wrong with him. I thought about how sheltered he had been all his life, and how unprepared he was for his current experiences. For the first time it occured to me how vulnerable this poor fellow was compared to me. But there was nothing I could do for him: he seemed beyond reach.

And so we lay there in silence.

The afternoon seemed to go on forever. When at last evening came, the wind strengthened, buffeting us as we crawled out of the haystack. But the rain had slackened, at least. We began to drag ourselves towards the Hungarian border. It took us at least three hours of struggling through the mud to arrive at the village the Yugoslavs had pointed out to me — halfway, they had said, to the border. It took another three hours of wading through mud to navigate a big circle around the village. At some stage during that detour I noticed that I had lost one of my boots. I had neither the will nor the energy to go back and search for the lost boot, so I removed the remaining one and threw it away.

By the time the village was behind us we were absolutely exhausted. We hauled ourselves to the nearest haystack and used the last vestiges of our depleted energies to pull out enough hay to create a hole large enough to contain us. Disappearing inside, we promptly fell asleep.

I awoke, hungry and wet, about noon the next day. The rain had stopped and the wind had abated. I could see the outline of the border village ahead, and the road leading to it. Traffic on the road was light but constant, so we could not move from our hole. It would have been nice to sleep the afternoon through, but our hunger and the cold would not let us.

As was always the case in times of trouble, my father came to mind. I remembered him telling us as children how terribly he had suffered from hunger in his youth. Father said it often happened that he went to bed without an evening meal, and at times he had nothing at all to eat for two days in a row. Many nights he could not sleep for hunger. Once he was so hungry he tried to eat the mud brick in the wall beside his bed.

I remembered vaguely the house that Father was born and raised in. Before our own decline into poverty we lived next door to it, in a better, larger one bought for us by my maternal grandfather. There was a huge backyard in my father's old house, perhaps 200 metres long. The family could have grown enough potatoes, beans and corn to feed themselves all year around. They could have planted fruit trees. But there was nothing.

My father could have been a teacher of Hebrew and Yiddish in one of the Jewish community schools, but he did not have the drive for it. And he was too proud to go begging. He used to quote old Hillel, one of the most revered sages of ancient Israel, who said, '*Pshot nevailtah bashook, valo tizdakek labriot*' — 'Skin dead animals in the market place, but don't put yourself at the mercy of people.' Thus did my father preach. Sadly, his actions hardly matched his rhetoric, for he did nothing if not put himself at the mercy of people, even if indirectly. Our frail, over-worked and undernourished mother had to provide for him too.

Mother often nagged my father to tell her

one of his stories — old Jewish legends and childish Chasidic folklore which she loved to listen to. One such story came back to me then, lying in my haystack just beyond the Hungarian border. It was about how greatly tzedakah (charity) was appreciated in heaven. There was a miserly rich Jew, my father used to tell, who never did any good deeds in his life, except one. He bought a tallith for a young man who was too poor to buy one. Now, this miser died and his funeral was very poorly attended. Among those few who did attend was a saintly rabbi. As they buried the rich man, the rabbi stood there looking intently into the grave, and continued to do so long after the grave was covered and the Kaddish recited. Those who accompanied the rabbi looked at each other, waiting impatiently for him to leave. Yet nobody dared disturb him or ask him what he was looking at. After a long time a smile appeared on the rabbi's face and he turned away from the freshly covered grave. Later, before the evening prayers, the rabbi told his congregation the following: 'As they put the old man in his grave, I saw a couple of shaidim [devils] coming up to claim him, but before they could reach him a tallith appeared, dancing around the dead man so that the shaidim could not get to him. For a long time the vile spirits tried to snatch him, but every time they got close the prayer shawl warded them off. After a long while they tired of their unsuccessful attempts and left, and the tallith wrapped itself around the body. By virtue of the only mitzvah he ever fulfilled, the man was safe.'

I remembered the only good deed my father ever performed for me: he had made me a toy — the shoe-polish box nailed to a stick — when I was three years old. As memories went this was a rather skinny one. But try as I might, I could not find a better one.

Dear Sabah,

I am sorry for the delay, but I just haven't had the opportunity to write. The army has kept me busy with a training course. For the first six weeks I had not one free hour in a day: physical training ten hours a day, and on top of that lectures, compulsory reading and essay writing! This is the first free weekend I have had, and after sleeping twelve hours straight I'm in top shape and in a better condition to reply to your letter.

I am glad to hear that your little foster child brings you so much joy. But I am sorry that you are making slow progress on your manuscript. Sabah, I exhort you to go on! I am so anxious to know what happens next. But it's not just for me that I urge you to write; it's for those who weren't as lucky as you — those who didn't survive. Listen to their voices: they demand that your story be told. How else will my generation know what occurred unless people like you tell it how it was? It's up to us to do our utmost to prevent anything of the sort occurring again.

So please, Sabah, don't stop until you have accomplished what you've started.

My love to both of you,
Esther

17

Holding On and Letting Go

I stared at my silent partner. He was continuing to lose his grip on reality — breaking down, giving up hope, withdrawing into himself. He has no chance, I thought; if I stick to him I'll be doomed. I knew I had got him into this mess, but I also knew that if there was any chance of saving myself, it wasn't with Peter. I contemplated leaving him behind but, unable to resolve my conscience, I did nothing. And then my old fear of the dark rose inside me and I thought, even as he is — useless for all intents and purposes — he is better than nobody at all. Besides, what would come would come, no matter what I did. I could only try to adjust.

As the afternoon wore on, the skies darkened again, the wind strengthened and the rain resumed. It was a mixed blessing: these conditions would make our life a little more miserable, but they might also help us avoid the border guards. When it became so dark that I could not see the road, I decided it was time to move. 'Well, Peter, this is it,' I said. 'We had better get out of here and get going.' No answer.

'Peter,' I said again, 'we had better get a move on.' Still he did not move. 'Come on, Peter, we cannot stay here. Put your boots on and let's go.' At long last he stirred and slowly started to pull his boots on, without uttering a word.

We crawled out of the haystack and began walking towards the village, though we could not see it any more. We used the familiar noises coming from it to guide us — dogs barking, the sounds of moving vehicles. To our right was the road, which could not have been more than 100 metres away. I could hear the odd vehicle passing along it. I decided to turn left and pass around the village that way.

After walking for several minutes I realised that Peter was not behind me. For a second I panicked and opened my mouth to shout his name, but came to my senses just in time and refrained from calling out. I tried to pierce the darkness with my eyes, searching desperately for his figure. But it was too dark and I could neither see nor hear him. I realised that to go and look for him would probably prove futile. I was also, by this point, more afraid of getting lost than of being alone, so I pressed on regardless. I leaned into the wind and driving rain and willed myself to continue. I could not feel my legs; machine-like, I pressed onward.

Eventually I saw the outlines of small guard houses, spaced every 200 metres. I lay low, watching. Now and again the door of one or another would open and someone would enter or leave. There was nothing else for it: I gathered all my willpower and the little energy I could muster and began wading through the mud as fast as possible between two guard houses, desperate to pass before someone came out again. When I drew level with the guard houses, the door of first one and then the other burst open and out jumped two huge German shepherds, dragging their keepers along. More guards came running, their rifles in hand, yelling '*Halt, halt!*'

I was finished. I had no energy and no fight left in me. I keeled over like a stricken animal. The dogs stopped short of me and stopped barking while their masters came closer to take a look. '*Was ist denn passiert?*' — 'What's going on?' I was numb, but I could still hear them. 'I don't know,' another replied in German. 'He just collapsed.' One of them prodded me with his foot, and I stirred. '*Er ist nicht tot*' — 'He is not dead'.

I was past caring about anything and was

only vaguely aware of what was going on around me. The soldiers stood over my hunched-up body, wondering what to make of me, then an NCO came along and ordered two of them to lift me up and put me in an open van. With two soldiers guarding me, the NCO drove the van through the rain towards the village police station. There the soldiers peeled my sodden overcoat off me, struggling with its waterlogged weight. Water streamed off me, forming puddles which stretched out across the floor. I was so hungry and exhausted I hardly felt the cold. We sat and waited for an interpreter. Although I could speak German fairly well, I had said that I only spoke Hungarian. Despite my physical exhaustion, my mind was still functioning well. An inner voice was warning me: watch it, Alex, you are swimming in perilous waters.

Soon an old man appeared, speaking broken Hungarian. He turned out to be a well-meaning Austrian. What he didn't understand he invented to make up a fairly reasonable story. I had a document (false, of course) depicting me as a sixteen-year-old refugee from Szolnok, a town in eastern Hungary that had fallen to the Russians a month or so earlier, but the paper was hardly readable after the soaking it had endured.

I told the Germans, through the inter-preter, that I was a refugee trying to reach the safety of Germany. When asked why I hadn't gone through the proper channels, and how it was that I was coming from Germany, the old man explained that I was a simpleton, as was obvious, and that I must have lost my way in the terrible weather. The policeman in charge seemed to be satisfied with this explanation, and proceeded to write out a short report.

Before he left, the old man asked if they were going to feed me. The policeman shrugged his shoulders indifferently, at which the Austrian protested, 'The poor fellow looks in great need of a good feed.'

'There is nothing here to feed him with,' the policeman replied curtly, then added, 'I would not say no to a good feed myself.'

The old man left and some ten minutes later returned with a thick slice of bread and a good slice of bacon. He gave it to me. This was the first meal I had eaten in two days, and it had been a much longer time since I had tasted something so nourishing. A starving dog could not have looked more gratefully at his master feeding him. I heaped all the blessings I knew on the old man, in a mixture of Hungarian and Hebrew.

As soon as I disposed of the wonderful food I was locked up in a cell. It had a bare concrete floor, not even a mat of any description. I lay on the cold floor and fell almost immediately into a sound sleep.

In the morning, despite having slept on concrete in my wet clothes, I felt no physical ill-effects, not so much as a sneeze. I sat there pondering my future. How many times had I found myself locked up, and how many times had I escaped? So long as I had my health and my wits I felt optimistic.

The door of my cell opened and two Hungarian gendarmes appeared, carrying rifles with bayonets fixed. (I must have seemed a very dangerous prisoner, I mused!) They promptly took charge of me and I was driven off towards Hungary. As soon as we were in no-man's-land, the senior officer turned to me. 'Now tell us the truth. How did you get here, and why?'

Here I made the mistake that probably saved my life. I thought to appeal to the gendarme's sense of common bond, so I told him that I had gone to Germany with a group of refugees and that they had taken us to Steyermark, where they put us in cramped and dirty accommodation, working us hard and feeding us next to nothing. So I had taken off, and decided to wait at home, in Hungary, for the Russians to be pushed back before I could go home to Szolnok.

This story wasn't entirely the product of my own imagination; in Budapest I had heard rumours of this sort of thing happening. My story stopped the gendarme dead. 'So!' he said, 'In that case we have to take you back!' At the time I thought that I had made a fatal error, but in retrospect I am sure that this mistake saved my life. Had I acted otherwise, I would most likely have been found out to be the Jew that I was and delivered to the Nazis, who would not have hesitated to shoot me. As it was, they took me back to the Germans and the senior gendarme told them my story.

The German officer turned to the gendarme in charge, saying, '*Vielleicht ist das ein Jude?*' — 'Maybe this is a Jew?' The senior gendarme, a big brute of a man, turned to me and asked, 'Are you a Jew?'

I straightened up and replied, 'No.'

The gendarme slapped me with an open hand across my face, and I fell to the floor. I got up and looked at my tormentor. He asked the same question again, and I answered again in the negative. He hit me again, and I fell, then pulled myself up without uttering a sound. I was hardly on my legs when he asked the same question yet again, and this time I answered angrily, 'I told you I am not!'

At that the gendarme said to the German officer, '*Das ist kein Jude*' — 'This is no Jew'.

The gendarme explained that a person who doesn't crawl and cry when threatened wasn't a Jew. I was grateful for the stupidity that this man so proudly and stereotypically displayed. (In Hungary at that time, if one wanted to depict someone as very stupid one would say that the person was 'as stupid as two gendarmes': the joke went that they always travelled in pairs, because only one could read and the other write.)

The German officer accepted the gendarme's conclusion. It was a small miracle. I was put back into the cell, and a couple of hours later delivered to the Gestapo and taken to Vienna.

My dear Esther,

Your letter brought me to tears. And I understand now what I must do. It will be enough if only you read this story. I thank you for having the courage to talk about death. You and I both have seen enough death.

You are right — if I do not complete this process, my story will die with me. The voices of those who did not make it cry out for me to speak for them. And the voices of those not yet born to our people, maybe your own children one day, cry out to be told. It is for these reasons that I will continue, no matter the difficulties. Whether the book is published now or not is irrelevant.

> *I thank you for your strength and your love.*
> *Your loving Sabah*

The train ride to Vienna was uneventful, but as soon as my guard and I arrived at the Austrian capital the air-raid sirens went off and we had to spend some three hours in a shelter near the station. As soon as the all clear was given we were taken to a bus which took us to the Rosauer Kasserne, a huge, L-shaped prison on the corner of two streets. Here I was given a shower and my clothes were deloused. My hunger and exhaustion aside, I felt triumphant to be rid, finally, of the lice. My spirits rose a little, and a tremor of hope moved through my blood.

As soon as I was dressed I was taken to Gestapo headquarters in Mortzen Platz. Sitting on a bench, waiting to be interrogated, I began to relax somewhat. The events of the last two days revolved in my head. That I was still alive was nothing short of a miracle. I remembered how, when I had first been brought into the police station at the border, a young SS man had come in to visit his friend and on seeing me had asked, 'What is this thing?', to which his mate had replied, 'Just some little bastard we caught at the border.' Then, as an afterthought, he added, 'Maybe you could take him outside a few hundred metres and finish him off?' The SS man scoffed: 'You crazy? In this weather? No thanks!' A miracle, I told myself.

The bench where I sat was on the fourth floor, and through a window I could see out over the metropolis. Most of the buildings I saw had been reduced to rubble, the result of systematic daily bombings by the Americans. I found myself hoping they wouldn't be coming again today — not while I sat at the Gestapo headquarters, at least.

From where I was seated I could see into an office where a middle-aged bespectacled man sat looking through some papers. He didn't fit the fearful image of the Gestapo man that most of us imagined. I wondered how he would treat me. After I had waited for about an hour, the man came out of his office and stopped in front of me. He was a tall, lean, fatherly figure, and I could see no malice in his features. After giving me a good looking-over, he asked, '*Sprichst du Deutsch?*' — 'Do you speak German?'

I gave him an uncomprehending look and shook my head, saying, '*Csak magyarul beszelek*' — 'I only speak Hungarian.'

'Hmm,' the Gestapo man grunted. 'Now what am I going to do with you? I have no interpreter. Never mind; I shall write something.'

He motioned me to come into his office and sit down. I waited while he rang home and spoke to a woman, probably his wife, asking how his child was. He didn't seem reassured by the answers he received. Eventually he said, 'Na *schön gut,*' and put the phone down, looking unhappy.

He sighed and took some papers out of a big brown envelope, probably the report about me. He must have had difficulty deciphering the handwriting, for he furrowed his forehead and peered closely at the paper, glancing back and forth trying to figure out what he was reading. While he was struggling thus, a younger man in SS uniform came in. When my interrogator looked up and saw him, his eyes lit up and he jumped up from his seat, hurrying towards the young man. '*Mein lieber Junge,*' he said, and father and son embraced and shook hands, then started talking, both at the same time. The Gestapo man looked at me and motioned me to get out. As I sat outside I mused to myself: well, well, even Gestapo and SS men can behave like human beings! At least towards each other.

After ten minutes the young SS man walked out of the office. His father stood at the door of his office, looking after his disappearing son. Some minutes later I was called into the office again, and the official, now in a much better mood, looked at the papers again then said, 'Ah, what the hell.' He began writing, occasionally pausing to throw me a thoughtful glance, before continuing.

When he had finished he pulled out an attaché case and took out a newspaper and a brown paper bag, from which he drew some sandwiches. My eyes almost popped out of their sockets and my mouth began watering. I had not eaten since the previous night. Seeing the food brought on the hunger which fear had almost made me forget. The Gestapo man suddenly looked at me, then at the sandwich, then at me again. '*Du armer Hund*' — 'You poor dog', he said, and threw the sandwiches into my lap. I was so hungry that it didn't occur to me to be surprised by his humane gesture.

About two hours later I was taken back to the Rosauer Kasserne. Yet again I had come through on the brighter side of things. Maybe what Rudi had said was true. Maybe I was a survivor.

18

Relativity

According to the papers that came with me, I was sixteen years of age. Accordingly, I was put into the children's cell, where the ages of the prisoners ranged from fourteen to seventeen years.

It was late afternoon by the time I got settled in the cell; lunch had been served more than three hours before I arrived. I consoled myself with the thought that it probably wasn't as nourishing as the sandwiches I had received from the Gestapo man. Around five o'clock the evening meal was served, consisting of 100 grams of bread, a few grams of margarine, the same amount of marmalade and a mouthful of a brew they called coffee. About an hour later, blankets were distributed, and thin straw mattresses were laid out under supervision by a guard.

In my six weeks at the prison I came to know some of the inmates. While the situation in which we all found ourselves was hardly enviable, for me, having endured so much in the last few weeks, it was in a sense a relief to

302

be in a place where daily life was not a struggle for survival. At least I did not have to labour with pick and shovel. I had a bed to sleep in, a weekly shower, and the food, while miserly in proportions, was at least regular. Moreover, for the first time in a long time I had the company of youths close to my own age and plenty of time to share with them.

A couple of days after my arrival a young man of about sixteen was brought in. He was tall, blond and blue-eyed — the very personification of a true Aryan. His name suggested a French origin — Kunoe de Peronne — but he was in fact an Austrian. On the first day he tried to keep to himself. He seemed bewildered and confused, and I guessed he had come from a good family and had never dreamed of being arrested and treated like a criminal. I soon learned that both his father and mother were under arrest and were somewhere else in the building. A very young sister was being cared for by a relative. Their crime had been to listen to enemy broadcasts. All this he told me on the second night as we lay beside each other, unable to sleep.

Just as I could recognise a crook from a mile off, I also knew a decent fellow whenever I came across one. I identified Kunoe as such a one and decided to trust him with my own story. Revealing my identity, I told him that I held great fears that I would be discovered a Jew. More in wishfulness than in seriousness, I told him I had decided to take the first opportunity to flee. Hearing this, he looked around to check that all were asleep and then unscrewed the heel of his boot. Out of its cavity he pulled some bank notes and gave me a fifty-mark note, saying, 'You'll need some money if you manage to escape. I have also managed to stash away two pistols at a certain spot. If you wish, tomorrow I'll draw you a map of the place. Take them to defend yourself. If I were you I wouldn't let them capture me; I'd rather die fighting.'

The whole scene was so unreal, as if it came straight from a spy movie. I questioned the young man further, curious to know where his passionate anti-Nazi sentiments came from. He explained that, in the beginning, his parents had believed the Nazi propaganda and had joined the Party after the inclusion of Austria in the Third Reich. It didn't take them long to become disillusioned with Nazism, however. After hearing horror stories from soldiers who saw or participated in the wholesale murders of Jewish men, women and children, they came to abhor all that they had previously embraced. But by the time they realised what was going on they were unable to oppose the Nazis openly, or even leave the Party. Young Kunoe had to join the Hitler Youth. He was even promoted. That was how he came to have access to weapons, and how he managed to stash away the pistols and ammunition.

'We thought we'd never be caught,' said Kunoe at the end of his story. 'I am sure it was someone my parents trusted who denounced us to the Gestapo.'

From the time we confided in each other, Kunoe and I became inseparable, always sitting together and talking softly about our past and our hopes for the future.

One morning the past caught up with me in a most unexpected way. I was in the washroom together with the inmates of another cell when I spotted Joachim, the young soldier who had offered me his rifle in Transylvania some months before. I guessed that the poor fellow must have deserted again, but now he was at the age where his life would not be spared. He had changed little — perhaps a bit thinner, a trifle older and somewhat sadder.

We could not talk in the washroom — it wasn't permitted. And there were too many guards to chance it. We just looked at each other with the surprise and delight of recognition.

There was another young man amongst us, a German of about sixteen, who was not well liked by any of the inmates. He was a faithful Nazi and was always trying to enlighten the company of the virtues of Nazism. The Ukrainians, of whom there were three in our cell and who wore their anti-Nazi sentiments smugly, often played cruel jokes on the poor fellow. One night they pulled his blanket off him and he, in his stupidity, called the guard. The guard opened the door and without listening to his explanation gave him a terrible beating for disturbing the peace.

This boy's name was Fritz and his story was a sad one. His father had been a member of the Tod organisation — a paramilitary force. This man was seldom home, working at times hundreds of kilometres away. While he was away, the boy's mother carried on with other men. Every time his father came home, someone would tell him about his wife's infidelities and he'd beat the daylights out of her. But as soon as he was away again, and the swelling around her eyes had disappeared, she was back in business for herself. Finally poor Fritz could take no more; he had had enough of watching this cycle of violence. He packed a few things and took to the road, whence he was picked up by the police for vagrancy and ended up in our cell. Even in

306

prison he remained a fervent Nazi.

The days in the cell were long, even for December's shortened days. At times, when there was nothing else to keep us lively, we played games. One of the games we made up we called 'arse-smacking'. The rules were simple. One player would hide his head in the lap of another player, then a third person would give him a smack on his arse. The recipient would have to guess who it was that smacked him. If he guessed correctly, the one caught would replace him and proffer his bottom to be smacked.

As soon as the game began we'd urge Fritz to strike. Sure enough, he would be caught, since we signalled each other, and Fritz would bend over to be smacked. If it had been anyone else's arse we would have held back, but with Fritz we let it rip. And he was never able to guess correctly. So we'd keep smacking him until we got sick of it and he couldn't sit down for days afterwards. To our bemusement, after a few days he was stupid enough to participate once again. The way I saw it, the master race was getting its arse kicked, and deservedly so.

It was also getting kicked in more serious ways by the Allies. Every day between eleven in the morning and two in the afternoon, American bombers appeared over the metropolis and sowed death and destruction on an even greater scale than before. Locked in on that fifth-floor cell of ours, we were sitting ducks while tons of bombs fell all around us, shaking the building like a tree in a storm. There were no bomb shelters for us, nor for our guards. I discovered this one day when a bomb fell very close to our building and shook it violently. Suddenly the door of our cell flew open: a guard stood with his machine pistol at the ready. I presumed he was going to shoot us if the building broke up. Miraculously, although bombs continued to fall all around us, our building remained unscathed.

The festive season brought no relief from the bombing. I am sure the soldiers on both sides of the fronts sang their Christmas carols and prayed for hope and good will, at least for their own. We sat in our cell, hoping the bombs would keep missing us. During the day raids I sometimes looked at the boys sitting by the wall like trapped animals, their faces distorted by fear, and wondered if I looked the same.

On Christmas night, two young fellows were thrown into our cell. There was a great deal of whispering for some time (new arrivals always excited interest: they were our source of news, good or bad, of the outside world). The next day it became known that the two newcomers were SA men.

One of the men sat in a corner and sulked. He spoke to no-one, making it clear that he did not want to be disturbed. Being a big, burly fellow, his wish was respected. If it hadn't been for his mate, who spoke freely, we would never have found out why they had been thrown into prison.

Apparently the two men had been guarding a temporary concentration camp for Hungarian Jews, at Bruk an der Leite — the camp I had escaped from. Among the inmates had been a rich Jew who wore a gold wristwatch, probably the last vestige of his wealth. One of the SA men fancied this watch and asked the Jew for it. The poor fellow was reluctant to part with it. He probably thought it might some day serve to buy his life with. What he didn't realise was that this was that day. Anyway, the SA man didn't wait for the Jew to make up his mind: he simply took the watch off him, and left.

The Jew, in his stupidity, complained to the commandant, who made the guard return the watch to its owner. Consequently, the guard took the Jew to the perimeter of the camp and shot him, reclaiming his watch. He filed a report asserting that the fellow had been attempting to escape. When the commandant investigated the incident he found that the reported escape attempt was false. The gold watch was found on the guard, and both he and his mate, who had signed the false report, were arrested.

The murderer said nothing to us, but his friend spared no particulars regarding the whole gruesome business. He expressed no regrets, although he was not too happy about being with us. Within days of their arrival the two men volunteered for the Waffen SS, and shortly afterwards they were gone. We did not miss them.

As time went by, our German captors became very edgy and nervous. People were arriving at the prison in droves, having been arrested for the most insignificant of reasons. Among these was a famous Viennese actor and singer by the name of Paul Hurbiger. We wondered what terrible crime he could have committed to warrant the incarceration of this highly esteemed man. One evening, during the changing of the guards, he was heard singing a song most appropriate to the times and our situation. Its refrain was, '*O du Freiheit, du wundershöner Traum*' — 'Oh you freedom, you wonderful dream'. From then on, every night when the guards changed the cry went out, 'Paul, sing us the freedom song,' and Paul would oblige.

It was clear to us that the Nazi regime was desperate, fuelling our hope of an imminent end to our predicament and a chance to survive. But we had to survive the bombing raids first. On the 20th of January it happened: a bomb fell on our building, cutting through all five floors and exploding in the basement. Incredibly, none of the prisoners were harmed, but fifty policemen died (the bomb, as if guided by a knowing hand, struck the wing where the policemen's quarters were situated).

I also had to survive my Jewishness. News reached me that Jews were being dealt with summarily. Now the fear of being found out further increased, playing terribly on my mind.

A couple of weeks after arriving at the prison I had made the discovery that the cell next to mine was full of Jews. They were being helped by the International Red Cross with extra rations of food and cigarettes, and for the time being they were safe under the protection of the charity. The two cells had a mutual waterway, serving both our toilets. One could climb up on the toilet and make contact with them, and I had done so, without giving my name, but identifying myself as a Jew by quoting the Shema Yisrael (the portions of the Scriptures repeated twice daily by adult Jewish males as a confession of faith). In this way I'd received a little something from them, now and again.

But now that the fear of discovery increased I stopped communicating with them. Even though the food they shared with me was of great value, my fear was greater than my hunger.

On the 25th of January, at six in the morning, I was called out of the cell. In the first minutes I thought, this is it, I have been found out, and now I have come to the end to my existence. But as the minutes passed and I waited in the corridor while others were called from their cells — but none from the cell in which the Jews were kept — I began to relax a little, especially when I spied Joachim amongst those coming to join me. Then I thought, oh no! Joachim is not a good omen. As a deserter, he is most likely for the chop.

My heart began pounding again. But as the company grew to some fifty or more, I relaxed again. They wouldn't do in so many people at once. No. We were most likely being transferred somewhere else.

We were told to line up in twos, and Joachim came to stand beside me. They handcuffed us together and marched us to the gate and into a prison van. Within minutes we were on our way. During the ten-minute ride, neither of us said a word.

As the van's door opened we saw that we were at a railway station, in front of a special carriage for transporting prisoners. We were seated on hard wooden seats with our feet chained to the floor and our hands to the seat. As soon as we were all loaded, the train took off, to where we could not imagine.

19

Mauthausen

Heavy clouds promised snow or rain. I looked around me: Joachim sat beside me, but otherwise I saw no familiar face. We were not allowed to talk, and our chains denied any kind of signalling. So we winked at each other. I felt reassured that wherever I was being taken, it was not as a Jew to be eliminated. (Eliminated I might still be, but not as a Jew!)

After a three-hour ride, the train drew to a stop and the guards began unlocking our chains. As I came out, I read the name of the station: Mauthausen. The name meant nothing to me. We were lined up three abreast and marched off — in the company of at least twenty SS men armed with submachine guns and holding guard dogs on heavy leashes.

It was a hilly area, cold and windy. The ground was covered with hard-packed snow. I was lucky to have the warmth of the overcoat I inherited from Erno; it offered some defence from the biting wind. But my feet weren't very comfortable in the wooden-soled boots I had been issued with at Rosauer Kasserne. I have been colder, I told myself.

Recent snowfalls were already crisp under our feet as we walked slowly towards the prison. If any of the prisoners tried to look around, he was kicked hard by the SS guard nearest him, and told harshly to keep his eyes straight ahead. I curbed my own curiosity.

The road sloped upwards and I lost my footing. A guard kicked me in the back, and I would have struggled to stand had not Joachim pulled me to my feet. He remained beside me to secure my footing as we carried on. We continued our ascent of the winding narrow road for about two hours until eventually we saw some sort of a compound ahead.

It was situated on a plateau at an elevation of some several hundred metres. It took us another half an hour to arrive at the gates of the camp. A huge wooden gate in a metal frame was flanked by stone walls. On either side of the gate stood a tower, each rising about 5 metres above the wall. Armed SS formed a welcome-guard. As the gates opened we could see a street stretching some 300 or 400 metres ahead of us, ending at a stone wall. On the left were two rows of barracks and a stone wall surrounding another row of timber buildings. On the right stood three large brick buildings, stretching the length of the street.

I could see people moving about on both sides of the street, undernourished, fear and desperation in their faces. Most of them were wearing thin prison garb with white and blue stripes. Some were dressed in normal street clothes, but these had a square patch cut out of each trouser leg and out of the back of their coats, and a piece of the prison uniform sewn into it. It was bitterly cold as we stood there waiting to be admitted.

We were taken to the second building on the right-hand side and led into a shower room. On our side of the wall were wooden benches where we had to leave our clothes. Along the opposite wall, two long tables were set up. Five men with pencils and paper sat behind them. After the shower, we had to appear naked before these clerks to give our particulars. They then assigned us barracks and identification numbers. This information was recorded on a piece of material, worn just below the left shoulder — number, nationality, prisoner's qualification: Jews had a yellow triangle, political prisoners had a red one, and criminals were denoted by green. Another set of numbers was worn on a tin bracelet on the left wrist.

As I waited, naked, in line, all my fears of

being discovered flared up again. This time I could see no way out. This time they would take one look at my circumcised penis and know I was a Jew. Was this how I was to die? I had an almost irresistible urge to run. Looking in every direction like a trapped animal, I could see no options. I found myself standing in front of a clerk, a bored-looking man in his thirties. He asked me my name. Without thinking, I told him the name I had given the border guards, and consequently the Gestapo, and all the particulars I had added. When I told him that I was a Roman Catholic of Hungarian nationality, he gave me a puzzled look. After thinking on it for several seconds — a lifetime to me — the clerk shrugged his shoulders and wrote down what I had said, then waved me on.

A miracle again! My feet trembled as I crossed to the other side of the room to collect my clothes. I am still alive, I said to myself. Before we dressed, a man with a mechanical shear came around and went through our short hair from the middle of the forehead down to the neck, creating a bald furrow to distinguish us from any normal human being — another measure to prevent successful escape.

As soon as we were dressed we were led into the barracks. Joachim and I were assigned to barrack number twenty-four, inside the quarantine division. Behind our barracks was another enclosed section which contained two more barracks. In those, Russian prisoners of war were held. This enclosure was permanently shut, and only the SS could be seen going in and out. There were two extra guard towers specifically guarding the Russians, and every now and then the guards on these towers sent a burst of machine-gun fire into the compound.

The quarantine section was also closed off from the main camp, but the gate was only guarded by an inmate, who as a rule didn't take much notice of the people going in and out. Thus there was considerable movement through that gate. If one had the courage to pass through as if one were entitled to, there was no problem. Only those who hesitated were questioned by the guarding inmate, usually a German criminal.

It must have been mid-morning when we arrived at our barracks. The other people assigned there were milling outside in the freezing cold. Eventually we were called in by a stubben ältester (a concentration camp policeman in charge of rooms in a barracks), who issued us with identity tags. Our clothes were cut as prescribed, and we were given the pieces of material to sew into the cavity.

Apparently it was left for us to find the needle and thread to do the job.

Minutes later we were turned out again into the biting cold with these gaping holes in our clothes. I began to wonder if I would freeze to death. I noticed that the more experienced inmates, in order to avoid freezing, had invented a method to share their body heat: two or three people would embrace each other; others would join them, forming a ball around them; then, layer after layer, people would attach themselves to the outside of the growing pack until a huge ball was formed. After a while, those whose backs faced the outside cold would begin to peel off and start a new ball. Then layer after layer of the previous ball would join the new one, until the old ball had unravelled, and then the whole system would start up again.

It was cozy and warm inside those human balls. Of course, the comfort didn't last, and the time spent on the outside was bitter. But there was constant movement all morning, and a spirit of survival and cooperation, if not camaraderie.

Suddenly all movement stopped and people scrambled to form a queue. Lunch had arrived. Six inmates carrying three milk cans, two to a can, brought the watery soup — the sum of our lunch. There were a few pieces of potato, and if one was very lucky he'd find scraps of horse meat too. Each of us received a ladleful of the brew, and we drew strength from its warmth, if not its nutrition.

Before the inmates were apportioned their ration, a big pot was filled from the bottom, dredging up most of the nourishment. This was for the bosses. Only then were the ordinary inmates given their miserable share. When all had received their measure, there was still some soup remaining in the can, and the hungry prisoners scrambled, shoving and kicking the weak out of the way. The German criminal in charge then lifted the milk can with its contents and hurled it at the fighting prisoners, who scrabbled wildly to save whatever could be lifted from the packed snow and their clothing. Joachim and I were too far away to participate, and watched the circus from a distance.

'This is no way to get food,' I said to Joachim.

'There must be a better way,' he agreed, 'and we had better find it, or there is no future for us here.'

A man standing near us warned us that the Ukrainians hunted in packs here, like wolves. They would attack any single person who had a scrap of food, he said. There was no chance for ordered sharing when they were around.

Looking at his identity tag I saw that he was a Slovak.

'Why are you here?' I asked him.

'I was caught with the partisans in the Tatra Mountains, near Banska Bistrica. And you?'

We told him our official stories and he looked us over searchingly. I was sure he didn't believe us. As for him, although he did not look particularly Jewish, I had a strong feeling he was just that. Those sort of feelings had never let me down so far. And yet I didn't dare trust him. In this place it was inadvisable to trust anyone.

We were lucky, that first day in Mauthausen. An hour or so after lunch we were allowed into the barracks. And even though the huge room was not heated, it protected us from the bitter wind; within minutes, in the crowded room, we were warm.

The Slovak, Joachim and I found a spot where we could sit with our backs to the wall. Only those quick enough found room to sit; the others had to stand. From where I sat I saw a roll of shaving soap under some furniture not far away. I wondered what would happen if I ate it. As if reading my thoughts, the Slovak said, 'Maybe one could get that roll of soap, but eating it would do no good. It would give you terrible cramps in the stomach; dysentery as well. And dysentery will kill you here.'

Perhaps I would have to eat the furniture instead.

'You see that chimney out there?' said the Slovak, pointing to the window opposite us through which we could see a huge brick structure. 'You probably can't see the black smoke from here. Do you know what it is?' We shook our heads. 'That is the chimney of the crematorium. It works day and night. Even so, they cannot manage to burn off all the bodies they have to dispose of.'

'What are you talking about?' I said, turning to him angrily. 'This is not one of the vernichtungs lagern [murder camps].'

The Slovak looked at me, a bitter smile on his lips. 'Isn't it? There are three ovens in that crematorium. If you have a chance, go out and you will see the hundreds of dead bodies neatly stacked in front of them, like railway sleepers. I hear they are going to recruit a group of people to bury some in mass graves.'

'I don't think I will volunteer for that job,' I said dryly.

'I don't know much about the whole business,' he continued. 'I have only been here ten days. But as a rule they get plenty of volunteers for jobs. They promise extra food.' Then he added, 'You know, a man won't last here more than five or six weeks without extra nourishment. Not that you'll see anyone dying of starvation: they come around every two or three weeks and select the weak and emaciated for the gas chamber.'

Joachim and I exchanged fearful glances.

That evening, as we were lined up outside for counting, a group of young Jewish boys arrived from Auschwitz. One of the inmates grabbed one of the boys, embracing and kissing him. A youngster amongst the newly arrived group asked his companion, 'Who is he?'

'He is my uncle,' the child replied.

The children were led into the barracks and kept there until the call for line-up came. A shout went out: *'Eintreten for appel'* — 'Fall in for inspection'. We were all lined up in five rows, a couple of metres apart, and made to stand to attention while an SS guard counted each row slowly. If he lost count, he went back and started anew.

On my first rollcall, there were no problems: the numbers tallied and we only had to stand there for some ten or twelve minutes in the freezing air. But on other occasions things did not go so well. If a man was missing we'd have to stay there at attention until he was found, alive or dead. If he was found alive, he was soon dead — beaten and kicked to death.

After the appel we were ordered inside our barracks. The criminal in charge of our barracks picked out the youngsters, myself amongst them, and sent us into a side room. There were blankets on the floor, and we were told to lie on our sides, head to foot like sardines. More blankets were thrown on top of us and we were told to sleep.

It was warm squeezed together like that. However, if one of us could not bear lying on a certain side any longer and started to turn, then everyone in that row had to turn with him. It was a disturbed night's sleep that I got.

A couple of nights later, when I missed out on being included in the children's group, I had the misfortune to experience how the other half lived. We were herded into the larger room, where there were no blankets, and instructed to sit down on the floor in each other's laps. After a short time we couldn't sit straight anymore and tried to lean on the man behind us. But the man behind could hardly hold himself, let alone another. Soon the man against the wall found himself crushed by the combined weight of many bodies. Thus fights erupted, and the seniors came in and beat us mercilessly with their rubber sticks. Then we were ordered to get up and stay up. Some of us found a way, supporting each other, to sit in a circle and doze for a while. There was little room to move, and we couldn't stay in our positions for long. Our legs and arms went numb and we had to get up to renew the circulation in our limbs. It was a long and uncomfortable night, and one I will never forget.

First thing in the morning we were driven into a washroom in the centre of the barracks. There we had to put our head and neck under a running tap — a very quick wash, and then out. I was not quick enough on the first morning, and one of the boss's henchmen struck me with his rubber stick across my back, causing me to throw my head up and hit my neck on the iron tap. I staggered out of the washroom and the pain in my neck troubled me for days afterwards. But I had learned my lesson.

20

Selection

Soon after we were counted, Joachim and I went off to familiarise ourselves with our surroundings. We had no difficulty getting past the inmate guarding the gate: we simply pretended to have business outside, in the main camp. First we went to the crematorium and saw the stacked bodies waiting to be burned, just as the Slovak had told us. We stood in silent amazement.

Finally we shook off this nightmare and I asked Joachim to look around on his own while I tried to make contact with any organisation which might exist among the Czech prisoners, some of whom had been there for several years. One of the prisoners introduced me to a man he thought might be able to help. I told him my story in as much detail as I could, and asked him if there was any way he could help me to survive. He let me say my piece without interrupting me; then finally he said, 'I don't know if I will be able to do anything for you. I am only a prisoner here, like yourself.' And with that I was dismissed.

I went to look for Joachim and found him watching a group of inmates carrying soup containers from the kitchen. He was deep in thought and I startled him when I called his name.

'The only suggestion I have,' Joachim said, 'is to ambush the soup train, dip our containers into the cans and run, each in a different direction. This way we have a chance of getting away with a good helping of soup.' Then he added wryly, 'Not that the soup contains very much nourishment.'

'Let's try it today,' I agreed.

About an hour later we were waiting on the corner of two paths where the soup train passed, our containers at the ready. As the people carrying the cans appeared, we rushed towards them, plunged our containers, each into a different can, and ran as fast as our legs would carry us, each in opposite ways. By the time the capo decided which one of us to chase, we were out of sight. We met a few minutes later, breathless and laughing.

'I wonder if we gained as much energy in our prize as we used up in running,' Joachim laughed. But our stomachs were full and it felt good.

When we finished our soup, Joachim said,

'There must to be an easier way to make a living.'

'The trick is to find it.'

'We will, my friend, we will,' said Joachim with confidence. 'If we keep searching for it. We have nothing to lose, do we? If we are caught, the punishment is death. If we don't try, we are going to die anyway.'

We ran back to our barracks to queue for our official share of soup. We were just in time.

In the afternoon we were out again seeking some elusive way to supplement our meagre diet. We came across a group of German prisoners who turned out to be Jehovah's Witnesses — a Christian sect I had never heard of. These people's faith forbade them to carry arms or engage in war. Refusing military service in Hitler's Germany was a major crime, and thus they found themselves in concentration camps. Joachim and I were fascinated by their beliefs. One of the men was happy to explain his religion to us, and though I cannot recall his explanation anymore, I remember vividly his hands passing to each of us a slice of bread, thinly spread with marmalade.

We learned that these people managed to get food parcels sent from their families, which enabled them to survive quite comfortably. In fact, they apparently had so much food that they could afford to spend a little of it trying to recruit a few souls. Now here was a religion worth subscribing to! We could hardly wait for the following afternoon to taste some more of the new gospel.

Alas, the man who talked with us was no fool. After a few days he realised we only came for the extra food, not the salvation of our souls, and he dropped us like hot potatoes. In response, we decided to knock off the pocket watch he guarded so jealously. We managed to pull off the theft without a hitch the next day.

We sold the watch for fifty cigarettes, the legal tender in the camp. And for that we obtained four loaves of bread, half a kilogram of margarine and the same of marmalade: enough to supplement our diet for two weeks.

When I first arrived at Mauthausen I was confounded to discover that there were Jews there who had come from various other camps. Did this mean that what I had heard about the way Jews were being dealt with was untrue? I soon learned the simple truth: there were indeed Jews who had been moved from other camps, and they had been treated no better or worse than the rest of the inmates, but none of these people were publicly known as Jews. All those who were known had disappeared.

A group of officially registered Jews from another camp arrived one evening. The poor wretches were lined up around the crematorium and then hosed down with cold water. The temperature was well below zero at the time, and these starved, weak souls froze to death within half an hour. We found them in the morning stacked neatly beside the crematorium. Any initial relief I had felt at discovering Jews living within the camp turned to a new terror when I witnessed their brutal elimination. But Joachim and I went on with the business of securing our survival by whatever means we could, and fear, like any other emotion, soon lost its edge. I recovered my fatalistic attitude: what had to happen would happen anyway, no matter what I did or didn't do. And so we continued our risky business.

There wasn't a great variety of punishments in the camp. For most crimes, the only punishment was death. All that differed was the means by which it was administered. During the time I was there I saw people gassed, shot and beaten to death. Many of the SS and most of the capos were sadists. They all enjoyed beating people, usually with the heavy rubber truncheons they carried, and needed little excuse to indulge themselves. Placing hardened criminals in charge of other prisoners was one of the Nazis' simple solutions to control in the camps.

Exploring the camp proper, I found that in other sections people lived in far more tolerable conditions than we did in the quarantine section. All had their own bunks, for a start. Most were political prisoners: some 200 Spaniards, some Poles, Yugoslavs and a few Bulgarians.

The latest bunch of political prisoners came from Hungary. As soon as the Nazis occupied Hungary in March 1944 they had grabbed most of the Hungarian intelligentsia (who had opposed the alliance with Germany). The Gestapo entered Hungary with lists of names and addresses, and picked their victims up before any of them had a chance to go underground. Newspaper editors were there, journalists unsympathetic to the German cause were there. Even the most moderate leaders of the Labour movement, tolerated by Horthy and his gang of right-wingers, were there. Members of the Kallay ministry had also been imprisoned, together with several members of the defunct parliament. Lawyers, university professors and other professionals had not escaped capture either. Even one of the leaders of the

Zionist movement in Hungary was among them. It was rumoured that he was being sent to Switzerland in a deal worked out between the Gestapo and the Hungarian Jewish leadership. Also among these Hungarian political prisoners was the man who had been the richest Jew in Hungary: Leo Goldberger of Buda, a friend of the now deposed ruler of Hungary. Goldberger was despised by his fellow prisoners for his arrogance and snobbishness. Even in his current circumstances he still clung to the notion of being a very important person. Mr Goldberger died only hours before the Americans liberated us. None mourned him.

Since my identity tag identified me as a Hungarian political prisoner, I had no problem approaching some of these people. When asked why I was in the camp, I said I was a communist. Like all prisoners in the camp proper, these people had a few lockers where their property was kept and watched. In my own barracks, one could not keep food anywhere, or hide anything of value. If the capos didn't steal it, other inmates would.

The Hungarian politicals had an elected committee running their affairs. I spoke to the leader of the committee asking for his help — in particular, to keep in their store whatever I could manage to acquire in the way of food or clothing, since I had no way of keeping anything in my present circumstances. He was very polite and offered his help in any way possible, since I was a Hungarian and a political. He wasn't fooled by my story of being a communist agitator; he said I looked too young for the job. 'But,' he said, 'we'll extend you every help we can, as long as we are all in the same boat.'

I cared little whether they believed me or not. I was just grateful to have gained their help.

I was only ten days in Mauthausen when I was caught in the first selekzia (selection) — a procedure they carried out periodically to weed out those who were ripe for the gas chamber. SS men would go from barracks to barracks and herd those we called musulmen — people who were all skin and bone, blankly staring — into the larger hall, lining them up on one side to pass naked before an SS official who would make the selection: right or left. Those sent to the left were allowed to put on their clothes, while those sent to the right had to stay naked. When all the prisoners had been checked, those on the right were taken to a storeroom where they were held till the selections in all the barracks had finished, then collected and marched off with the rest to the gas chambers.

Why I had been selected I had no idea. Although I was skinny, I was not on my last legs. I moved slowly along the line, shivering as much from fear as cold, my hands clasped in front of my penis. The officer looked me up and down momentarily, then, glancing back at his book, called simply, as an inspector might reject an unripe apple, 'Right'.

I was momentarily stunned. My usual impulse to save myself was frozen — not that there would have been many options to consider anyway. I felt no sorrow, no regret, just exhaustion and hunger. It didn't occur to me to cherish these last minutes on earth. I was numb.

A few minutes later, the door of the storeroom opened and a man came in, escorted by two capos. He was a doctor and he began to check to see if those assembled were really in such bad shape. I and another man were plucked out and sent back to join the other inmates, having been declared not ripe for the last shower.

Although I have read of other cases like this, this was the only instance I knew of in my whole time at Mauthausen that a person selected was returned. You cannot imagine how many times in my life I have relived those miraculous moments.

21

Potatoes

Joachim and I made many forays in our efforts to gather the food we needed to survive, but never, on those occasions, did we steal food from any individual, knowing that it meant shortening that person's life as sure as physically injuring him would have done. And neither I nor Joachim was a murderer. We were not prepared to kill another, even at the peril of our own survival. In my case I adhered to a Jewish tenet which states that a Jew must, if necessary, forfeit his own life rather than disobey the commandments. One of those commandments is '*lo tirtzoch*' — 'thou shall not murder'; and at that time, in that place, there were many men who had no such scruple.

After the known Jews had been eradicated from our barracks, there was enough room for us to sleep on the floor, like sardines. This was an immense improvement on the previous arrangement. The Slovak told us, in confidence, that he had found a source of bread, enough for the three of us. We were touched by his generosity, which enforced my belief that he was a Jew and that he sensed that I was one too. It turned out that the Spaniards, who were the official distributors of bread, always kept a certain amount for themselves. But the bread would never last more than two to three days, and when it went off they threw it out, near the fence behind their barracks. This was where the Slovak made his find. We went along with him and found large pieces of bread, green, yellow and blue with mould. Not very appetising, and probably not very nourishing either, but in our situation bread of any colour was bread; we held no prejudice.

After two weeks in quarantine, Joachim and I were transferred to barrack number twelve in the camp proper. But the last night in quarantine was a memorable one. Around midnight we woke up to the sound of gunfire coming from the closed-off section where the Russians were held. The SS came running and cursing from their barracks. The yelling, shouting and firing went on for about an hour. Now and again a bullet came crashing through the wooden panels of our barracks. After a while, only a few cries could be heard, and they were quickly stifled by a bullet or the butt of an SS rifle. Then all was quiet, and remained so for the rest of the night. In the morning, cartloads of dead Russians were wheeled out: nearly 600 of them, to be stacked in front of the crematorium.

Rumours as to what had happened flew around the camp. Three days after the incident I heard a reliable account of what had occurred. (The Czechs had a radio receiver, and they were able to pick up an Allied station that told the story of the Russians.) They had decided to try and break out of the camp while they still had the strength to attempt the effort. Of some 600 Russian prisoners, six managed to escape and find their way to the Russian lines. The rest were slaughtered mercilessly — we had seen the bodies to verify that much. And that was the end of the Russian prisoners of war in Mauthausen. Strangely enough, the enclosure they had been kept in remained shut and out of bounds to all, just as it had been while the Russians were there.

In barracks number twelve we experienced conditions which were almost humane. Here we had bunks. Mine was situated above Joachim's and we were allowed to stay inside during the day if we wanted to. One still could not keep food safely; its theft was guaranteed, one way or another. I remember the first night I was there a fellow tied some food, wrapped in a rag, to his leg as he went to sleep. In the morning his parcel was gone. But we counted our blessings, particularly when the weather was foul.

Towards the end of February the weather improved somewhat. The hard-packed snow began to thaw. New arrivals came to the camp. They were Italians — partisans, we were told, though we thought they must have made poor partisans to have been caught in their hundreds, virtually without putting up a fight. The Germans apparently still considered them dangerous, however, for they began executing them a few days later. By then, even some of the most ardent fascists had stopped believing in their final victory. Whatever was left of the Italian fascist units disintegrated through desertion. Some of them turned partisan as a means of redeeming themselves in the eyes of the new anti-fascist regime.

Prior to the executions I had befriended one of the youngsters among the Italians. He could not have been older than eighteen, maybe even younger. He spoke very little German or any other language, and I spoke no Italian at all. So we could talk very little. He had a wonderful pair of alpine boots, and when his turn came to go before the firing squad — for whatever reason, they shot the Italians rather than gassed them — he changed his wonderful boots for my timber-soled cotton shoes. He explained his generosity to me by telling me that where he was going he wouldn't need his boots.

It never occurred to me at the time, but years later, when I recalled those times in Mauthausen, it struck me how peculiar it was that people went to their death without the slightest fuss. Men who were marched off, either to the gas chambers or the firing squads, usually knew where they were being taken, and yet they went quietly, resigned, almost willing. During my five months at Mauthausen I saw hundreds of men march knowingly to their deaths, and I never saw one scene of a desperate struggle, or pleading for life — not the slightest attempt at escape, nor any endeavour to resist. Even today I have no explanation for this phenomenon. In most cases they were led by just a single SS man. A group of ten or more could easily have overcome that one guard and then used his weapon to try and fight their way out. They had nothing to lose. And yet they never tried to resist.

Every morning a group of fifty or so prisoners went out to a nearby field where our potato stock was stored in deep straw pits. Their job was to bring in the daily ration under heavy guard. One day I made a deal with a man detailed to go. In exchange for a day's rest from a job which entailed a long walk and hard labour, we swapped IDs. My hope was that I would be able to steal a few potatoes. Potatoes were also a form of currency in the camp: four of them were worth one cigarette.

It was not cigarettes I was after; I had stopped smoking as soon as I saw that that vice led only to addiction and ill-health. I had watched men sell their precious food for cigarettes and die of starvation, or end up being sent for selection because they were not eating. Our idea instead was to barter potatoes for cigarettes, an easier currency to keep and exchange for other necessities.

So on the morning of my mission I tied down the ends of my trouser legs and pulled the socks above them, and as we filled the bags I put a good number of spuds through holes in my pockets into the trouser legs. As we finished piling up the bags onto the carts, an SS man noticed my bulging legs and called me over. Knowing the usual punishment for thieving, my heart went cold. I stood frozen to the spot. Then, realising that disobedience would most certainly be the end of me, I slowly went to the guard, walking with difficulty, stepping with my legs widely spread. The guard looked at me with scorn.

He said, '*Mufs das sein?*' — 'Does this have to be?' He struck me hard across my face and turned away, leaving me with my potatoes.

I could hardly believe my luck. Not only had he spared my life, he had left me with my priceless booty! There was still the danger that the guards at the gate would notice my deed. However, I had long ago made up my mind that if I had to die I didn't want it to be a drawn-out affair, and the difference between being killed for stealing or dying slowly by starvation wasn't worth considering.

As we neared the gate to the camp it began to rain. By the time we were at the gate it was pouring, and the guards opened the gate without bothering to search any of us. We ran for shelter. Joachim was anxiously waiting for me. We examined my spoils: I had forty-two potatoes — a small fortune. Of these, we exchanged thirty-two for cigarettes. Ten potatoes we boiled and ate with a little margarine we still had from the proceeds of the sale of the Jehovah's Witness watch. Perhaps their god had been watching over us after all.

22

Three Ways to Leave

A newcomer arrived at our barracks, an American army captain. At that time my English was rudimentary, to say the least, but I tried to engage the captain in a conversation. I had very little success, however. He just wouldn't talk.

Mauthausen, in the middle of February 1945, was still pretty cold, particularly late in the afternoon when the sun fell from view. At night the temperature fell to several degrees below freezing, but there were so many of us in the dormitory that it was not cold.

Joachim and I landed a job, and a prime one too, working in the SS storerooms shifting various items from room to room. Among other things there was a huge quantity of civilian clothing here: overcoats short and long, some of very good quality, hundreds of suits, shirts and underwear. Joachim and I managed to knock off a good pullover each, and lifted various items of value to exchange for food.

One morning, just before we were supposed to go to our jobs, we were ordered into our barracks. I heard the fearful word selekzia. Sure enough, I was again sent to the side destined for the gas chamber. My brain worked fast. I eased my way to an open window where, shielded by the people in front, I quickly slipped through, pulled on my clothes while crouching low on the verandah encircling the barracks, and ran to the other side. I found a window in front of which those who had survived the selection were standing. I tapped on it lightly, to attract the attention of the man standing beside it. He looked at me, frightened and confused. For every second he hesitated my life hung in the balance. After some moments he opened the window. I threw him a glance of gratitude, slipped in without notice and was safe, for the moment. It took me some time to stop my heart from banging against my ribcage.

When the selection was over and I sought out Joachim, he looked at me as if I was a ghost.

'Great God,' he exclaimed, 'how did you manage that?! I saw you being sent to the other side. I was sure I'd seen the last of you. Oh God, am I glad to see you again!'

'The feeling is mutual, Joachim,' I replied. 'I really thought I'd had it this time.'

A few weeks later I found myself sent for the third time to the wrong side. This time I pretended to misunderstand the order and went to the left, fearing with every step that the SS guard would call to one of the capos to send me to the other side. But the SS were so arrogant in their role that they could not imagine anyone defying their order, and so didn't check how it was carried out. I reached the surviving group without trouble, and was again safe. Thankfully, that was the last selection. And just as well: I was running out of tricks.

It did not occur to me then, but years later I wondered why it was that I was persistently selected to go to the gas chamber. The purpose of those selections was supposed to be to weed out those on their last legs. But although I was not in the best shape, I was nowhere near as bad as those called musulmen. And yet I was always sent to the wrong side. Eventually it dawned on me: passing naked in front of the SS selectors, they could see I was circumcised, and therefore a Jew.

One day our American captain found his tongue. Somewhat haltingly he told me he had diarrhoea for the second day in succession, although he had not eaten anything the previous day. Diarrhoea was almost as dreaded as the selections. It usually ended with death. Joachim and I were still working in the storerooms, and I remembered having seen some coal powder — a good cure for the runs — amongst the medicines. I promised to try and get it.

I managed to grab some of the powder for the captain and he was most grateful. From then on, he often sought me out for a chat on neutral subjects. He never asked any personal questions, and ignored any such coming from me. He recovered from the diarrhoea, and survived to become the deputy commander of our camp after the Americans liberated us nearly three months later.

The fronts must have hotted up as the winter drew to a close. The Allied air forces increased their activities: we often saw their aircraft passing overhead, at times dipping their wings to us in greeting. They apparently knew what the place was. Linz, an industrial town some 30 kilometres from our camp, was now bombed daily, and the ground shook under our feet as the bombs fell on the town. Labour commandos were organised to travel there to clear the debris from the wreckage.

Not long after the Russian break-out a small group of Russian officers was brought in. One of them, a slim, well-built man of about thirty, was placed in my barracks. His name was Yevgeny and he was a major in the Red Army. Though my Russian wasn't very good, it was sufficient for a simple chat. I learnt from Yevgeny that he had been slightly wounded in an engagement near Budapest and was knocked unconscious. When he came to, he found himself in a makeshift prisoner-of-war camp. He was apparently brought in by some other Russian prisoners of war, all wounded to some degree. They were held in that makeshift camp for ten days, during which time many of the wounded died for lack of medical help. They were kept in atrocious conditions in the open, without any washing facilities or access to medications. Only those with lighter wounds pulled through. After some days the officers were transferred to Mauthausen.

The major and I enjoyed each other's company enough to talk regularly. He used to laugh at my mistakes in Russian and good-naturedly correct them.

Yevgeny was most anxious to escape and return to the fighting. He explained to me that this was the time when he had a chance to make big strides forward in his career. Although we all hated being where we were, he hated it with a striking intensity. He still had the energy to hate, being relatively fresh to the camp. And although he talked little, he was an eager listener, especially if one talked about possible ways of breaking out of our death trap, as he called it.

I knew of no feasible opportunities, but tried to invent some to amuse or please him. He was not fooled. Still he kept pressing me about the place and its surroundings, and I shared my rather limited knowledge with him. Political prisoners were not allowed to go out of the inner camp. (The Germans, in their wisdom, considered me a dangerous political prisoner.) The only time I had ventured outside was on my trip to the potato store.

I did know that apart from the potato collectors there was another group that worked a few kilometres down the valley, building a railway line from north to south. It was hard work, and one would have no difficulty in finding people willing to swap their ID tags in order to escape a day's work on the line. For some reason, though, I did not tell Yevgeny of this possibility for a long time, perhaps because I knew he would be unable to resist this opportunity to escape. I had some pretty strong reservations about this method and was unwilling to let him judge his chances of escaping that way, since it involved endangering the innocent person with whom he changed identities. That person would almost certainly have been killed for his part in Yevgeny's escape.

At this point I did not consider joining the major in any break-out attempt he might make, because somehow I believed that I was destined to survive the war without resorting to such desperate actions. My many miraculous escapes only strengthened this belief, and my confidence grew by the day.

But it was soon shattered when one day Joachim, together with some other army deserters, was called, taken to an enclosure behind the administration block, and executed by firing squad. For days after that, scores of people, mostly political prisoners, were taken away and shot. Now I began to worry again. I wondered whether my turn was soon to come.

I remembered an old joke about a forest being suddenly deserted by all the animals living in it. A rabbit watching the panicky exodus stopped a hare and asked, 'Why all the panic?'

'Didn't you know?' the hare replied, 'There is a huge expedition coming to hunt and destroy all the panthers.'

'But surely you and I have nothing to fear. We are not panthers. We look nothing like them.'

'Try telling them!' said the hare, and took

off after the other animals.

I knew I was not much of a political prisoner, but it seemed that, as the end of the war loomed, the Germans were taking no chances.

I missed Joachim terribly. He had been a real friend and companion in the worst of conditions. But now this new fear focused my energies towards the future, and I began to think about escape with Yevgeny after all. It seemed to me that the chances of survival in the camp versus pulling off a successful escape were about equal. After thinking on the subject for several days, I decided to attempt an escape with Yevgeny. First, I decided, we would have to join the railway gang and go out and examine the layout and conditions of the surrounding area, then we could make some plans and prepare rations to effect an escape.

When I approached Yevgeny with my thoughts on the subject, he was most enthusiastic. 'It's a terrific plan,' he said, looking at me with admiration. 'We cannot be more than 150 kilometres from our lines. We'll be able to make it in three days, at most. We'll make it for sure.' I wished I could share his certainty.

After long discussions we decided to be ready to flee on our first day out, if the opportunity arose. Having made that decision, preparations had to be made, like eliminating the 'street' on top of our scalps, acquiring civilian clothes and whatever provisions were possible for three days. We had few illusions about being able to take much food with us. I had a couple of cigarettes with which I could buy a little food. We had our heads shaved, and managed to get hold of some clothes to wear under our prison garb.

In three days we were ready to try our luck. It was not hard to find two people to change our identity tags with, but as we were put on the truck to take us out, new orders arrived. We were to be taken to Linz to clear the wreckage from the previous night's heavy bombardment. We looked at each other as we heard the news. 'We'll play it by ear,' whispered Yevgeny, and I nodded.

In Linz, we didn't have the slightest chance to slip away. There were hundreds of people there, not only from Mauthausen but from some other camp in the vicinity, as well as a large group of zwang arbeiter (forced labourers), mostly from Poland. Guards were as thick as flies — mainly young villains, no more than fifteen years old, armed with rifles they were only too happy to use.

When at long last we were back in camp,

completely worn out and glad to be back, out of reach of those sadistic teenagers, we shook our heads. 'Maybe this isn't such a good idea after all,' I said. Yevgeny just looked at me without saying a word. During the next few days I made every effort to avoid him. I don't know why, but I felt uncomfortable with him after the Linz experience. He must have felt the same way about me too, for he seemed happy to avoid me.

I then tried to contact the Czech who I believed to be in charge of their underground organisation, but he would not talk to me either. I found out later that he took me for a Hungarian and he hated the Hungarians, as did every self-respecting Czech nationalist. Several days passed, and Yevgeny came up to me saying, 'This is ridiculous, we are behaving like children. We have to think again about our plan. What happened a few days ago was sheer bad luck. I still believe that your original plan was sound. Let's give it another try.'

I was far from enthusiastic. I wasn't one to be superstitious, but what had happened the last time seemed like a bad omen to me. Yevgeny laughed nervously and said I would have to give him an answer in three days.

I felt very lonely without Joachim. There was nobody to talk to, and nobody I could rely on for cooperation in acquiring the extra food I needed to survive. Together we had been a terrific team, able to sense each other's thoughts, acting in perfect harmony when the need arose. I was still fairly well off, but I had to give thought to the future, a future measured in days in this place.

I liked Yevgeny, and even trusted him to some degree, but my sixth sense told me to be careful with him. For example, he did not strike me as a suitable partner in the business of gathering food. Joachim and I had shared a sense of principle about never hurting an individual by stealing his portion of food. We only stole from stores, which seldom, if ever, were justly distributed. We may have relieved some well-off individual of some of his luxuries, but never of his basic necessities. For some reason I feared that Yevgeny might not have such scruples in this regard. He seemed a decent enough fellow, but like all of us he was a product of his environment. And where he came from, there were no holds barred where survival was concerned.

Since I had left quarantine I seldom saw the Slovak who had befriended me when I arrived. Now I decided to seek him out, to see if he would replace Joachim as my food-finding partner. I was still convinced that he was a Jew who, like me, had managed

352

somehow to fool the Nazis by hiding his real identity, for I had no doubt that I wasn't the only one to manage it. I found him in apparently good health; fuller in face and body than I had ever seen him. I was quite surprised.

'How did you manage to fatten yourself up so nicely?' I asked.

'Oh, I have been doing all right lately,' he said, then added, 'I get plenty of bread, even some of better quality than before. On top of that, I organise something extra now and again.'

I was pleased to see him doing so well. I told him about Joachim, and asked whether he wanted to team up with me. He agreed and we shook hands. But the next morning when I went to see him to discuss our plan of action I found him dead in his bunk. He had not been fat at all: rather, he was distended, and had died of starvation. There could have been very little nourishment in that bread he had filled himself with, and it seemed he had not found anything extra, as he had boasted. I stood and stared. Poor fellow, at least he died peacefully in his sleep, believing he would pull through.

The Slovak's death depressed me to the extent that I decided to try once more to implement the escape plan with Yevgeny. I approached him and suggested we make another attempt via the railway gang. He was delighted, asking simply, 'When?'

'The day after tomorrow.'

He shook my hand vigorously, saying, 'I promise you, we will make it. You'll see.' I worried about his motives, and wondered whether the Soviet system he was so eager to rejoin would make him the hero he wanted to be. I decided that I would be wise to part company with him once we had escaped.

The sun was already warming the earth when we set out with the railway gang. After a forty-minute ride in a lorry we arrived at the work site. Yevegny and I were set the task of unloading the gravel arriving in open carriages. It was necessary to lift the heavy sliding doors and place a stone as high up underneath them as possible to hold them open. Then we would shovel the gravel out. I had been at it for maybe fifteen minutes when the stone I had placed slipped and the heavy door fell on two of my fingers, ripping off my finger nails.

The SS guard nearby noticed the accident and, to my amazement, took me aside and dressed my wounded fingers with great care. He then told me to sit beside him and rest. I sat there, musing on the ironies of fate. The unexpected humanity of an SS man was going to prevent my escape. The wounds by themselves would not have done that.

I spent a reasonably happy day basking in the sun, my spirits lifting despite the pain in my fingers. Again I was filled with the conviction that I was destined to survive. I made up my mind, there and then, not to try escaping again. Twice I had planned to escape and had twice been foiled by chance — I was not going to force the issue. Yevgeny was not given a chance to escape alone, and we returned to camp without event.

Before returning to my barracks I said to Yevgeny, 'That's it, my friend. I will not try it again. Find yourself another partner.' He just nodded. A few days later I heard that he had escaped. He was recaptured some days later and shot.

★   ★   ★

The Nazis now began scraping the bottom of the barrel. Not only were they recruiting fifteen-year-old children, but most of the criminals in the concentration camps were invited to join the SS if they were willing to fight for the Fatherland. A group began training in Mauthausen.

Then hope arrived in the form of Red Cross trucks. They stopped at the main entrance to the camp and a huge supply of food parcels, destined for us prisoners, was unloaded. Suddenly it began to rain and people were sent to carry the parcels inside into one of the SS stores. I was lucky enough to be one of those so engaged. There was no need to rip parcels open; many had already burst from the pressure exerted on them. Like most of those around me, I managed to steal some sugar cubes, some chocolate and a piece of cheese before the job was over. This was a huge haul, enough to sustain me for another fortnight. The next day, parcels were distributed — one to every two inmates. I was a rich man. Would this food be enough to keep me alive until the war ended?

It is hard to describe the impact these Red Cross parcels had on the inmates of Mauthausen. People who had long given up any hope now realised that they were not forgotten by the outside world, even if that outside world was still too far from reach. They began to dare to hope that they might yet come out of this alive. Some spoke of seeing justice done and vengeance wrought on their long-time tormentors. Everywhere, ghosts came to life, throwing off some of their pathetic appearance, taking an interest in their appearances again, even smiling.

Of course, by this time all known Jews had

been eliminated from the main camp. A small group were kept in a tent camp, just outside the perimeter of the old camp, in the most miserable conditions possible. They were joined by a large group of Hungarian Jews who had recently been brought in. Why and for what purpose they were kept there we had no idea. It was possible that the outside world, through the Red Cross, knew of those people's existence. We wondered if the Nazis were reluctant to commit any more mass murders as the end drew near. There was also the possibility that there were simply too many bodies to dispose of. The two crematoriums were working day and night, and a special detail was burying hundreds in mass graves, but there was still a huge pile of bodies in front of the crematorium — growing, rather than shrinking, by the day. And the weather was becoming milder, threatening rapid decay of the bodies out in the open.

At any rate, they were there, those poor Jewish wretches. I could see them faintly, moving about around their tents. No Red Cross parcels for them. Even the meagre soup that was carried down from our kitchens was ladled out in the most miserly fashion to them.

One night we woke to a loud explosion nearby. We were shocked, since the Allies had not dropped bombs anywhere near us, knowing who inhabited the camp. In the morning we found that a single bomb had been dropped directly onto the tent camp. We wondered if an Allied plane could have mistaken the camp for a military target. A rumour circulated that the Germans had done it. Whatever the cause, the only sure thing was that several hundred Jews who might have otherwise survived died as a consequence of that bomb — some instantly, many slowly, writhing out their agony over the following days. They were not given medical aid or assisted in any way.

I believed it was a good sign that I could now feel some compassion for others. Ever since Joachim's death I had thought of no-one else besides myself. Perhaps it was because my belly was now nearly full that I felt reassured of my own destiny. I could believe that with every passing day the end of the nightmare was nearing. I was convinced that after all of my trials I was going to make it through. With these thoughts in mind, I felt bitterly for my fellow Jews in that terrible place. What more could I do for them in these circumstances than tell their story?

We could feel a thaw in the harsh atmosphere in Mauthausen. Perhaps it was an illusion, but even the SS didn't seem as hostile. Some executions still continued, but not many. And there seemed to be fewer SS around. Vienna had fallen to the Russians, so it was rumoured through the camp. We believed it. Someone had seen Viennese firemen being billeted in vacated SS barracks just outside the camp. The Russians had to be close.

Many of the inmates grew apprehensive at the possibility of being liberated by the Russians. Most concerned were the Ukrainians, many of whom had initially volunteered to come and work for the Germans and had only recently fallen foul of their masters. The rest of us had nothing to fear from the Russians; they were certainly the lesser of two evils. Still, we held out some hope that we would be liberated by the Western Allies.

The group of criminals who had volunteered for the SS left the camp to be sent into battle against the Russians. Rumours went flying in the camp that the Germans were abandoning their positions in the face of the Western Allied advances and pouring all they had left into stopping the Russian advance. They had good reason: they knew they had little to fear from the Americans and the British, but the Russians would exact a tremendous revenge for the innumerable atrocities the German forces had committed on their soil. The likelihood of being liberated by the West increased. It was a sweet prospect to savour.

We became aware of an eerie silence. The Allied bombing raids on Linz had stopped. Was it because they had managed to destroy everything? Or were their own armed forces so close that they didn't want to endanger their own men and equipment? Work on the railway line stopped. The inmates who had worked on that project were happy instead to laze in the sun. Everything pointed to an end to our horrors.

Still, we were apprehensive.

23

Endings and Beginnings

Spring! Beautiful spring was upon us. The sun warmed our bodies and souls. For days there was no rain and the skies were cloudless. The SS had relinquished the administration of the camp to the Viennese fire brigade. They still manned the guard towers and the gate, but they stayed out of the camp. Even the twice-daily rollcalls stopped. Anyone who managed to escape was not missed. Not that anyone wanted to escape now — we were too close to redemption to take the chance.

However, rumours circulated that the Nazi leadership in Berlin had ordered the camp and its inmates destroyed, to wipe out any proof of what had taken place. I heard from the Czech underground that there was a fierce argument raging between the commandant of Mauthausen and his deputy, a war-crippled officer of the Waffen SS, over Himmler's latest edict. The commandant was keen to carry out the destruction, while his deputy disallowed it. A couple of days later I heard that the commandant had fled and left an instruction to carry out the infamous Himmler decree. We were all on edge, expecting to be blown sky-high at any moment. But nothing happened.

The following day, on the 4th of May, the SS disappeared. The gate was now manned by unarmed members of the Viennese fire brigade. We could hear sporadic gunfire around the camp. There was nothing to be seen, but by the sound of the exchanges they could not have been more than a couple of kilometres away. This continued for most of the day.

That night nobody in our camp slept. We prayed that our liberators would come through the gate at any moment. On the 5th of May the tension in the camp was almost unbearable. Most of us stood near the gate. Some forgot to come to their barracks for lunch, such as it was, and eyed the gate with its unarmed guards. They in turn eyed us, visibly nervous.

Early in the afternoon the gate opened and in rolled armoured vehicles. American soldiers walked behind them, rifles at the ready. For minutes we watched them silently, unable to move or make a sound. Then, all at once, people surged forward towards them, shouting, crying and laughing. Imagine, if you can, how the soldiers reacted to seeing these emaciated people, starved and sunken-eyed, in tattered rags, mobbing them in their thousands. They retreated behind their vehicles, some firing their weapons in the air. The tanks quickly positioned themselves, barring the big gate, and after firing a few machine-gun bursts into the air turned their weapons on us threateningly. The movement of the mob stopped. We all looked confused, our energy spent, our enthusiasm blunted.

Then, out of the multitude, stepped our fellow inmate the American captain. He approached the leading vehicle, out of which stepped an American officer. They saluted each other and exchanged a few words. Then another officer came out with a loudspeaker and, in good German, told us to relax.

'You are now free and soon will be able to return to your homes. First we will have to fatten you up a little before letting you go. But from now on there is no danger to your lives or your wellbeing. Our soldiers will be here to protect you, if necessary. No-one can harm you in any way. You frightened some of our men a few minutes ago; now everything will be okay. So please let us in to set up an administration and see to your needs.'

The captain was appointed Deputy Commandant of the camp. The armoured vehicles left, but a small detachment of soldiers remained behind under our captain's command. For the rest of the day the camp was like a disturbed ant hill. People walked around as if in a dream, milling around in groups, talking excitedly of the day's events and their hopes for the future.

Quite a few died that night, adding to the huge pile of bodies awaiting disposal. The morning brought with it the first day of reckoning: all the German criminals who had served as enforcers and standover men, beating and torturing us at the behest of their German masters, were dragged to the centre of the camp and there beaten and kicked to death. American war correspondents filmed the whole grizzly affair. Soldiers watched the spectacle, some with glee, others with disgust, but they took no action to stop it.

Most of the second day after liberation was taken up by this crude method of meting out rough justice to the capos. I took no part in the execution of these men. I watched one or two, and that was enough. But during the afternoon, as I was walking between the barracks, I got caught up in a big commotion which erupted in front of me. I saw a couple of Czechs holding onto a stocky little fellow who could not have been an inmate, judging from his rosy cheeks and nice little pot belly.

The Czechs said he had been in charge of the gas chambers. I watched the colour drain quickly from the man's face, his little eyes darting from one Czech to the other. He must have seen that he was not going to get any mercy from them, and there seemed to be no way to escape. Already, many people were milling around, and more joined by the second; soon there would be hundreds encircling him.

The man pleaded with his captors to spare his life, saying that he had only done his duty, as ordered. Naturally this cut little ice with these people.

I noticed a silver chain with a watch sitting in the man's vest pocket. It occurred to me that where this little Nazi was going he wouldn't be needing a watch. I grabbed the silver chain and pulled it and the watch from him, then turned away from the crowd. I had never had a watch before, but I did not keep it long. I did as I had done as a child when my father gave me my one and only toy: I exchanged the watch for food.

Now I had time to reflect on those who had perished. Joachim, Joachim, how I missed him, poor friend! The Nazis made sure he did not escape their punishment. Gone too was the Slovak, and the poor Russian. The American captain, on whom I had practised my English, was now a busy man. I had nobody to talk to. I wandered around the camp aimlessly, thinking about the past and wondering about the future.

Slowly, people grew tired of the carnage. And although the Czechs continued the hunt for Nazi sympathisers, few people bothered to take part in the killings.

On the third day of our liberation a group of Hungarians approached me, greatly agitated. 'Please help us,' they begged. 'The Czechs have grabbed one of our people.' There was panic in their eyes. 'They claim he was a Nazi and are going to kill him. He was a high-ranking official in the Kallay government; he is no Nazi. You have good connections with the Czechs, please help us to save him.'

I could not refuse, even though I was not sure I could sway the Czechs. It turned out that this man had been held incommunicado in one of the single cells in the camp. The Czech underground was a well-organised unit; they had more than a reasonable knowledge of who was held in the special cells and why. If they now wanted to destroy this Hungarian, on the pretext that he was a Nazi, what was I going to say to stop them?

A crowd gathered, knowing nothing of the dispute nor caring. All they could see was a well-dressed man, not as terribly undernourished as they themselves were. They quickly concluded that the Czechs were right and moved in to help.

'Please, let this man go,' I called to Prchallo, the Czech man who was trying to pull the terrified Hungarian away from the protective embrace of his countrymen. Hungarians and Czechs had hated each other for many generations. This circus seemed about to play out an age-old rivalry. 'He is not a Nazi.'

'Fuck off,' Prchallo responded tersely. 'Don't meddle in things which are none of your business.'

I ran to the American commandant's office. The captain asked why I was so agitated. 'Please come quickly,' I said, 'and bring a few soldiers with you. I'll explain on the way.'

As we arrived at the scene, the Czechs were just gaining the upper hand, having managed to tear the Hungarian away from his supporters with the help of some onlookers. They were dragging the poor fellow towards the killing grounds. The man's face was ashen and he trembled with fear. On the captain's orders the soldiers intercepted the mob, stopping them in their tracks. Seeing there were only two soldiers, some of the mob began making threatening moves towards us. But several more soldiers arrived, their weapons drawn, indicating no nonsense was going to be tolerated.

The Czechs stopped, angry, frustrated and confused. Some of the people who had been backing them began drifting away.

'What is going on?' the captain asked dryly.

Prchallo, still clutching his prey, replied, 'A Nazi.'

'So? Who appointed you judge and executioner?' said the captain. The Czechs stood there, stunned. This was the first time our liberators had intervened in these acts of retribution. The air was tense. What did the Americans know about how we had suffered at the hands of these Nazis? Why should they defend them now?

'Release that man,' the captain snapped.

The Czech complied without so much as a murmur.

'We will take this man,' the captain continued. 'If he is a Nazi, as you claim, he will be dealt with accordingly. But if he is innocent, as the Hungarians claim, he'll be set free like the rest of us. Either way, justice will be done, by those who are authorised to mete out justice. We have tolerated your revenge until now, for obvious reasons. But it will not be tolerated any more. Nobody will be allowed to take the law into their own hands again. If you suspect anyone, come and disclose your suspicions to me and I will make sure they are investigated. No Nazi will be allowed to escape justice, I assure you. I was one of you and I know what you went through here. You can trust me. Now, all disperse.'

Within minutes the crowd melted away, and I followed the soldiers and the Hungarian we had saved to the office. The man was on the verge of tears, squeezing my hand as he thanked me, over and over again, until I had to ask him to stop. Half an hour later the whole issue was cleared up and the man was free to leave, surrounded by a Hungarian committee elected to represent the Hungarians before the American military. I was supposed to be represented by the Czech committee, but right now I was not very popular in that circle.

Now that the initial thrill of our liberation had settled, we realised that we were still prisoners. Our conditions had not changed greatly, except for the fact that our lives were not in danger any more. The food had only improved slightly and was still insufficient. It was explained to us that we must be fed carefully so as not to overload our delicate stomachs. Letting us eat as much as we wanted could be fatal for some of us, they said. I did not know to what extent this explanation was sincere, and I had my doubts.

Still, all explanations had no effect on our circumstances. We had to keep queuing up three times a day for our meagre food, though we did so in a more dignified, less desperate manner. Gone was the cruel pushing and shoving of the capos. If there were second helpings to be had they were given away in an orderly manner, according to a prearranged system.

Now, for the first time, boredom began to be a problem. So many people shut up in such a limited space with nothing to do but wait for someone to decide their fate meant that quarrels flared up regularly, some developing into fist fights. In most cases they were one-sided affairs, where a stronger man beat a weaker one. Often these quarrels were about some material possession the weaker one had and the stronger one wanted. It became imperative for the weaker people to seek the protection of strong ones, especially if they had something of value. I had one of my two blankets taken off me by a big Hungarian. I had enough sense to avoid a fight, and that way saved the remaining blanket. I knew that I could have gone to the commandant and complained, but I did not want to bother him with every triviality. I also knew he could not be around to defend me every time I was attacked. I had to find a way to protect myself without falling back on the captain's goodwill.

Most of us began worrying about our future. There were no bright prospects. Our pasts, we knew, were more or less dead and buried, but we had good reason to fear the uncertainty of the future. Most of the Ukrainians would not even consider returning to their homes. They were terrified of the treatment they were likely to receive from the regime that would not forget their betrayal, or what was perceived as such. The Poles, most of whom were high-ranking officials in the army of the pre-war regime, realised that Poland was now essentially under Russian occupation, which meant that there would be no positions for them to occupy. Not only that, but they would not be well-received by the Russians. The majority of Hungarians were in a similar situation, or even worse. Their government had gone along with the Nazis, and most of them had supported that government.

I had no past that I cared to remember, but my future seemed to be just as empty and threatening. I held no hope of seeing my parents again, or any of my brothers or sisters, and I had no desire to return to the place of my childhood. Budapest seemed the most logical place to return to. I had taken plenty of time to consider my relationship with Olga, the girl from the Zionist underground, and had decided that there was no future in that relationship. There was no point in seeking her out. I hoped she had survived; that was all.

As soon as the Americans told us we were free to go, I was among the first to put my name down to return to Budapest.

24

Budapest 1945

The train arrived at the western railway station. The passengers, mostly Soviet soldiers, streamed out of the wagons, hurrying to wherever they were bound. I stood, staring at the wrecked station which had been hastily patched up to enable it to function. From this same station I had been shipped to Austria some seven months prior — to the concentration camp from which I was meant never to return.

In Mauthausen, although death was certain, I was surrounded by comrades, or at least fellow sufferers. Now, alone on this platform, the pieces of my life scattered like papers to the winds. The value of finding myself alive was much less certain than the sense of loss I now had to face. My parents? Certainly dead. Five brothers? They were young; perhaps some of them had survived. Three sisters? Pretty, perhaps *too* pretty.

I walked through the city. In whichever direction I looked there was not a building untouched, scarcely a glazed window unbroken. There were enormous holes in the walls from the many shells that had been lobbed into the city. Many a roof was damaged, if not destroyed. I had not been prepared for this almost total destruction. In one sense it was a depressing sight, but in another it was balm to my heart to see that these people who had wronged my brethren and me so terribly had not escaped unpunished.

I wandered aimlessly, not knowing where to go. Suddenly I remembered the Jewish Welfare Society on Bethlehem Square. I didn't know if it still existed, but it was the only place I could think of to go for help. I caught the tram to the eastern railway station, which would take me to the square. It was late afternoon by the time I got there. I hadn't had anything to eat that day, and very little the day before. First of all I had to find some food and a place to sleep, and then I would inquire about the fate of my family.

The rambling building which housed the welfare society was damaged but still standing. Temporary repairs had been made to facilitate its use. The offices were full of people, young and elderly, seeking help and inquiring about relatives. A babble of languages rose from the throng. It took me some time to find an official to tell my problem to. I was given a voucher to go down to the kitchen, where I received a meal; upon returning, another voucher took me on a tram to an address at Zuglo, an outer suburb, where I would be able to stay for the time being. The official also looked through his lists of survivors but could not find the names of any of my brothers or sisters. 'But,' the man said, 'you may try your luck with the International Red Cross; maybe they have some fresh lists.' I did this, but they were unable to uncover anything.

However, by an amazing stroke of luck, next day as I was walking back towards Bethlehem Square I saw my sister Leah on the other side of the street. Running across to her, oblivious to traffic, I was almost run over by a cursing Russian soldier in a jeep. Leah and I laughed and cried, embracing each other and talking excitedly while the Russian hollered abuse in the background. After the initial excitement I let go of my sister, a little embarrassed by our display of affection — after all, we hadn't seen each other for over ten years, and hadn't kept in touch. Both of us had been so busy with the business of survival that we had had no time for one another.

I took my sister back to the home at Zuglo, where I had a room all to myself. There we sat down and began to make up for a decade of separation.

'Were you at home when the deportation began?' I asked.

Leah shook her head. 'No, I was at Ujlak, working as a maid for a well-to-do Jewish family. I was deported with them.'

'What about Bassia? Was she at home with Mother and Father?'

'I don't know, but I don't think so.'

'So you don't know any more than I do about what's happened to our parents?'

Again my sister shook her head. 'I'm going to the Red Cross to check the lists they have of survivors from the various camps.'

'I can save you the trip, Leah. I've already been there. Nothing. Not even your name was on their lists.'

'What about you?' she asked.

'Well, I used a false name . . . '

As my voice trailed off, Leah shook her head. 'Our parents wouldn't have liked to see you like this: eating bare-headed, living in this place where there is no kosher food.'

'Well, our parents are not here, are they? Nor anywhere else. They, and God, are long gone.'

Leah said nothing. I studied my sister's weary face. 'I'm thinking of going to Chust to see if any of our family have returned,' I said.

376

'Or if anyone there knows something about their fate.'

'Take me with you,' she said.

'Too dangerous,' I responded, 'especially for women. All those drunken Russian soldiers roaming around. And anyway, there is nothing two can do that one can't accomplish.'

Leah made no answer, and we studied each other's eyes in silence.

The next day I put on the only suit I had, a summer uniform of unknown origin that I had found in the huge store of the German army in Mauthausen, and took the train to Chust.

Walking into town I was surprised by the lack of any sign of fighting: no ruins, no signs of the war that had raged in the area not so long ago. Only an eerie silence. Turning into the street where my parents' house stood, a street that used to be lively and boisterous with children, I was shocked that there was not a child to be seen, not a sound to be heard.

Suddenly, further up along the street, a head appeared out of a gate, as if checking to see who was disturbing the silence of this graveyard. Just as quickly it disappeared. I passed the house of Dr Wasserman, a stocky little man with a goatee beard. He would have been in his seventies had he survived. He had come from Bohemia and had difficulty understanding his Yiddish-speaking patients, but he battled the language barrier and treated everyone who came to him with equal care. Opposite the doctor's house was the home of my mother's cousin. His name was Shaye Kaufman and he had been a leather merchant, owning a shop on the main street. A little further on was the building of the Hebrew school, a private school that was host to the better-off and less religious children. Now it was neglected and desolate. The school had been banned soon after the Hungarians took over the region in 1938. As I passed it, in my mind I could still hear the noises of children playing in the yard. Where were those children now? How many had survived?

I stopped at Ackerman's grocery shop where my poor mother used to shop for the little she could afford, mainly the weekly measure of maize flour, a little yeast and very little sugar. Some weeks she didn't have the money for these basic necessities and Ackerman would let her take them on credit. Ackerman and his wife had come from Hungary, and unlike the majority of Jews in Chust spoke Hungarian rather than Yiddish. They had two grown-up sons, both dentists and both brilliant soccer players. I wondered if either of them still lived. Their shop stood high on the corner of a small street. Now it looked as if its owners had shut it only temporarily, perhaps for a holiday.

It was on this spot some years back, I recalled, that I, together with my little sister and even smaller brothers, had caught up with my father after he had been offended by my mother and tried to leave home. The memory of their quarrel was painfully acute.

A few metres away was the last pylon and the last of the electric street lights. This was where I used to stop at night coming home from cheder and wait for the policeman for fear of walking alone in the dark.

Further along there was the huge garden once owned by a man people called the Bulgar, though he was Czech. This once immaculate plot with thriving vegetables was now overgrown with wildflowers and weeds. Several metres down the street, just before my parents' house, stood a big, rambling place that had belonged to a Hungarian family. There had been two girls a bit older than me. Every time I passed their house the girls used to sing me a little song which went something like: 'Jew boy Muriel — tomorrow be your funeral.' They sang in Hungarian, so it wasn't until years later, when I learned to

379

speak that language, that I understood what they had been saying. As it turned out, it was the older girl's funeral not long after: she died of chicken pox. It seemed that that family was gone, too. Their house looked as deserted as any on the street.

My parents' house stood as I remembered it; only the low fence in front was missing and the small gate hung on one hinge. Most of the windows were broken and the front door stood wide open. The weeds in the yard reached up to my neck. Inside there was no trace of the little furniture that had once been there. My father's shtreimel was lying on the floor in its tin box. Some of the holy books were strewn around, but nothing else remained to remind me of those who had once lived here.

It didn't occur to me then, but later on I recalled that my father wrote the birthdays of all his children in one of his holy books. This was my chance to find out my exact date of birth, according to the Jewish calendar, at least. But I didn't take the book. At the time, birthdays were the last thing on my mind.

Heaving a deep sigh, I turned and left the place. No tears: I had given up crying a long time ago. And anyway, I had known in my heart for a long time what had happened to my parents and most of my family. The time for crying had long passed.

I turned and went back the way I had come. Somehow Budapest, with all its terrible destruction, hunger and Russian military brutality, did not depress me as much as this town did. Its body was untouched but its soul was utterly destroyed.

I walked back to the railway station I had arrived at only a few hours earlier, not knowing when the next train west was due. I only knew I wanted to get away as fast as possible from this place of desolation. I had no fond memories of it, and now no emotional ties.

Skinny and shrunken-eyed, I stood and stared ahead.

Dear Esther,

Here ends my story, but not the carousel of my memories. I can still see that boy standing there. Locked in that moment in time, he is standing there still. This stringy specimen, this old man and frightened boy, this living ghost, is me. Although I am now more than three-quarters of a century old, I am still that figure, still standing there on that platform, trying to decide what I should do. And at the same time I feel that I could not possibly have been that person, could surely not have seen, tasted and experienced that nightmare.

Everything in these pages is true — the truth as I experienced it. What we call history is only the prejudice of one person. I am sure other people saw things differently, but I have tried my best to give you an accurate picture of what I saw and experienced.

It has taken me fifteen years to learn enough English to write this autobiography. Even so, language has often remained a barrier. But perhaps no language, no matter how rich, can truly describe what I endured. I know for certain that if a person has never experienced real hunger, hunger which has no chance of being satisfied, then words are not enough to help him imagine it. If you have never experienced mortal fear, then even the most exacting description will not give you a taste of it.

I have spent much of my life side-stepping memories, pulling down blinds and closing shutters in my mind. But you, my dear grand-daughter, have given me the strength to revisit the past and complete my journey.

This is the end of the story so far. It is also the end of our struggle for our home, the sum total of fifty-two years of sweat and toil. We have been thrown out of our home. Luckily we have good friends who have taken us into their home, so we haven't had to go into the street. We will find a solution, eventually. I always did. But Savta suffers. I hope to be able to help her rise from the depth of her depression, in time, and start anew for the who-knows-how manyeth time.

Now we must find some other subjects to deal with. You, I am sure, will have plenty to keep you busy.

My best wishes be with you always.

Your loving Sabah,
Alex Sage